Quality of Life for Persons with Disabilities

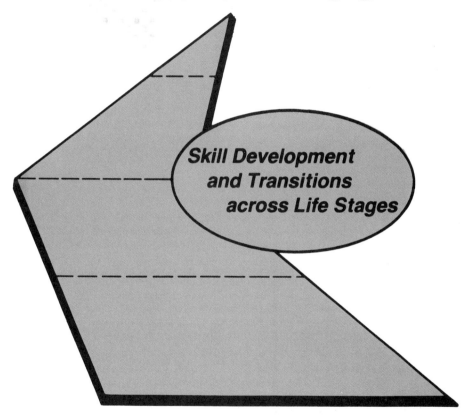

**Skill Development
and Transitions
across Life Stages**

Robert A. Weisgerber
*American Institute for Research
Palo Alto, California*

AN ASPEN PUBLICATION®
Aspen Publishers, Inc.
Gaithersburg, Maryland
1991

ALBRIGHT COLLEGE LIBRARY

Library of Congress Cataloging-in-Publication Data

Weisgerber, Robert A.
Quality of life for persons with disabilities : skill development and
transitions across life stages / Robert A. Weisgerber.
p. cm.
Includes bibliographical references and index.
ISBN: 0-8342-0221-2
1. Vocational guidance for handicapped—United States.
2. Handicapped children—United States—Vocational education.
3. Handicapped—Employment—United States. I. Title.
HV1568.5.W44 1991
331.5'9'0973—dc20
91-527
CIP

Editorial Services: Jane Coyle Garwood

Library of Congress Catalog Card Number: 91-527
ISBN: 0-8342-0221-2

Printed in the United States of America

1 2 3 4 5

Contents

Preface

As the reader approaches this book, it would be appropriate to keep in mind a particular orientation toward persons with disability and the design of services that facilitate their learning and living that have evolved during the author's 20 years of study and research in the area of disability. That orientation can be expressed in the following three observations.

First, disabilities, whether occurring at birth or at some other point in life, cause each affected individual to have a unique perspective on life. That perspective can be shaped in a positive way through experiences in which the individual is encouraged to interact with others in social situations and develop his or her functional skills. The extent to which the individual becomes self-sufficient in life is not merely a consequence of the severity of the condition but is very much influenced by the availability of opportunities to develop friendships and competence. It is also a reflection of highly personal qualities such as self-esteem, persistence, patience, and socially acceptable risk-taking behavior.

Second, the person with a disability has worth and value and should be afforded understanding and support without smothering his or her individuality. Day in and day out, the individual with disabilities faces challenges and barriers. Understanding and support on the part of others can help to address these factors, but it is unlikely that they will eliminate them altogether. By the very circumstance of a disability that adversely affects daily functioning, each person with a disability must rely to some extent on coping strategies in order to gain a reasonable level of independence and quality of life. This suggests that the nature and form of understanding and support that are supplied by others can play an important part by guiding the individual toward self-reliance in needed skill areas. In other words, interventions should be designed to develop self-sufficiency to the extent possible and, where it is not possible, to facilitate and assist the individual's functional performance through human assistance or technological means.

Third, quite obviously, the individual with a disability changes in many ways over the life course (as do we all), but the disability itself induces a continuity of challenge that transcends any particular life stage. For most persons with disabilities, there is no corresponding continuity in the provision of services. Intervention is usually transient, occurs within a particular life stage, and comes from different service providers who are addressing specific needs. Similarly, social support involves family, friends, coworkers, or others whose own life courses intersect with the person with disabilities only for a limited time.

This book focuses on how, at different life stages, the quality of life of persons with disabilities can be enhanced and supported. It points to the importance of linking services during transitions across life stages, and it attempts to describe the range of strategies and services that are being employed by service providers as they help persons with disabilities reach their individual potential and discover the satisfaction that comes with self-sufficiency.

It is hoped that this book will help to coalesce the energies and skills of service providers to permit greater independence and a better quality of life for persons with disabilities, regardless of their levels of disability or their current stages in the life course.

Disability and the Concept of Quality of Life

This chapter examines the general concept of quality of life as it applies to human needs and wants over the life span. It provides a rationale for how the term "quality of life" will be used in this book. We present a general model that examines the concept of human development in relation to major life stages: birth, infancy, and early childhood; the school years; the productive years; and the senior years. We also introduce a model for functional skill development, particularly with respect to social competence and employability. We discuss some of the factors that influence success in learning and living with disabilities. Finally, we make clear that coordination of services at various life stages, such as the transition from school to work, is essential if the potential for quality of life for many persons with disabilities is to be fully realized.

THE CONCEPT OF QUALITY OF LIFE

The definition of the concept of quality of life varies from individual to individual and changes for each of us over our life spans. It comprises a personal valuation of what is important in our lives and, in large measure, accounts for how we expend our energies. The Panel on the Quality of American Life, one of nine panels of the President's Commission for a National Agenda for the Eighties, defined quality of life as

a sense of well-being, a dynamic blend of satisfactions, which presumes:

First tier: Freedom from hunger, poverty, sickness, illiteracy, and undue fear about the impact of the hazards of life . . .

Second tier: Opportunity for personal growth, fulfillment, and self-esteem, which includes

- Opportunity to establish and maintain social bonds with family, friends, community, and co-workers.

- Opportunity to participate in and derive meaning from religious, civic, family, and work activities.

- Access to sources of esthetic and intellectual pleasure, including museums, concerts, the use of public parks and libraries, participation in educational and other activities.

- Access to activities pursued for recreational purposes, such as hiking, athletics, reading, and TV viewing." (Panel on the Quality of American Life, 1980, pp. 14-15)

Efforts to measure quality of life were initiated in 1960 by President Eisenhower's Commission on National Goals. At that time definitions of quality of life were based on a broad consideration of environmental and social factors, including education, concern for individual welfare, defense of the free world, health, and economic growth. Others who have examined the factors associated with well-being include Andrews and Withey (1976), Campbell, Converse, and Rodgers (1976), and Kamman, Christie, Irwin, and Dixon (1979). The latter study was noteworthy in that it called for participants' subjective reportings of happiness over a day, a week, and a month, with the self-assessments in longer time periods yielding a more "stable" impression of their actual happiness level.

John C. Flanagan, the founder and now-retired chairman of the American Institutes for Research, has long studied the way that people have defined quality of life. Based on interviews with 1000 people (500 males and 500 females) at the ages of 30, 50, and 70, Flanagan (1979) identified 15 areas that generally constitute quality of life. In no priority order, they are

1. health and personal safety
2. material comforts: good home, food, conveniences, security
3. close relationship with spouse or person of opposite sex
4. having and rearing children
5. close friends and sharing of activities
6. relationships with relatives
7. helping and encouraging others
8. participation in local and national public affairs activities
9. work that is interesting, rewarding, and worthwhile
10. learning and improving your understanding
11. understanding oneself and knowing one's assets and limitations
12. expressing oneself in a creative manner
13. socializing and meeting other people
14. reading, listening to music, or observing events
15. participation in active recreation

How do Americans prioritize the elements of their quality of life? It is possible to get some idea by examining the percentages of males and females at the ages of 30, 50, and 70 who identified the components in the list above that were most important to them (see Table 1–1).

Consistent with what we know about the aging process, placing a high priority on work drops off with advancing years. However, attention to health and well-being remains high for all age groups. The data in the Flanagan study (1979) are on a representative sample of the general population. As such, they establish a reference point against which the quality of life priorities of persons with disabilities may be compared. No comparable data have been collected from persons with disabilities, unfortunately, and research on this issue needs to be carried out.

In examining Flanagan's (1979) findings we can observe that some components of quality of life remained stable and highly valued over a 4-decade period, from age 30 to age 70. This should not be taken to mean that the same components apply in the first 3 decades, ages 0 to 30. Clearly, "having and raising children" is an adult expectation. Instead, we should assume that the value systems of children, youth, and young adults will undergo significant change as they mature and encounter different life experiences.

Table 1–1 Important Components in the Quality of Life for Adults

Components	Percent Identifying Quality of Life Component	
	Males	Females
Sample of 1000 30-year-olds		
☐ Health and personal safety	98%	98%
☐ Work	91	89
☐ Close relationship–opposite sex	90	94
☐ Having and raising children	84	93
☐ Understanding oneself	84	92
Sample of 1000 50-year-olds		
☐ Health and personal safety	96	97
☐ Work	90	86
☐ Close relationship–opposite sex	91	81
☐ Having and raising children	84	92
☐ Understanding oneself	84	90
Sample of 1000 70-year-olds		
☐ Health and personal safety	95	96
☐ Material comforts	87	84
☐ Having and raising children	82	87
☐ Understanding oneself	80	88
☐ Having close friends	75	89

Source: Adapted with permission from *Life's Last 20 Years: How To Improve Them,* by J.C. Flanagan, from a paper presented at the American Psychological Association, September 1979.

This latter point has special significance for individuals with disabilities because their life experiences are likely to be constrained (as compared with nondisabled individuals) as a result of two factors:

1. Functional limitations imposed by the disability: For example, mobility impairments *may* restrict movement and build dependency on others at the expense of personal independence, and sensory impairments *may* preclude gaining experience vicariously through television or other media.
2. Restricted social interaction: For example, parental "protectiveness" *may* lead to social isolation of the child with a disability, and peer and societal

rejection *may* lead to an absence of friends, role models, and other esteem-building social bonds.

The Relationship of Health to Quality of Life

The World Health Organization (1980) presented a model that differentiated among the terms "disease" or "injury," "impairment," "disability," and "handicap." In this model

- *disease, injury, or congenital malformation* (the intrinsic pathology or disorder) leads to
- *impairment* (loss or abnormality of physiological, anatomical, or psychological structure and function), which leads to
- *disability* (inability to do alone or do alone without difficulty tasks of everyday life, including physical disability in movements, strength, and mobility and social disability in "whole" tasks of daily living), which leads to a
- *handicap* (disadvantages with respect to social roles and the physical environment), which restricts opportunities to accomplish desired goals or tasks.

Quality of life for a child, a teenager, or an adult cannot be attained unless the individual thinks and acts positively toward himself or herself. The individual who makes the best of the situation and the nature of the disability and strives to improve his or her circumstances will be more likely to experience quality of life.

Self-abuse, either in terms of physical self-abuse or substance abuse, including excessive habits of eating or drinking and drug use (other than as prescribed for a specific medical condition) are attempts at gratification that are counterproductive to quality of life. This is equally true for persons with disabilities and those who are not disabled. Substance abuse leads directly to a deteriorating physical and mental condition and increases the risk of early death. More is said about substance abuse in Chapter 2.

Quality of Life for Persons with Disabilities

In understanding the implications of these findings, it must be kept in mind that the sample of persons interviewed in the Flanagan study was randomly drawn and thus is representative of the general population at the ages specified. As such, the study provides a reference point against which the lives and values of persons with disabilities can be compared.

Flanagan (1982) recognized this problem when he suggested that the categories having to do with material comforts, work, health and personal safety, active recreation, and learning and education would need to be subdivided. Additionally, he suggested that this subdivision should occur based on further research in which up to 1000 critical incidents from persons with disabilities would be analyzed. As mentioned previously, research of the type suggested by Flanagan has not yet established whether there are differences in the valuations of persons with disabilities and those who are not disabled.

Judgments about the quality of life for persons with disabilities can, in some instances, have implications for survival. Gartner and Lipsky (1987) have noted that critical judgments are involved in the making of medical-social determinations for newborns. They cite the Gross, Cox, and Pollay (1983) report in *Pediatrics* in which the University of Oklahoma Health Sciences Center applied a formula for quality of life (QL). The formula was $QL = NE \times (H + S)$, where NE meant natural endowment, H meant contribution from the home, and S meant the contribution from society.

The effect of intervention based on this distinction can be dramatic (Hentoff, 1985). The newborns classified as "high" in terms of QL were given "active" medically oriented treatment; those with "low" QL did not get this "vigorous" treatment. All of the high-QL infants survived (although one died in an automobile accident), but none of the low-QL infants did. This suggests that medical intervention (or the lack of it) based on assumptions about the quality of life can be an ethically important issue, raising serious questions about the effect of "disabling attitudes" on the performance of service providers at the earliest stage of life.

Madeleine Will (1984a), former assistant secretary for education and head of the Office of Special Education and Rehabilitative Services, was once questioned by the editorial staff of American Education concerning her views on the "very poor" quality of life of persons born with multiple disabilities. She responded by quoting from a letter she had received from a severely disabled individual:

> Who stops to figure out why being disabled is such a horrible fate? Most disabled people (we can assume we're experts in this) will tell you that despite what everyone thinks, the disability itself is not what makes everything difficult. What causes the difficulty are the attitudes society has about being disabled, attitudes that make a disabled person embarrassed, insecure, uncomfortable, dependent. Of course, disabled people rarely talk of quality of life. But it has precious little to do with deformity, and a great deal to do with society's own defects.
>
> The public talks about that kind of life as though it is simply inevitable for deformed infants. What they should be asking is: Why is it inevitable?

The real issues of this debate have not surfaced yet. The debaters have spent no energy trying to find out just how decent a disabled life could be, if it were allowed to be decent. (p. 5)

Typically, when the term "quality of life" is used, we are concerned with the individual who is living the life. However, we also need to take into account the effects of disability on the quality of life of significant others, particularly the immediate family (Bendell, Stone, Field, & Golstein, 1989; Frey, Fewell, & Vadasy, 1989). With early intervention programs for very young children with disabilities, discussed at length in Chapter 2, a great deal of emphasis is placed on family services.

This is true for two distinct reasons: First, the family bears most of the responsibility for the care and nurturing of the young child with disabilities, and it is a difficult, often frustrating challenge to those family members. Having a newborn infant, toddler, or child with a disability in the home places the family members under considerable stress, and their ability to cope and make adjustments in their own lives is by no means assured, potentially leading to a degradation in their own quality of life. Second, knowing that the child has a disability is a great emotional burden for the parents, and to some extent for siblings (Gallagher & Powell, 1989), and many of them experience feelings of guilt, failure, and lowered self-esteem. It is no small matter to overcome these negative feelings with the necessary love, continual support, and patience that the child needs.

It is important to note that interventions that address human capacity should be based on assessments of both strengths and needs. As Kaiser and Hemmeter (1989) pointed out in connection with family intervention, a needs-based model of intervention is deficit centered and has limitations (e.g., it does not facilitate conflict resolution when family members' values diverge). In contrast, an intervention model that emphasizes family strengths leads toward making choices among alternatives, building involvement and the sharing of responsibility for outcomes among family members— including the child with a disability.

Certainly deficits should not be ignored, for they are real and they are limiting to functionality. However, the *way* in which they are addressed should be oriented toward capacity building, either through the development of relevant, essential (enabling) skills, compensating behaviors, or the use of assistive technology and support systems.

One thing is clear— quality of life is intensely personal. But it is also a matter of importance for society as a whole. One of the characteristics of a civilized society is that it cares for the individual members of that society. This book takes the position that each human life has worth, each person has potential (that is often unrealized), and each person can be a contributing member of the larger social system.

These fundamental assumptions underlie our discussion of human development across life stages. They help to focus our discussion on critical life stage transitions, where the influences of the larger society significantly influence the opportunities available to persons with disabilities. Figure 1–1 summarizes these major life stages and lists just some of the areas of transitional need that are associated with each.

Transitional needs, as listed in Figure 1–1, represent classes of events in which the particular skills and behaviors that are required differ substantially from what the transitioning individuals have experienced previously, necessitating an adjustment of some kind (e.g., psychosocial, developmental, economic) in order to accommodate the new circumstances in which the individual must function. For example, caregivers at the beginning of life are necessarily medically oriented. Consequently, infants' needs are identified in terms of deviations from "a healthy state." Developmental specialists come into prominence when it is apparent that the deviation, if unaddressed, will lead (in all probability) to an obstacle to the further mental or physical development of the child. The medically oriented team relinquishes its central role to parents as the latter take on major caregiving responsibility on a day-to-day basis. Parents, in turn, eventually "release" or delegate caregiving responsibility to persons in day care or other centers organized for purposes of child supervision and development. Each of these mini-transitions is facilitated to the extent that the specialists are familiar with one another's roles and take the time to explain to the parents how these roles are complementary and important to the child's current stage of development.

Important transitions occur upon entry and advancement in educational environments. Too often we assume that the school system operates "systematically" and that teachers and specialists share information in meaningful, relevant ways as the child progresses from grade to grade. Certainly, that is the intent of the individualized education plan that is supposed to be developed and maintained on each child. But there are numerous mini-transitions that can influence the continuity of services, such as transitions from the intermediate to the secondary grades. While both are academically oriented environments, the transition typically involves going to a new school (often farther away from home); adjusting to new teachers, rules, and expectations; and mixing socially with many new classmates in a postpuberty, competitive environment.

The transition from school to work is, of course, a major experience for the child with a disability. But there are many mini-transitions that occur throughout the productive years, such as changing companies or jobs, having to adjust to a change in supervisors or adding new responsibilities, and relocating to new communities with different travel and living requirements.

Retirement is an important transition that marks a change in lifestyle. In addition, there are other mini-transitions subsequent to this life change that are

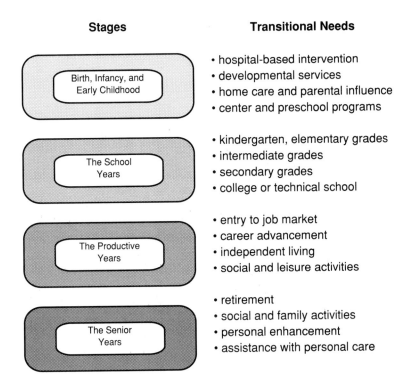

Figure 1–1 Life Course Transitions

induced by marked changes in health and economic independence. These are likely to follow (but can be coincident with) retirement.

HUMAN DEVELOPMENT ACROSS LIFE STAGES

From birth to death, we are all individuals with unique characteristics and potentials. Each of us begins life with a complex genetic make-up. Our development as functioning human beings is conditioned in part by this genetic make-up. For example, it helps to explain differences in physical and mental capacity among siblings. As we grow, we encounter a range of favorable and unfavorable situations and events, and positive and negative influences and relationships. We experience achievements and failures, and we respond to these with a range of emotions and behaviors. We are different when we start life, and what happens to us as we pass through life further establishes our uniqueness.

We can distinguish several life stages that act as major influences in the course of our lives. The first time frame involves the life stage from pregnancy through birth, infancy, and early childhood.

The *prenatal* period is critical because our well-being and development are dependent to a substantial degree on the age, general health, and habits of our mothers, including their nutritional, smoking, and drug habits. Certainly, damage to the fetus during pregnancy can lead to adverse, even irreversible, consequences that will limit functioning after birth.

The *perinatal* period covers birth and the immediate 2-week period thereafter. Physical damage during birth, especially if it involves trauma to the brain, can be irreversible. Prematurity, with attendant low birthweight, can lead to potentially serious complications since undeveloped organs may not be able to develop properly.

The *neonatal* period spans the first 2 months of life. It is a crucial period in which health and nutritional needs are paramount. In the case of the preterm child, it may be coincident with the child's term of stay in a neonatal intensive care unit.

Infancy and early childhood are times of rapid learning and times during which at-risk children need special attention. There is ample evidence that environmental influences have a powerful effect on the development of infants and toddlers. An environment characterized by deprivation inhibits human development, while a rich, nurturing environment is likely to enhance development. An essential element of environmental influence during these formative years is the nature of social interaction with family and significant others, such as child care providers.

The Council of Chief State School Officers (1988) has issued a call for action:

> Our concern is for young children and what society must do to assist them in their infinite capacities. Our focus is on the partnership of family, health and other care givers, and educators who need to help each child develop those capacities. Our challenge is to assure the partnership is in place and prepared to nurture each child from the earliest moments of life. (p. 1)

The second life stage spans the school years. These years, when activities are largely centered around structured learning in a social context, require a continuous assessment of one's personal performance in comparison with that of others. The school environment in which this learning and assessment take place strongly shapes the individual's self-esteem. Personal characteristics that are often shaped at this time, such as the determination that a young person with disabilities displays in the face of challenges, may be at least as important as acquisition of knowledge and skills.

Society recognizes that dropouts, who shorten their schooling, typically function at a disadvantage throughout life, while those who extend their school years by enrolling in postsecondary education are taking steps to gain a professional level of knowledge and skills. It is also worthy of note that the narrow time frame of the years 17 to 22, when nondisabled youth are engaging in high-risk activities (motorcycling, diving), is a period when a number of these able-bodied individuals become handicapped due to tragic accidents.

The third life stage encompasses the productive adult years. This is the time of life that assumes productivity in daily living, whether in terms of becoming successfully employed, starting a family, utilizing leisure time, or otherwise contributing to the society of which one is a part. Implicit in this period are the twin concepts of self-sufficiency and independence. These are primary objectives for persons with disabilities. It is a time frame in which responsibilities are encountered and accepted, and individual accomplishments, however small, become milestones toward increasingly challenging goals.

The fourth life stage is often referred to as the senior years. Personal ambition, the acquisition of goods and property, the raising of families, and other patterns associated with the productive years are replaced by an increased awareness of mortality, concern for health and well-being, and a concern for the preservation of capital. Frequently, the senior years are characterized by modest personal requirements and a willingness to become an observer and to vicariously enjoy the accomplishments of others. They are also years in which loneliness begins to replace socialization and the need for assistance in matters of daily living increases.

This four-stage life continuum helps to place in perspective the psychosocial and physiological changes that we go through over the years. Each of these stages is the focus of much attention and concern unique to that life stage.

In the first stage, it is a matter of national concern that irregularities in the development of the fetus are often attributable to improper health habits on the part of the mother. Birth, the transition from the prenatal stage to infancy, can be crucial—termination of pregnancy at substantially less than full-term growth presents the prospect of serious medical complications for the newborn, whose lungs, eyes, and other organs are not yet developed. Brain damage or other traumas occurring at the time of delivery can result in lifelong disabilities.

The infancy and early childhood period is often the first time that we become aware of emerging hearing and vision deficiencies or any delayed development in speech, physical growth, or learning, as well as motor and chronic health problems. It is in this critical period that at-risk children need multidisciplinary attention and the close, caring relationships that can be provided in a family setting.

The Council of Chief State School Officers (1988) has summed up the need for strengthening the capacities of families in this way:

> The family is the focal point in fostering and sustaining a child's positive growth and development. The family "curriculum" in the earliest years is more important than the school curriculum. However, increasing numbers of families need assistance in providing experiences which lead to the positive development of children. (p. 5)

During the school years we are greatly concerned with ensuring that individuals with disabilities benefit from schooling. We place a premium on providing the assistance and accommodations necessary to provide appropriate education or training in appropriate instructional settings. Too frequently, however, we focus on near-term issues (such as minimum academic competencies for graduation) and lose sight of critical longer-term issues (such as employability and self-sufficiency) that become paramount the day that schooling (secondary or postsecondary) is left behind.

During the productive years we look for fulfillment of individual potential and the attainment of personal goals. These include such factors as financial security, parenting, and family health, as well as recognition by peers on the job or in one's chosen profession and acceptance in the community. In large part the productive years are a period in which the individual with disabilities makes a contribution to society through the expression of his or her abilities.

During the senior years, individuals usually reduce their commitments to employers or retire altogether. Depending on the state of their health, they may become more dependent on assistance from others. To the extent that the nature of their disability is associated with physical well-being, the time for transition from the productive years to the senior years may be accelerated for persons with disabilities. As is true for nondisabled persons, the more that elderly individuals with disabilities are able to stay active and enjoy friendships, the more they will be able to enjoy those senior years.

A MODEL OF FUNCTIONAL SKILL DEVELOPMENT

Disability can be defined in many ways. Most commonly, it is thought of as one or more physical, mental, or emotional conditions that interfere with or prevent "normal" capacity to function. This approach, which is reflected in the definitions of disabilities used by the Department of Education, is based on an assumption of deficits from the norm. It stems from the medical model, in which diagnosis is based on organic disorders. It leads naturally to the use of labels to categorize specific types of disability. However, the categorical approach is not always easy to apply. Questions about appropriate classification often arise when a person is either marginally disabled or multiply disabled.

Rather than thinking of disability according to the type of disability, a better way to think about it may be to focus on whether the person or persons are able to function effectively in particular skill areas. In this approach there is a shift from labeling and group categorization (and stereotyping) toward a characterization of individual performance in terms of what the person can do (or can learn to do). The emphasis shifts from static descriptions of disability (sometimes observed but at other times only inferred) to dynamic descriptions of performance and ability.

Clearly, in order for this functional approach to classification to have consistent meaning, attention must be paid to the context in which the individual is expected to function. To illustrate, assume an individual with a disability has reason to travel using public transportation in the community. Assume also that the community is fairly large and that it is sometimes necessary to deal with strangers *en route*. In this situation, the kinds of barriers and problems confronted by visually handicapped persons are likely to be different from those confronting persons who are mentally retarded, deaf, or physically disabled, yet they all have something in common. All of these individuals with different disabilities have to exhibit an ability to interact with others in order to successfully navigate the route, to reach and return from a destination. How well they can interact with others in the course of this travel is a social skill, which they either (1) lack, (2) are moderately but inconsistently effective at utilizing, or (3) are independently able to perform.

Individual Differences

When we encounter identical twins, we tend to be impressed by how much they look alike, share similar mannerisms, and otherwise behave in similar ways. The reason that we are so impressed is that we are quite unaccustomed to seeing duplication of characteristics in different individuals. In fact, it is the differences in people that make for diversification in societal roles, such as careers, and that lead us to selectively develop friendships and deep, lasting relationships.

While we recognize and value these individual differences, it is also true that we function in a society that has certain expectations about the extent of variation that is contextually "appropriate." For example, we know that not everyone is equally punctual, and to some extent we make allowances for this variation. However, any individual who is habitually late clearly operates outside the range of social acceptance and will encounter negative reactions from those persons who are affected by the consistent tardiness.

Personal development that occurs during the growing years involves three inter-related factors: (1) learning desirable patterns of social behavior, (2) conforming to acceptable boundaries of behavior consistent with societal expectations, and (3) adjusting learned behaviors according to contextual demands. Individual differences reflect the degree to which these factors are mastered.

Levels of Functioning

Generally, the terms "low functioning" and "high functioning" are used by special educators and rehabilitation counselors to differentiate students or clients whose potential for skill development is low or high as judged through observation. It is important to note that the terms are descriptive of performance, not diagnosis, in which case the terms "severe" and "mild" are appropriate.

Severely mentally retarded individuals, for example, typically function at a low level in academic skills, in daily living skills, and in social skills. Mildly mentally retarded persons can be expected to function at a somewhat higher level in general, but not necessarily in all specific skill areas.

There is likely to be an interaction between the type of disability and the functional level in certain skill areas. Thus emotionally disturbed students are likely to be low functioning with respect to a number of social skills but can vary considerably in their level of functioning in academic skills and daily living skills.

When we examine the performance of individuals within any disability group, we find that the range of performance with respect to a given skill area is likely to be very large. We can find blind persons with high musical talent, some with modest or just-developing musical skills, and others with little or none. The same can be said for other disability groups, and for that matter, the same can be said for nondisabled persons.

Similarly, the individual with a high level of skill in one area will not necessarily be skilled in all other performance areas. He or she will likely be mediocre in some and not very good in others. Thus the skilled musician may be an adequate public speaker but a poor mechanic. This diversity is what makes the human race so interesting, gives rise to differentiation of work in society, and creates a challenge as we strive to reach different goals.

If the goal for persons with disabilities is to develop their individual potential to the fullest possible extent, as it should be, then it is important to establish the baseline skills they need to improve in order to reach their potential. A basic model for growth in self-sufficiency has been described by Weisgerber, Dahl, and Appleby (1981) that generalizes well across skill dimensions and across disabling conditions. As shown below in Figure 1–2, the model recognizes three stages of personal growth: dependence, semi-independence, and independence. Applied to vocational skills, the dependent stage involves tutorial, "hands-on"

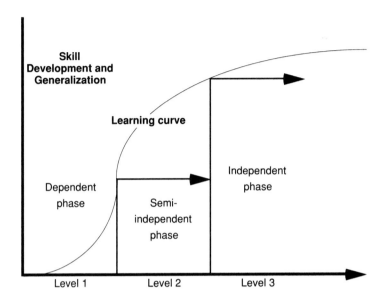

Figure 1-2 Basic Model for Growth in Self-Sufficiency.   *Source:* Adapted from *Training the Handicapped for Productive Employment* (p. 84) by R. Weisgerber, P. Dahl, and J. Appleby, Aspen Publishers, Inc., © 1981.

assistance because the low-functioning individual has not yet shown the ability to accomplish targeted tasks. The phrase "spoon-fed" is often used in a figurative sense to mean doing something for people who are unable to do it for themselves. It is important to realize that for almost any skill, whether general or specific, we begin at a spoon-fed stage, (hopefully) rapidly progress toward semi-independence, and eventually become self-reliant.

In the semi-independent stage, the individual with a disability may be able to do the tasks with some success, but performance is inconsistent, sometimes requiring intervention by another person to get things right. In the third stage, the individual with a disability can perform the tasks satisfactorily (allowing room for unintended error) in most contexts.

In a second example, involving daily living skills, an individual at the lowest stage would be cared for by society, unable to accomplish the routine activities that are fundamental to independent living. In the second stage, the individual with a disability may begin to exercise the necessary skills, though not perform them completely independently. He or she might be a candidate for cooperative living in a supervised setting. In the third stage, the individual with disabilities has reached a functional level of competence that warrants independent living, perhaps in a shared apartment, and needs assistance only under unusual circumstances.

SIGNIFICANT FACTORS THAT INFLUENCE SUCCESS

If we discount the elements of luck and timing, then most of what we are able to accomplish we can either lay claim to as a result of individual initiative, drive and determination, or as a result of instruction, assistance, and support from another person, or (as is usually the case) a combination of the two. Individual effort and commitment, together with external guidance and support, play important roles for persons with disabilities who are striving to achieve quality of life.

The Impact of Significant Others

Family members, teachers, friends, and mentors play an important part in shaping the lives of persons with disabilities. So do events and circumstances. The interplay of people and events, and what happens in particular situations, can become an important influence on the person with disabilities.

Critical incidents are those events that by definition make an important difference to the individual and to the attainment of his or her goals. Weisgerber (1991) has studied the critical factors that influenced persons with disabilities to enter, advance, and succeed in the fields of science, mathematics, engineering, and other technical specialties. Critical factors were identified in four areas; selected frequently cited factors are listed below in each area.

1. understanding or discovering one's interests and abilities
   - having outstanding teachers and courses
   - being encouraged by instructors, deans, parents, and significant others
   - self-satisfaction from doing good work
   - receiving positive or negative advice about a career field
   - observing adult role models, mentors, and parents
2. interacting effectively with others
   - being able to deal with negative communication
   - interacting with admissions officers and college counselors
   - interacting with teachers, students, and other friends
   - dealing with requirements imposed by instructors and institutions
   - getting assistance from teachers and from enablers at disabled student services offices

3. addressing barriers
  • coping with the limitations of disabling conditions
  • overcoming physical barriers
  • arranging adjustments in note taking and lectures
  • arranging adjustments in test taking
  • acquiring needed equipment
4. finding quality of life as an adult
  • being able to deal with work problems, stress, and disappointments
  • being aware of personal accomplishments and contributions
  • being asked to consult, speak, or publish
  • receiving promotions, raises, and outstanding performance evaluations
  • being actively involved in finding the first career job

Not surprisingly, the single influence most often cited in the Weisgerber (1991) study was an outstanding teacher or course that "turned them on" to the subject of science. Many persons felt that mentors had been critically important to their gaining entrance to and advancement in college or in a job. Many others expressed deep appreciation for the encouragement and support they received from their families.

Individual Determination To Get Things Done

Disability is not synonymous with inability. Persons with disabilities can do lots of things that nondisabled people do, but they may have to do them differently. Many persons with disabilities learn how to accomplish things by working around them, as evidenced by several nationally prominent personalities who have achieved positions of power and prestige in spite of their learning disabilities—which they admitted to after reaching their goals.

Weisgerber (1980) gave a number of examples of individuals who have demonstrated competence though they were disabled in some way. Newspapers, film, and television remind us of people with disabilities who have overcome their limitations to a remarkable extent:

• The young woman who started in television as a singer at the age of 10 and overcame her reading disability, which interfered with reading scripts, to become a popular lead actress.
• A deaf mute young man who earned a private pilot's license.
• An armless woman who functions fully as a homemaker— she drives to the market, selects vegetables, signs a check at the checkout counter (with her toes), cooks, serves, cleans up, and carries out numerous other activities of daily living.

- A blind man who received a state commendation for his effectiveness as a public information officer— he tells others how to get from place to place and reads the necessary printed material with an electronic device. On his off-duty hours he jogs, plays golf, bowls, swims, and water skis.
- A mentally retarded young man who has proved to be an asset in working with a team of archaeologists at an excavation site— he is a general helper, but he also plays an important role in labeling specimens.
- A one-legged man who climbed to the top of Mount Rainier and later founded a one-legged soccer team.

When one has a disability, the development of competence is no small accomplishment. It takes a lot of extra effort, not only due to the limitations imposed by the disability itself but also because of limitations imposed by external sources. Persons with disabilities who want to develop and apply their skills often find that one of the most serious difficulties they encounter is the attitudinal barrier imposed by others who choose to focus on their problems rather than their potentials.

Understanding Individual Strengths and Weaknesses

Whether disabled or not, we are all unique beings. Each of us has strengths and weaknesses, which take on varying degrees of importance depending on the context. Often, strengths can be built upon and weaknesses can be accommodated in one way or another. But before one can build on strengths and begin to overcome weaknesses, they must be identified and understood. Obviously, the presence of a disability may act as a limiting factor on skill development and its application. This can be important in certain situations, but in others it can be irrelevant.

Strengths can be thought of as skills that have been developed to a level that permits the individual to perform particular tasks efficiently, effectively, and independently. In the case of basic skills, such as reading, many kinds of day-to-day tasks can be affected. Skills can be described in general terms, such as "social skills," or very specific terms, such as "able to initiate, sustain, and end conversations."

We can think of weaknesses as undeveloped skills. They may have never been learned, or they may be partially developed but performed inconsistently. If they have not been developed by the time the individual leaves school, general skill deficiencies (such as the inability to read or socially interact with others) can severely limit job opportunities and effectiveness in daily living in the community.

To put this latter point in perspective, consider the fact that the activities that students engage in during their school years are determined by, and continuously monitored by, the teachers, counselors, and administrators in their school. If the individual has trouble in carrying out the activity, he or she can usually get help or advice from the teacher, counselor, or administrator. During the preadolescent period, and up until the mid-teens, out-of-school activities are often determined and monitored by responsible adults, usually family members. If the student doesn't exhibit appropriate behaviors or fails in some way, he or she can look to the parent, grandparent, or older sibling to lend a guiding hand.

In contrast, when young adults leave school and enter the community, there is no longer a requirement that they be directed and monitored closely. Nor is anyone obligated to constantly prompt them in specific social skills that may be lacking or supply them with solutions to social problems that they encounter, such as disagreements, teasing, and the like. Now success will be measured by how well each individual is able to function on his or her own.

Social Competence

It is a major thesis of this book that quality of life in the various life stages depends in large measure on the interactions we have with others. In the early years that interaction is built around the family; later it is built around peers and teachers, then coworkers and friends, and finally, around family and friends. Unless the individual with a disability has developed functional social competence, this aspect of quality of life will be difficult to attain.

In developing a definition for social competence, Meyen and Schumaker (1981) noted that it has been variously defined as

- a complex ability to emit appropriate responses, both verbal and nonverbal, to environmental events
- an effective response to specific life situations
- the ability to interact with others in particular situations in such a way as to produce positive effects for all who are involved in the interaction
- the ability to read social cues, understand consequences, and respond appropriately in different situations

Clearly, these definitions have much in common. Consistent with that commonality, *we will define the socially competent person as one who can adjust his or her response to newly encountered situations or actions of others, reacting in socially acceptable ways and bringing about desired consequences.*

The term "social skills" is frequently used in the course of this book. We use it to refer to a range of specific interpersonal behaviors that commonly occur in (1) routine situations in school, work, community, or home settings, and (2) unanticipated situations that may occur less frequently but with potentially important effect.

"Employability" refers to the possession of those social skills that are considered relevant to getting and holding jobs. Employability skills are many and varied. They are typically characterized by appropriate, overt actions in work settings but sometimes involve conscious nonperformance of a negative action. For example, an individual needs one set of social skills when called upon to interact with a supervisor who is giving instructions, but needs quite a different set of social skills if directed by a stranger (such as a customer) to perform an action that is not tolerated in the workplace.

ORGANIZING FOR SERVICE DELIVERY

The development of social competence and employability skills is neither automatic nor quick. In infancy and the early childhood years, coordinated effort on the part of parents and service providers helps at-risk infants and toddlers by providing prompt intervention whenever medical, therapeutic, or social services are required, and, more generally, by providing a climate of support and training in varied, experience-building environments.

During the school years, coordinated effort on the part of the school staff, related services staff (e.g., psychological and health professionals), and parents facilitates the child's realization of goals that are established, written, and evaluated annually in joint planning meetings. The composition of this joint planning team can change over time. For example, coordination between school personnel and rehabilitation staff is particularly appropriate at the secondary level because the responsibilities of the school staff will be phased out as the young person leaves the school environment.

During the productive years, when the individual with disabilities is in a productive, working environment, the frequency and nature of service often change and there may be a consequent change in the extent of coordination that is required among service providers. For example, with low-functioning individuals, coordinated ongoing support may be required among an employer, rehabilitation personnel, social services, and the family or significant others.

In the senior years, the need for coordination between social services and health services staff increases substantially. So too does the need for increased social support from other volunteers or friends who can help the individual with a disability enjoy his or her senior years with companionship, security, and dignity.

In order to effectively coordinate services at transition points and within each life stage, service providers need to be broadly aware of the relationships between federal and local efforts, current trends in patterns of service provision, and the different concerns affecting persons with disabilities over the life course. The balance of this book addresses these issues.

Chapter 2

Supporting the
Developing Child

LIFE STAGE: BIRTH, INFANCY, AND EARLY CHILDHOOD

Lerner (1981) described the formative years of birth, infancy, and early childhood as an especially critical time for any child who deviates from the norm in physical, mental, behavioral, emotional, developmental, or learning characteristics. Her definition of deviation included children with "established risk" (medically diagnosed handicapping conditions, such as cerebral palsy, spina bifida, and Down's syndrome), "biological risk" (a health history of developmental problems in the prenatal, perinatal, postnatal, or early development years), and "environmental risk" (early life experiences such as adverse family care, health care, nutrition, and limiting patterns of social stimulation).

Birth, infancy, and early childhood for children with disabilities are especially complex periods, partly because many players are involved and because the child is particularly sensitive to the extent, form, and coordination of external intervention by service providers and the family. Figure 2–1 shows some of these complex inter-relationships.

Time Frame	Service Delivery Team	Services Delivered
Prenatal period Perinatal period Neonatal period	Physician and nursing team with concurrence of parents	Intervention for at-risk children, parent training, and support
Infancy 1 to 36 months	Social services and therapist team assisting family	Therapy, family training and support
Early childhood	Educational and child care services collaborating with family	Educational readiness, socialization, transition help

Figure 2-1 Birth, Infancy, and Early Childhood: Inter-relationships and Dependencies

Direct interactions between service providers and the child and family are influenced by policy at the federal, state, and local levels and by emerging professional knowledge about what works (and doesn't work) in practice.

It was mentioned in Chapter 1 that the development of functional competence is neither automatic nor quick. In the early years, coordinated effort on the part of parents and service providers helps at-risk infants and toddlers by prompt intervention in instances where medical or social services are required, and, more generally, by providing a climate of support and training in experience-building settings. Coordination *between* service providers is critical at transition points bridging different life stages (Hanline & Knowlton, 1988). It is no less true that coordination is necessary *among* service providers within a particular life stage. Nowhere is this need for coordination more important than in the infancy and early childhood years, before formal schooling begins (Fowler, Hains, & Rosenkoetter, 1990).

Coordination of Federal, State, and Local Efforts

In 1965 Congress expressed its intent to help care for severely handicapped children by specifically including them in the form of Public Law (PL) 89-313, in which Title I (subsequently changed to Chapter 1 by the Education Consolidation and Improvement Act of 1981) focused on severely handicapped children in state-operated or supported schools. These children could be 0 to 21 years old, determined to be a state responsibility, and placed in a state-operated facility. Recently, the United States General Accounting Office (GAO) (1989c) determined that a greater diversity of children were being served in this program than was originally intended, including children not so severely handicapped (mainly in preschool programs). The GAO argued that this program, costing $151 million for the 1988-1989 school year, should be combined with the Education of the Handicapped Act, PL 94-142.

PL 99-457, the Education of the Handicapped Act Amendments of 1986, encouraged state and local governments to increase and enhance their services for young children with handicaps. Part H—Title I concerns infants from birth to 2 years of age. Section 619—Title II concerns preschool and the ages of 3 through 5. PL 99-457 is an entitlement act; that is, it recognizes the right of every child to receive service. The states are responding in different ways and with different time tables.

Meisels, Harbin, Modigliani, and Olson (1988) surveyed the childhood inter-vention policies of all 50 states and the District of Columbia. As of the date the survey was completed (May 1986), a variety of state agencies were involved in service delivery at these ages.

What agency generally takes the lead in delivering these services? According to the survey results,

- for the age band birth to 3 years, the public health agency led the state effort in over half the states
- for the age band of 3 to 6 years, 73% of the state education agencies served as the lead agency

What program components require substantial coordination? Case management services, which are mandated in the law, were identified by 40 states, staff training was named by 36 states, diagnostic/assessment procedures were named by 34 states, and intervention programs were named by 34 states. Bailey (1989) analyzed the evolution of case management in early intervention and described various studies that were intended to assess its effects. He pointed out some of the complications that can arise, including, among other things, a perceived lack of clout on the part of case managers and possible conflicts between the parents and the case manager.

What problems prevented coordination by the states? The nine most-named problems were

1. low funding
2. inconsistent eligibility criteria
3. lack of interagency coordination
4. limitations on use of funds
5. inconsistent regulations
6. duplication of services
7. lack of program evaluation
8. absence of accountability
9. overlapping mandates

It is important to realize that just as the Meisels et al. study (1988) was completed, the new PL 99-457 was coming into effect. It is likely that passage of the law will lead to a resolution of many inconsistencies across the states.

TEAMWORK AND TRANSITIONS IN CHILD CARE

From conception on, we all begin life totally dependent on others for our survival. We acquire survival skills gradually, and significant others play a major part in our development. Clearly, maternal and paternal influences are instrumental, but the effects of interventions on the part of others should not be underestimated. Health care specialists, of course, play an important role in the natal period, as do other professionals and volunteers who are involved in providing social, educational, and other support. Exactly how these helping professionals and volunteers interact with (1) the child, (2) the parents and other family members, and (3) one another has much to do with the effectiveness of the intervention. Further, this teamwork must be maintained as the child ages, different types of intervention and support are needed, and the members of the helping team change.

Transitions for Infants and Toddlers

A central concept within PL 99-457 is teamwork by professionals with complementary skills. However, as pointed out above, the composition of this team should change as children grow and their needs change—in other words, at critical transition points a different team should assume responsibility. Coordination is necessary, though all too frequently overlooked, among both the exiting and receiving professionals (Thurlow, Ysseldyke, & Weiss, 1988).

Kilgo, Richard, and Noonan (1989) provided insights concerning three transition points in the early childhood years. According to them, the minimum transitions for children with special needs during these years are (1) from the hospital's neonatal intensive care unit and follow-up clinic to the home or community infant/toddler services, (2) from these to public and private preschools, and (3) from these to primary-level public schools. Interestingly, data collected in Hawaii from 77 mothers and 31 fathers show an inverse relationship between the level of severity of the child's condition (at-risk, mild, severe) and parents' readiness to begin "thinking about the next educational program." Nevertheless, thinking and planning ahead are useful activities that parents should be involved in.

Issues involved with the first of these transitions, from the hospital to the home, have been explored by Hanline and Deppe (1990), Bruder and Walker (1990), and Odom and Chandler (1990).

Hanline and Deppe (1990) identified 14 issues in five areas that surround the birth of a premature child and suggest the service implications for each (see Table 2–1). Bruder and Walker (1990) reported on an intervention study involving the delivery of services to children who were "graduates" of a neonatal intensive care unit. They found that "the mothers who perceived the need for more support and received greater intervention exhibited greater responsiveness to their child, felt more competent as caregivers, and expressed more personal control over their child's outcomes than did their control group counterparts." Unfortunately, in reviewing the findings from a survey of 18 hospital nurseries and 34 home health care agencies, it was found that 17 of the hospitals did not have written procedures for parent involvement or formal plans

Table 2–1 Family Issues and Implications for Intervention

	Family Issues	Implications for Intervention
Confronting the premature birth	Emotional reaction to premature birth	Individualize support: Capitalize on family's resources and coping style
	Feelings of isolation	Meet parent-identified needs
	Understanding implications of premature birth	Provide parent-to-parent contact before and after hospital discharge
	Receiving adequate information from professionals	Provide accurate information for families
		Allow time for family to adjust
Assuming responsibility at home	Ambivalent feelings regarding discharge	Provide in-hospital contact with parents by professional who will assist parents to transfer hospital training regarding infant's care to home and who will assist parents with issues that arise after infant's discharge
	Infant's lingering vulnerability	
	Losing hospital staff support	Develop family support based on emerging parent-identified needs
	Unanticipated caregiving demands	Assist parents to understand their baby's unique behavior
	Understanding and managing the infant's atypical behavior	
Regaining control	Reestablishing control over own life	Focus intervention on utilizing family strengths
	Developing confidence in parental role	Enable and empower parents to make decisions for child before, during, and after hospital discharge
Making decisions about community-based resources and services	Locating services	Provide comprehensive in-home follow-up support services after discharge by professional who had established a relationship with family prior to discharge
	Evaluating appropriateness of services	
	"Going public" with infant's special needs	As needed, refer families to appropriate community-based resources and services

Source: From "Discharging the Premature Infant: Family Issues and Implications for Intervention" by M.F. Hanline and J. Deppe, 1990, *Topics in Early Childhood Special Education, 9*(4), pp. 15-25. Copyright 1990 by PRO-ED, Inc. Reprinted by permission.

to meet with parents prior to discharge of the child, and only three of the agencies made a visit with the family prior to discharge. Moreover, 12 of the agencies reported that inadequate discharge summaries had created obstacles prior to their initiating care for the high-risk infants, and only five of the agencies said they were familiar with the neonatal intensive care unit setting! It is obvious that this lack of coordination leaves much room for improvement.

Parents of technology-assisted infants experience major stresses during and after the child's birth and have substantial emotional adjustments to make when the child comes home (Odom & Chandler, 1990). In addition, they have greater stress in providing basic care, such as bathing a child who is attached to a ventilator or feeding a child who requires a gastrostomy tube or who has had a tracheotomy. In such cases, the inclusion of a home health care nurse in the intervention team is essential.

Issues involved in the second major transition, from the home and community service program to the preschool, have been examined by Spiegel-McGill, Reed, Konig, and McGowan (1990). In their view, parent education is central to successful transitioning. They proposed that a series of six parent-training workshops be undertaken, initiated 6 months before the child exits the infant program. The topics they suggested be covered include the following:

- the effects of transitions on our lives—in which parents are encouraged to reflect on transitions in their own lives
- knowing your child—in which parents are encouraged to organize their impressions of their child's functional abilities in cognitive, self-regulation, communication, sensorimotor, physical, and social development areas
- program options and services—in which parents develop criteria they want to see in a preschool program and attempt to locate one that best meets these criteria
- effective communication—in which parents learn how to describe their child's needs and abilities to school personnel
- educational rights—in which parents' legal rights are reviewed in terms of PL 94-142 and PL 99-457
- putting the puzzle together—in which parents learn the importance of preparing for upcoming multidisciplinary meetings

Intervention at Birth

PL 99-457 specifically addresses the need for service provision to children who are at risk of developmental delay in the critical period of 0 to 2 years of age. PL 99-457 was passed in 1986, and all states have begun to implement its provisions. Each state is charged with developing its own definition of developmental delay and setting the criteria for when a newborn or infant is deemed to be at risk. For example, low birthweight is typically a factor associated with potential developmental delay, but the criterion cutoff for eligibility differs across states.

What happens in a perinatal center designed to provide intensive care? One example is the Northeast Tennessee Regional Perinatal Center at the Johnson City Medical Center Hospital. The center provides inpatient and outpatient care for infants and mothers, treatment teams operating interactively with families, consultation services for parents, access to affiliated care services and transportation, and regional coordination.

The center describes the team approach to patient care as follows:

> At the Perinatal Center an interactive team approach is used to the maximum benefit of the patient.
>
> We seek input to patient care and family relations from referring physicians and nurses, our own medical and nursing staff, social workers, educational coordinators, administrators, respiratory therapists, and the clergy.
>
> The medically complicated pregnancy is addressed by a team of physician and nursing specialists from the fields of perinatology, cardiology, neurology, surgery, gastroenterology, hematology, nephrology, oncology, ultrasound, and genetics.
>
> Intensive newborn care is in the equally capable hands of our hospital-based neonatologists, nurse experts, and respiratory therapists who work only in our special care nurseries.
>
> They have immediate access to other members of the perinatal team, including a pediatric surgeon, pediatric neurosurgeon, orthopedic surgeon, pediatric cardiologist, and fully staffed genetics and birth defects unit.
>
> Hearing testing and other specialized evaluation services and a follow-up clinic for the "graduates" of our special care nurseries are provided.*

The relationship between early intervention with low birthweight infants and their subsequent cognitive development has been documented (Infant Health and Development Program, 1990). According to a study of 1000 infants at eight medical schools, significant gains have been found: Infants in the range of 4.4 to 5.5 pounds at birth have improved their IQ scores 13 points by age 3, while infants who weighed less than 4.4 pounds at birth improved an average of 6.6 points.

---

*Source: Courtesy of the Northeast Tennessee Regional Perinatal Center, Johnson City, TN.

The Individual Family Service Plan

The Handicapped Children's Early Education Program, within the Office of Special Education Programs in the Department of Education, has supported a variety of demonstrations designed to facilitate cooperative arrangements among the school, child care centers, and the home. The primary tool for ensuring coordination is the Individualized Family Service Plan (IFSP).

Bailey, Winton, Rouse, and Turnbull (1990) reviewed materials received by the Office of Special Education and Rehabilitative Services in response to a call to the field for materials related to the IFSP process. Included in these diverse materials were 24 IFSPs that were analyzed in detail. Of the 123 goal statements in these IFSPs, it was found that 41% centered on the child, 17% centered on medical/diagnostic information services, and 14% centered on family enrichment. Thirty-five percent of the goals focused on the parents, 15% on the clinician, and 10% on parent-professional collaboration. Bailey and his associates stated that

> the written product is possibly the *least* important aspect of goal assessment, goal planning, and service provision. The interactions between families and professionals *prior* to goal planning are of critical importance in establishing a positive, trusting, and collaborative relationship with families. (p. 25)

In the view of Krauss (1990), the IFSP sets a precedent for the federal government in the services it provides for families. The IFSP is the procedural tool for identifying and meeting the needs of the infant and the participating family. PL 99-457 directs the development of the IFSP by a multidisciplinary team and the child's parents. For this collaboration to be maximally effective, Kilgo et al. (1989) suggested that particular skills the parents need include

- awareness of the child's needs
- ability to describe those needs
- awareness of placement alternatives
- knowledge of legal rights
- familiarity with a preparatory curriculum
- knowledge about the IFSP process

It is appropriate to note that these skills are closely related to the target competencies developed in the six workshops proposed by Spiegel-McGill et al. (1990) and mentioned previously. Kilgo et al. also suggested that the following skills are critical for the professional staff:

- communication skills
- awareness of referral timelines
- knowledge of community resources
- knowledge of a preparatory curriculum
- knowledge of skills required in subsequent settings
- teaming skills

Parents can have a very substantial advocacy role when interacting with the case manager who is assigned to the child's case. Weil and Karls (1985) stated that an important goal is to help clients (such as parents) become as independent and self-sustaining as possible. Dunst and Trivette (1989) argued for a "client empowerment approach" to case management. This model provides "enhancement of the client's capabilities as a way of improving their capacity to negotiate service systems and obtain resources in response to their needs" (p. 92). Dunst and Trivette (1989) operationally define empowerment as "family identification and recognition of needs, the ability to deploy competencies to obtain resources to meet needs, and self-attributions about the role family members played in accessing resources and meeting needs" (p. 94).

The Family Enablement Project emphasizes assistance to lead agencies, interagency coordinating councils, and early intervention programs and provides technical assistance, consultation, and training for practitioners in seven states (Family Enablement Project, 1989). Materials are available at nominal cost to others involved in early intervention programming. For example, their outreach activities include several documents that are useful for initiating new programs. They produce a quarterly newsletter and calendar announcing upcoming events, and 1300 copies are sent across the country. The January 1990 edition of the newsletter, for example, clarifies seven misconceptions about needs-based family-centered intervention practices.

The Department of Education and the Department of Health and Human Services (1988), in a joint report to the Congress, stated that early intervention services include:

- family training, counseling, and home visits
- speech instruction
- speech pathology and audiology
- occupational and physical therapy
- psychological services
- case management services
- medical services for diagnosis and evaluation

- early identification, screening, and assessment
- health services necessary for the child to benefit from other early intervention services
- other services that support development in accordance with the definition of early intervention (e.g., nutritional services, social work services, special instruction)

The intent is to ensure multidisciplinary coordination among special educators, occupational therapists, physical therapists, speech and language pathologists, paraprofessionals, nutritionists, nurses, social workers, and families. This is much easier to say than to put into effect, because these professionals operate under different administrative rules, have different restrictions on who they can and cannot serve, and have varying budgetary constraints.

McCubbin, Sussman, and Patterson (1983) pointed out that family learning environments can provide for adaptive, growth-enhancing experiences or can increase risk through physical or psychological abuse, inadequate diet, unsanitary or disease-ridden living conditions, or deprivation involving father absence or non-normative family transitions.

Landerholm (1990) argued that for children in the 0 to 3 age range, a transdisciplinary approach should be used rather than a multidisciplinary (probably the more widely used term) one. She reasoned that the transdisciplinary approach has three characteristics: (1) the team performs services jointly, (2) individual team members with particular expertise actively train other members of the team in that skill, and (3) there is role release, wherein roles and responsibilities are shared among team members. After the initial evaluation is completed, this reduces the need for all the disciplines and makes it possible for one designated member to provide service continuity for the team as a whole.

Is it always true that a team approach is needed? Hume and Dannenbring (1989) reported on a longitudinal study of children in the Arrowhead Area Education Agency, Iowa, who were referred for screening (349 in 1976-1977 and 333 in 1980-1981), using the Marshalltown Developmental Profile (Standardized Revision) to determine eligibility for special preschool services. The children were then followed until they had reached the third grade, or age 8. The total number of students on whom data were available up to age 8 included 279 students who were deemed eligible for services and 177 who were screened and found ineligible for special services. Evaluations for the earlier group were done by one speech-language clinician, while the 1980-1981 evaluation was done by an early childhood special education teacher and a multidisciplinary team conducted the evaluation. It was found that both the one-person and the team approaches matched closely the later identification of students' identified disability category by grade 3. According to Hume and Dannenbring, "This finding would indicate that staff time spent on evaluation of young children might be better spent dealing with programming recommendations rather than determination of disability category" (p. 144).

Hutinger (1988) presented a model for assessing and linking services for families of handicapped children. Calling for multidisciplinary assessment, her multistage model calls for 6-month reassessments. Where possible, she suggests videotaping child performance in selected representative situations over time, then analyzing changes using one of several observational scales that she includes in a comprehensive review of instruments.

In the process of carrying out the evaluation, it is important to keep in mind that the father and mother are good sources of information about the child's performance and needs. Sexton, Hall, and Thomas (1984) examined the question of whether parents' evaluations of their child and those of the professional staff differed substantially and in what way. They found that the multiple sources of data (mother, father, professionals) are highly correlated, but that the mothers tended to rate the child's functioning highest, closely followed by the fathers; the diagnosticians were lowest in their ratings of the children. Sexton et al. pointed out that it is not a question of who's right or who's wrong but rather that this variation indicates the need for discussion between parents and service providers and a team approach to decisions on how best to meet the child's needs.

Model Services in the Early Childhood Period

The United States GAO (1989a) prepared an extensive bibliography of the literature on child care. This review, which is highly recommended for those not familiar with the literature, gives citations and brief abstracts covering 21 different areas (e.g., child abuse, industry-kinder care, policy and issues, licensing and regulations, and parent-oriented studies).

Karnes and Stayton (1988) studied 144 projects funded as demonstrations under the Handicapped Children's Early Education Assistance Act of 1968 (PL 90-538). Of the 144, 29 were no longer in existence at the time of the survey, 96 responded to the survey, and 67 reported that they provided services to infants and toddlers. The survey revealed a number of interesting patterns in assessment and service delivery. Twelve of the projects that responded to the study were termed "model projects" and described by Karnes and Stayton (Exhibit 2–1).

The San Bernardino City Unified School District (California) believes it is not too early to start planning for transition even while the child is in the womb (Winget, 1989). Program Specialist Debbie Warren explained, "Transition is the umbrella for all our children from birth through adulthood starting with our parent-infant program. It's helping the neonatal baby with special needs transition from the hospital by helping the parent to obtain services" (p. 5). That is just the beginning. The 3500 San Bernardino special education students are supported as they move from home, to preschool, to kindergarten, to special day class, to classes or activities with their general education peers, and from the campus to employment, further education, and social activities in the community.

Exhibit 2–1 Some Model Early Education Projects (Karnes & Stayton, 1988)

- The Developmental Education-Birth Through Two Project (DEBT), Lubbock Independent School District, Lubbock, Texas

- Supporting Extended Family Members (SEFAM), University of Washington, Merrywood School for the Handicapped, and the Advocates for the Retarded Citizens of King County, Washington

- Early Childhood Day Care Model Project, Region XIX Education Service Center, El Paso, Texas

- Tuesday's Child, Chicago, Illinois (initially associated with the Children's Memorial Hospital in Chicago)

- Adolescent-Infant Development Program, Department of Pediatrics, Howard University Hospital, Washington, DC

- Project Linking Infants in Need with Comprehensive Services (LINCS), Missouri Department of Mental Health and Missouri Department of Health, Columbia, Missouri

- Program for Children with Down Syndrome and Other Developmental Delays, Child Development Center, Sumner, Washington

- Macomb 0-3 Rural Project, McDonough County Rehabilitation Center and Fulton County Rehabilitation Center, Illinois

- The Coping Project (Children's Optimal Progress in Neurodevelopmental Growth), Johnson Rehabilitation Institute, John F. Kennedy Medical Center, Edison, New Jersey

- Multi-Agency Project for Preschoolers (MAPPS), Developmental Center for Handicapped Persons, Utah State University

- The Family Day Care Project, Child Care Coordinating and Referral Service, Ann Arbor, Michigan

- Children with Hearing Impairments in Mainstreamed Environments (CHIME), Nassau County Board of Cooperative Educational Services, Westbury, New York

---

For over a decade the Dallas Independent School District implemented a comprehensive intervention model for handicapped youngsters called Project KIDS (Kindling Individual Development Systems). Wilson, Mulligan, and Turner (1985) reported that by 1985, over 2000 children from a wide range of economic and cultural backgrounds had been served by this program. Offering a continuum of service and assistance from birth to age 6, Project KIDS includes

- home-based programming for "students" from birth to 2 years of age
- an option of home-based or center-based programming for children in the 2 to 3 years age range, with the option being dependent on the functioning level of the child and the family's ability to transport the child to the classroom
- a full-day, 5 days per week, center-based program, including transportation, for children aged 3 to 6

Intervention in the Project KIDS model begins at birth or from the point at which the child has been identified as at-risk for developmental delay. If the child qualifies, services are provided at no cost to the family. (These services may even be provided in Spanish, the second most common language in Dallas.) Planning for programming and assistance is jointly arrived at between the primary caregiver and the primary decision maker. This frequently requires clarification of the complementary roles of the parent and teacher. Attention is given to working cooperatively with the family, placing a priority on cultural values that sometimes conflict with the program objectives as set forth in instructional objectives. An example of a potential area of conflict may be seen in the degree to which discipline and behavior management techniques are applied differently by families from different cultures.

An important transitional stage within this early childhood model is the bridge from home-based to center-based instruction, which often occurs when the children are 2 to 3 years old. Murphy and Vincent (1989) surveyed 23 day care centers in Madison, Wisconsin, to determine day care teachers' perceptions of the "critical skills" needed by children entering day care if they are to perform successfully. They identified five areas (listed in descending order of importance): communication, independence, social interaction, compliance to rules/routines, and preacademics. Of 57 different behaviors/skills that were rated, the five most important were in the areas of communication and independence. In particular, day care teachers rated highest in importance those communication skills allowing the child to communicate wants and needs and to know when to ask for help.

Guralnick (1990b) argued that "participation in mainstreamed programs is an essential component for improving the peer social competence of young handicapped children" (p. 11). At the same time, he pointed out that "interactions [with nonhandicapped children] tend not to be overtly hostile, but disagreements in which delayed children are involved are quite common, much more so than when only nonhandicapped children interact" (p. 7).

It is important that the child not be "turned over" by the parent to the child care staff without some agreement as to what kind of child development plan will be put in place for each child. If the child with disabilities will be in an integrated day care center, that is, one with nondisabled children, parents should be aware that there is some evidence that placing the child with a disability in nonoptimal, practical situations poses some risks and drawbacks (Smith & Greenberg, 1981).

One approach to coordination is for the teacher of infants to meet with the parent and new teacher in the center, or for the teacher to visit in the home. The outcome of these initial meetings is a tailored plan for instruction that will be followed (and modified) until the child is ready to enter the regular school program.

Quality of Care in Child Care Programs

It is essential that the child care program into which the child is placed meet quality standards (Raymond, 1990). It is regrettable that quality standards vary considerably from state to state and that, irregular as they are, they have not been enforced with the consistency and regularity that these young, fragile children deserve. Binder and Shapiro (1988) reported the licensing require-ments, including child-to-staff ratios, for the 50 states and the District of Colum-bia (Table 2–2). According to these 1988 data, the staffing requirements in day care centers in the 0 to 12 months age range vary from 1:3 (Maryland, Massachusetts) to 1:12 (Idaho). In the 12 to 18 months range, the same discrepancy in ratios holds true (Maryland, Idaho). In the 18 to 24 months range, 13 states require a 1:4 ratio, while Florida, Idaho, Louisiana, Mississippi, and South Carolina require only a 1:12 ratio. At 24 to 30 months, 4 states require a 1:4 ratio (California, Connecticut, New York, Rhode Island) while 9 allow the 1:12 ratio. At 30 to 36 months, Rhode Island requires a 1:4 ratio, while Hawaii requires only a 1:16 ratio. For family day care homes a similar variation in licensing requirements exists. In Arizona the requirement is a ratio of 1:4, while in Arkansas it is 1:16. Further, in some states the ratios are affected by whether there are children with disabilities being served.

Given these extremes, it is clear that a state license is not a guarantee of quality. Other considerations include the nature of the activities in which the children are engaged; the caregivers' training in child care, educational cre-dentials, and familiarity with the special needs of children with disabilities;

Table 2-2 Licensing Requirements and Child-Staff Ratios in the 50 States and District of Columbia

	Day Care Centers — Child-to-Staff Ratios									Family Day Care Homes		
	Ages up to 12 months	12 to 18 months	18 to 24 months	24 to 30 months	30 months to 3 years	3 to 4 years	4 to 5 years	Corporal punishment prohibited in all circumstances	Liability insurance required	Number of children allowed in home	Corporal punishment prohibited in all circumstances	Liability insurance required
Alabama	6:1	6:1	6:1	10:1	10:1	20:1	20:1	√		6	√	
Alaska	5:1	6:1	6:1	10:1	10:1	10:1	15:1		√	6		
Arizona	5:1	6:1	6:1	10:1	10:1	15:1	20:1		*	4	†	†
Arkansas	6:1	6:1	9:1	12:1	12:1	15:1	18:1			16		
California	4:1	4:1	4:1	4:1	12:1	12:1	12:1	√		12	√	
Colorado	5:1	5:1	5:1	5:1	8:1	10:1	12:1	√		6	√	
Connecticut	4:1	4:1	4:1	4:1	10:1	10:1	10:1	√		6	√	
Delaware	4:1	7:1	7:1	10:1	10:1	12:1	15:1	√	√	6	√	
DC	4:1	4:1	4:1	8:1	8:1	10:1	15:1			5		
Florida	6:1	8:1	12:1	12:1	15:1	20:1	25:1	√		5	√	
Georgia	7:1	7:1	10:1	12:1	15:1	18:1	20:1	√		6	√	
Hawaii	P	P	P	8:1	16:1	20:1	20:1	√		5	√	
Idaho	12:1	12:1	12:1	12:1	12:1	12:1	12:1			6		
Illinois	4:1	5:1	8:1	8:1	10:1	10:1	20:1	√	√	8		√
Indiana	4:1	5:1	5:1	7:1	10:1	12:1	15:1	√		10		
Iowa	4:1	4:1	4:1	6:1	8:1	12:1	15:1	√		6		
Kansas	3:1	5:1	7:1	7:1	12:1	12:1	14:1	√	√	10		*
Kentucky	6:1	6:1	6:1	10:1	12:1	12:1	14:1	√	√	12	√	√
Louisiana	6:1	8:1	12:1	12:1	14:1	16:1	20:1	√	*	‡	‡	‡
Maine	4:1	5:1	5:1	8:1	10:1	10:1	10:1	√	√	12	√	
Maryland	3:1	3:1	6:1	6:1	10:1	10:1	13:1	√		6	√	
Massachusetts	3:1	4:1	4:1	10:1	10:1	10:1	10:1	√	√	6	√	
Michigan	5:1	9:1	9:1	12:1	12:1	14:1	16:1	√	*	6	√	
Minnesota	4:1	7:1	7:1	7:1	10:1	10:1	10:1	√	√	14	√	
Mississippi	5:1	9:1	12:1	12:1	14:1	16:1	20:1			15		
Missouri	4:1	4:1	8:1	8:1	10:1	10:1	16:1	√		10	√	

P   Prohibited
*   State requires liability insurance for transportation only.
†   State regulates only government-subsidized day care homes.
‡   State does not regulate.

Source: Reprinted with permission of *Parenting Magazine*, September 1988, pp. 72–73. Chart compiled by Amy Binder and Bill Shapiro.

Table 2-2 continued

| | Day Care Centers — Child-to-Staff Ratios | | | | | | | | | Family Day Care Homes | | |
	Ages up to 12 months	12 to 18 months	18 to 24 months	24 to 30 months	30 months to 3 years	3 to 4 years	4 to 5 years	Corporal punishment prohibited in all circumstances	Liability insurance required	Number of children allowed in home	Corporal punishment prohibited in all circumstances	Liability insurance required
Montana	4:1	4:1	4:1	8:1	8:1	10:1	10:1	√	√	6	√	√
Nebraska	4:1	4:1	6:1	6:1	10:1	12:1	12:1	√		8		
Nevada	4:1	6:1	6:1	6:1	7:1	7:1	7:1	√	√	6	√	√
New Hampsh.	4:1	5:1	6:1	6:1	8:1	12:1	15:1	√		6	√	
New Jersey	4:1	4:1	7:1	7:1	10:1	10:1	15:1	√	√	5	‡	‡
New Mexico	6:1	6:1	10:1	10:1	12:1	12:1	15:1	√		12	√	
New York	4:1	4:1	4:1	4:1	6:1	7:1	8:1	√	√	6		
N. Carolina	7:1	7:1	7:1	12:1	12:1	15:1	20:1	√		5	√	
N. Dakota	4:1	4:1	4:1	5:1	5:1	7:1	10:1	√	√	7	√	√
Ohio	5:1	6:1	7:1	8:1	12:1	14:1	14:1			12		
Oklahoma	4:1	6:1	6:1	8:1	12:1	15:1	15:1	√	*	5	√	*
Oregon	4:1	4:1	4:1	10:1	10:1	10:1	15:1	√		5	√	
Pennsylvania	4:1	4:1	5:1	5:1	10:1	10:1	10:1	√	√	6	√	
Rhode Island	4:1	4:1	4:1	4:1	4:1	7:1	10:1	√	√	6	√	
S. Carolina	8:1	8:1	12:1	12:1	15:1	20:1	25:1			6		
S. Dakota	5:1	5:1	5:1	5:1	10:1	10:1	10:1	√	√	12	√	
Tennessee	5:1	7:1	8:1	8:1	10:1	15:1	20:1	√	*	7		*
Texas	5:1	6:1	9:1	11:1	15:1	18:1	22:1			12		
Utah	4:1	4:1	7:1	7:1	15:1	15:1	20:1	√		6	√	
Vermont	4:1	4:1	4:1	5:1	5:1	10:1	10:1	√	√	6	√	√
Virginia	4:1	5:1	5:1	10:1	10:1	12:1	12:1	√	√	9		
Washington	4:1	7:1	7:1	10:1	10:1	10:1	10:1	√	*	6	√	*
W. Virginia	4:1	4:1	4:1	8:1	8:1	10:1	12:1	√	√	7	√	
Wisconsin	4:1	4:1	4:1	6:1	8:1	10:1	13:1	√	√	8	√	√
Wyoming	5:1	5:1	8:1	8:1	10:1	15:1	20:1	√		6	√	

P Prohibited
* State requires liability insurance for transportation only.
† State regulates only government-subsidized day care homes.
‡ State does not regulate.
Source: Reprinted with permission of *Parenting Magazine*, September 1988, pp. 72–73. Chart compiled by Amy Binder and Bill Shapiro.

the food provided; and arrangements for medical care, special equipment, and safety provisions.

Hartley, White, and Yogman (1989) used Massachusetts data to illustrate the difficulty faced by parents who seek quality care for their child with a disability. With a total day care enrollment in 1988 of 94,919 children, only 2,211 slots were allocated to children with special needs, which means that for parents in many parts of the state, it would be very hard to find a suitable placement for their child.

Affordability and quality are two terms that are hard to reconcile in the provision of child care. Young families in which the mother is working are necessarily concerned with finding day care services. They must find care for their children that they can afford, especially those in the lower income brackets. They want care that is high quality, but they are limited in what they can pay. They are forced to settle for what they can get at the price they can pay, which often means a compromise at the child's risk.The fact is that a number of parents can afford no child care at all, or very little—far from what an ideal service would cost.

The United States GAO (1989b, 1990a) has examined the cost implications of high-quality programs for early childhood education. In response to a request by Senator Edward Kennedy in connection with S.123, the "Smart Start" bill, the GAO sent questionnaires to 265 full-day, full-year preschool and early childhood education programs accredited by the National Association for the Education of Young Children, and 208 responded (a 78% response rate). Findings are summarized in Appendix 2-A.

Given the ratio of children to care providers and the need for keeping costs down in order to attract customers, day care centers pay their staff wages or salaries that are far below what should be earned by service providers with appropriate training and skills. (See subsequent discussion of recommended training for purposes of certification.) This leads to difficulty in attracting skilled staff members and contributes to a seemingly perpetual turnover and loss of qualified staff members, who often see no prospect of significantly increased wages in the future. The turnover leads inevitably to a diminished level of quality in the remaining staff as a whole. Of course, the children bear the consequences when the persons in whose care they are placed are at low skill levels.

In describing the need to be flexible in order to find a suitable integrated day care setting, Hartley et al. (1989) pointed out that the challenge to the service delivery team is to find a satisfactory match between the child and the program. Hartley et al. stated that "some disabled children, as well as nondisabled children, thrive in family day care centers and not in large day care centers. The warm, more family-like environment of the family day care center may indeed be the 'least restrictive environment' for the many children" (p. 9).

The integration of moderate to severely handicapped children into integrated day care settings has been evaluated by Templeman, Fredericks, and Udell (1989). They noted that "while 'whole program' placement presents a number of important challenges that must be worked out if it is going to be a quality placement for the special needs student, it also avoids many of the problems associated with partial placement options" (p. 317).

The Council of Chief State School Officers (1988) proposes the following criteria for quality programs of child care:

1. a child development approach that exemplifies what is known about how very young children learn in an environment uniquely fashioned to their needs for physical, emotional, social, and intellectual growth
2. staff prepared for the special field of early childhood education and benefiting from networks and supervision that provide constant renewal
3. adult-child ratios appropriate for the age and needs of the child and meeting standards established in the child development field
4. a length of program day and year and a continuous learning environment that are matched to family need
5. evaluations, both of programs and the progress of individual children, that are based on developmental goals and reflective of the uniqueness of early childhood education

Bailey, Palsha, and Huntington (1990) reported on a telephone survey of a random sample of 20 personnel preparation programs and a mail survey of 49 infancy-focused programs and 70 early childhood-focused programs, all in institutions of higher education offering special education certification. Table 2–3 shows selected data adapted from Bailey et al. and contrasts the average training time for undergraduate versus graduate and infancy versus early childhood programs.

Table 2-3 Mean Hours of Training Time by Program Type

Content Area	Under-graduate	Graduate	Infancy	Early Childhood
Normal infant development	14.0	4.7	33.1	26.9
Family assessment	5.2	7.1	12.4	11.5
Interdisciplinary team process	13.5	15.2	14.9	12.6
Case management	9.3	7.9	8.8	8.2

Source: From "Preservice Preparation of Special Educators to Serve Infants with Handicaps and Their Families" by D. Bailey, S. Palsha, and G. Huntington, 1990, *Journal of Early Intervention, 14* (I), pp. 43-54. Copyright 1990 by Journal of Early Intervention. Adapted by permission.

Bailey and his associates (1990) found that most of the clinical site training time was spent in center-based sites (50.8% for the infant-oriented programs and 60.3% for the early childhood–oriented programs) followed by home-based sites (32.7% and 19.8%, respectively), and relatively small amounts of time at NICU sites (9.7% and 4.9%), developmental evaluation centers (4.2% and 8.9%), and other sites (2.6% and 5.8%). Casting doubt on the notion that clinical practice can be greatly affected by training workshops, they concluded that the quantity of persons receiving formal training needs to rise and that quality and effectiveness of the training needs to be emphasized.

McCollum, McLean, McCartan, and Kaiser (1989) developed recommendations for certification of early childhood special educators. In their view, personnel preparation programs should deal with the following major areas:

1. *Educational foundations*
   Social and philosophical
   Life-span human development and learning
   Professional orientation and development

2. *Foundations of early childhood special education*
   Historical and philosophical basis of early childhood special education
   Child development from birth to five
   Atypical development from birth to five
   Survey of exceptionalities

3. *Methods in early childhood special education*
   Families of young children with special needs
   Assessment of the young child
   Curriculum methods: Birth to two years
   Curriculum methods: Three to five years
   Physical and medical management, including health management
   Environmental and behavior management
   Interdisciplinary and interagency teaming
   Organizational environments for early intervention*

Source: From "Recommendations for Certification of Early Childhood Special Educators" by J. McCollum, M. McLean, K. McCartan, and C. Kaiser, 1989, *Journal of Early Intervention, 13*(3), pp. 202–203. Copyright 1989 by Journal of Early Intervention. Adapted by permission.

Assessing Effectiveness

The question arises as to whether participation in early childhood programs "really helps" the child with special needs. Hartley et al. (1989) cited a paper by Anderson reporting on a longitudinal study on effects of public day care in "high quality" centers in Sweden. According to this study, "Swedish children entering high quality group care prior to age 1 did better on cognitive and socioemotional outcomes at age 8 than children staying at home or entering group care later" (p. 3).

The Early Intervention Research Institute at Utah State University has been examining the efficacy of early intervention with handicapped, at-risk, and disadvantaged children using meta-analysis, a technique that has been controversial. Beauchamp (1989) summarized research findings by White and Casto (1985) and Casto and Mastropieri (1986) pertaining to the handicapped and at-risk as follows:

- Early intervention has moderate immediate benefits for handicapped, at-risk, and disadvantaged children with benefits of one-third to one-half standard deviations in a variety of areas, including IQ, language, and academic achievement. (White & Casto, 1985)

- The question of long term impact of early intervention for handicapped children cannot yet be answered, because so few data are available. (White & Casto, 1985)

- Program intensity/duration is not related to program effectiveness for disadvantaged children. (White and Casto, 1985) However, longer, more intensive programs appear to be more effective for handicapped children than shorter, less intense programs. (Casto & Mastropieri, 1986)

- Programs for handicapped children using parents as sole or major intervenors are no more effective than programs with little parental participation. (Casto & Mastropieri, 1986)

- Although there is a slight advantage for starting disadvantaged children in intervention earlier, few data are available to support a similar advantage for handicapped children. (Casto & Mastropieri, 1986)*

Source: From "Meta-Analysis in Early Childhood Special Education Research" by K. Beauchamp, 1989, *Journal of Early Intervention, 13*(4), p. 378. Copyright 1989 by Journal of Early Intervention. Adapted by permission.

Campbell (1989) has taken the position that quality of services in early intervention is in the eye of the beholder. She suggested that a team consisting of representatives of the family, the staff, and the administration decide on the form and timing of the evaluation. She further suggested the use of the FCLC Quality Indicator Checklist, consisting of 72 items in the following areas:

1. family-centered services
2. curriculum content
3. integrated classroom interactions
4. planning
5. integrated methods
6. child outcomes
7. facilitating strategies
8. team management

FAMILY ROLES

McDonald, Kysela, Siebert, McDonald, and Chambers (1989) conducted a study of parental perspectives concerning a timeline for the transitioning of infants with disabilities into preschool. Twenty-five families were involved in this study; 24 mothers and 6 fathers were interviewed. The children ranged in age from 27 months to 35 months. Summarizing the parents' perspectives, most held to the following opinions:

1. Transition planning should begin 6 months to a year prior to the change in programs.
2. Parents should be involved in planning, including being provided with written program descriptions, tours, meetings with parents whose children attend the school, meetings with teachers, and a chance to examine the curriculum.
3. It is important to avoid surprises when the transition actually takes place.
4. The home teacher should provide follow-up support by visiting the new program in the preschool after the child has started to attend.

Specific steps have been identified that preschool teachers can take to facilitate the difficult transition into school (Hanline, Suchman, & Demmerle, 1989). First, teachers need to recognize parental concerns. Teachers need to put parents at ease and make them feel welcome. Second, parents should be invited to participate. This is especially useful at first, when there is a period of adjustment. Later, the formation of a parent group is helpful. Third, the preschool classroom should be as much like a regular preschool classroom as possible.

This suggests such things as displaying the children's work and providing privacy for the parents in matters relating to the child's Individualized Education Program. Children should feel that they can explore their environment, make choices, express themselves, and solve problems. Fourth, teachers should allow ample time for adjustment to the new situation.

Research on the readiness of developmentally delayed children and normal children to transition into different preschool environments has been summarized by Sainato and Lyon (1989). They suggested that the use of a structured interview can be a cost-effective way of gathering information about the receiving educational environment—information about the schedule of activities, the type of instruction, the grouping of children, and the behavioral demands of regular preschool environments.

Hamblin-Wilson and Thurman (1990) examined parental satisfaction and involvement in the transition from early intervention into kindergarten in Philadelphia. While there was a low response rate to their questionnaire, casting some doubt on the generality of the findings, selected findings are of interest. Sixty-eight percent of the parents visited the receiving school, and 58% were participants in program planning. Parents who were most satisfied with the transition process were more educated and believed they had had more support.

A considerable body of research exists on the relationships among family variables, child development in Home Start and Head Start programs, and long-term effects in educational settings. Peters (1988) analyzed Head Start's influence on parental and child competence. According to Peters, the research substantiates the potential of short-term benefits of regular participation for low-income children, and to some degree for handicapped children on some measures of cognitive and social development. Also, longitudinal analyses document the intermediate and long-term effects of Head Start and similar early childhood intervention programs: "It appears that early intervention has a strong and continuing effect on children's ability to cope with the basic demands of schooling right through the completion of high school" (p. 73).

Gallimore, Weisner, Kaufman, and Bernheimer (1989) applied family ecology theory to the study of family behaviors and roles for developmentally delayed children. They found that the "sustainability" of everyday activities is a better predictor of child and family outcome than is the measured "stimulation level" or quality of the home environment. In other words, daily routines that are as hassle-free as possible and clear roles for family members to play contribute to positive outcomes.

Whether families are effective or not is influenced in part by the kind of help they receive *apart* from those services provided to the child with disabilities. For example, there is a mixed body of literature that suggests that the siblings of the child with disabilities may present a special problem to the extent that they exhibit negative feelings toward the brother or sister with a disability (Johnson

& Murphy, 1990). Feelings of anger, embarrassment, resentment, jealousy, fear, guilt, and sadness and a perception of being overburdened are different forms of negative feelings that the sibling may feel and need help in overcoming. The same literature also indicates that other siblings can develop intense feelings of joy and pride in the accomplishments of their brother or sister, or that feelings may fluctuate depending on family experiences.

Fuqua, Hegland, and Karas (1985) studied the linkages between preschool teachers and parents and found that teachers were more satisfied with parent involvement if parents were viewed as capable of interacting with their children in productive ways. Parent attendance at meetings was positively related to parents' abilities to "take the lead" in interactions with teachers. Communication between parents and teachers was considered to be at its best when it was direct, informal, and personal in nature.

Parents and service organization staff do not always interact effectively. They often interact in inconsistent and unplanned ways that may or may not be helpful to the child.

Winget (1990) cited two sources as providing useful guidelines for family services:

1. *Guidelines and Recommended Practices for the Individualized Family Service Plan*, National Early Childhood Technical Assistance System (1983): Ten principles for family-focused services

2. *Early Intervention Tailor Made*, L. Kjerland (1986): comparison of traditional child-focused services and family-focused services at intake, in assessment, in the Individualized Education Plan, and in intervention

It is clear that families of handicapped children need to rely on a network of support systems across the life span (Dunst, Trivette, & Cross, 1986; Espinosa & Shearer, 1986; Fewell, 1986; Mallory, 1986; Stagg & Catron, 1986). Unfortunately, support systems are not always available, nor are they always as helpful as one might wish.

Rimland (1985) is the parent of a child with disabilities and the author of *The Furies and the Flame*, a book that describes her struggle to rear her son. Speaking to attendees at a convention on learning disabilities, she expressed the anger and frustration that parents often feel in seeking appropriate services for their children.

> Special parenthood made me inherit an array of social workers, administrators, teachers, doctors, psychologists, counselors, and volunteers who all know better than I do what is good for my handicapped offspring. . . . If I want the best that life has to offer anyone for my child, don't shred my dream, don't say I am "rejecting" of his limitations.

Parents of children with disabilities understandably are concerned for their welfare and future. In giving their love and attention, many parents "do" for their children, and in so doing lose an opportunity to teach the child that he or she can accomplish many things on his or her own. This is not to say that children with disabilities should not receive extra attention, but rather that their parents should recognize opportunities that can help them test what they can do independently. The intent is that they discover themselves and reach the maximum potential of functioning that their disability allows.

Interviews with successful adults with disabilities frequently point to their childhood and their parents' support as an important contribution to their independence as adults. Consistently, what they say is that they were challenged by their parents to try things on their own. It might have been as simple as learning how to get up after falling, or as complex as learning how to take responsibility for a household duty.

Parents may feel comfortable teaching their child basic survival skills, but they may feel ill-equipped to support "school-like" learning.

The Center for the Study of Reading (no date) suggested 10 ways that parents can help their preschool children become "good readers." The suggestions, stemming from a report of the National Commission on Reading, are not restricted to the preschool years but apply as well to any of the years in which the child is encountering and becoming familiar with the printed word. They include

- reading aloud to the child
- encouraging independent reading
- helping the child acquire a wide range of knowledge
- encouraging thinking about events
- talking about their experiences
- providing the preschool child with writing materials
- encouraging the watching of television with educational value
- monitoring how much television is watched
- monitoring school performance
- continuing your own involvement and encouraging leisure reading

Whatever the activity, it can be facilitated by parents through a combination of positive attitude, patience, and support. From the children's perspective, if they perceive that the parents believe in them and expect them to develop new skills, they are much more likely to do so than if they are protected from possible failure. In effect, the youth with a disability needs to develop a sense of self-awareness and self-actualization that says, "I can and I will."

The long-term result is a young adult who is ready to make the transition from secondary education into higher education, accepting the challenges of further academic study, or to enter into the mainstream of community life and employment, participating fully and actively within the limitations imposed by the disability. In either case, the essential characteristic is that the young person with a disability is not passive or indifferent but has learned to be actively involved in his or her own life.

Obviously, there will be disappointments and mistakes, but the patience and support of the parents mean a great deal to children with a disability and play a major part in helping youngsters recognize the difference between what they cannot do and what they cannot *yet* do. They need to learn that with practice and persistence, they can improve on their present status. They *will* succeed if they are *determined* to succeed.

Parents as Consumers and Planners

Barbara Bush is well known for her support of programs to promote literacy. Less well known is her awareness that learning the basic skills of reading and writing depends on the quality of parent participation and the help of others. Referring to the experiences of the President, herself, and their son Neil, she said, "We found how frustrating and challenging a learning disability can be, and how important it is to have specialized help for learning disabled children and their families" (Bush, 1989, p. 1).

The California State Board of Education has stated, "The inescapable fact is that consistently high levels of student success are unlikely without long-term family support and reinforcement of the school's curriculum goals" (Winget, 1989/1990). Keying on that premise, the State Department of Education in California developed a policy for parent involvement that establishes six areas in which educational programs should involve parents:

1. parenting skills
2. learning strategies
3. coordinated community services access
4. school-home communication
5. school instructional support with training
6. decision making

In the California plan, the first four of these areas are to be addressed in the proposed IFSP. Patrick Campbell, the director of special education, envisions the IFSP as a "unifying piece" (Winget, 1990, p. 1) for all the individualized plans—Individualized Education Program, Individualized Program Plan, and Individualized Transition Plan.

In thinking about parent involvement with the early development and education of the child, it is natural that the mother-child dyad comes to mind. In view of the birthing process and the bonding that takes place in the first few months following birth, this is not surprising. However, there is also a strong argument for involving the father in the development of at-risk children, such as those that are premature, retarded, or otherwise handicapped (Bristol & Gallagher, 1986). Parke (1986) pointed out the greater stress on parents of these children and the greater need for care, whether it is provided in a mother-child dyad, a father-child dyad, or a triad of all three.

Yogman (1984) found that over the first 18 months, fathers of preterm infants engaged in more caregiving tasks than fathers of full-term infants. There is some evidence that involvement by fathers of retarded children is low. However, with nonretarded handicapped children their participation is relatively high, if the offspring is a boy (Tallman, 1965). A more recent investigation by Gallagher, Scharfman, and Bristol (1984) did not show role differences for the mother or father of developmentally delayed children when compared with those of the parents of nonhandicapped children.

What is the reaction of the parents of handicapped and of nonhandicapped children to preschool mainstreaming? Green and Stoneman (1989), citing Bailey and Winton (1987) indicated that parents of handicapped children generally favor preschool mainstreaming. These parents feel that the benefits of integration are "exposure to the real world" and the chance to be accepted in the community, but they also see possible drawbacks in the instructional effectiveness in these settings, particularly as regards "the level of training of preschool teachers and day care staff in issues related to the mainstreaming of handicapped children." The attitudes of parents of nonhandicapped children in mainstream settings seem to reflect the extent to which their own child receives a quality preschool education.

Parents as Advocates

When the person with disabilities is a minor, parents or guardians play a key advocacy role. Parents practice advocacy when they actively represent, in their view, the best interests of their child. In the context of disability, advocacy can be defined as the process of being proactive on behalf of a person with a disability, disability group, or all persons with disabilities in areas where rights and opportunities are not fully available. Advocacy has been a major contributor to all the major advances in public awareness of the needs, capacities, and rights of persons with disabilities in the last 30 years. Advocacy is not radicalism but rather an affirmation of the rights of every citizen. It is an effort to bring to a higher level of social consciousness specific areas in which change should be made.

Parental advocacy is typified by several kinds of actions on behalf of their children:

- If the child is in infancy or early childhood, the parent acts as an advocate by noting any unusual delays or imbalances in the development of the child and by seeking the professional assistance mandated under PL 99-457, the Education of the Handicapped Act Amendments of 1986. By 1991 each state should have put in place a statewide comprehensive service delivery system for handicapped children from birth to 5 years of age. Parents can and will play an important role in each state as this comprehensive plan is being formulated.

- If the child is enrolled in a program run by the school district, the parent can serve as an advocate on behalf of the child by actively participating during school-initiated meetings convened to approve an Individualized Educational Program (IEP), which guides the instructional program for the child during each school year. In cases where there is disagreement, the parents are entitled to appeal school-based decisions. For example, they might insist on school services appropriate to their child's capacity to benefit from those services.

- Parents can become involved in the monitoring process that takes place periodically when the Office of Special Education Programs (OSEP) periodically reviews the states' implementation of the Education for All Handicapped Act (PL 94-142) (Toombs, 1989b). They can do this directly by informing OSEP about areas of special concern in implementation of the state plan, by proposing schools and state-operated programs for on-site visits, by encouraging OSEP to hold on-site hearings, by encouraging parents to attend any public hearings, by commenting on matters addressed in the hearings, by requesting a copy of the Corrective Action Plan (CAP) that directs any needed corrections, and by analyzing and monitoring the state's response.

- Parents have also played a central role in lobbying legislators on behalf of bills introduced to address the needs of persons with disabilities. They have been widely credited not only with getting major legislation passed (such as PL 94-142) but also with forestalling the cessation of existing legislation when it comes time for renewal.

Toombs (1989a), writing as the Chairperson for Advocacy Services for the Association for Children and Adults with Learning Disabilities, indicated that being assertive (not passive or aggressive) is the key to preserving the rights of the parent and child. Toombs stated that assertiveness is

- knowing and understanding your rights.
- knowing and understanding your child's rights.
- asking questions whenever you need clarification.
- repeating a question until it is satisfactorily answered.
- insisting that all persons who should be at an IEP meeting are actually there. This includes someone who has the authority to make decisions.
- keeping a paper trail of all communication regarding your child's ed-uca-tion, sending copies to the appropriate people, and requesting copies of school records and documentation.
- monitoring to be sure that your child's IEP is followed.
- knowing that you are a full partner in planning your child's education program and being treated as such.
- letting people know that you intend to resolve issues and are willing to go to due process as a last resort if necessary.
- learning all you can about your child's disability and needs, strengths and weaknesses.
- knowing about available resources and using them.
- knowing who the key people are, finding out the right person to talk to, and trying all avenues.
- praising and thanking people when appropriate.
- above all, NEVER SAY, "I'M JUST A PARENT!"*

SPECIAL ISSUES SURROUNDING AT-RISK CHILDREN

The term "at-risk" has taken on a good deal of importance due to its use in legislation and its association with the onset of poor health, disabling conditions, and low functional performance. We will discuss some of the important issues surrounding the at-risk child. At the same time, we know that there are other considerations that need to be studied, such as environments in the home that clearly put a young child at risk of injury or death.

Source: From "Being an Effective Advocate in the Educational System" by M. Toombs, 1989, *ACLD Newsbriefs, 24*(4): 11. Copyright 1989 by Association for Children and Adults with Learning Disabilities. Adapted by permission.

Defining "At-Risk"

In commenting on a report, *Status of the States' Progress Toward Developing a Definition for Developmentally Delayed as Required by P.L. 99-457, Part H* (released by the Carolina Policy Studies Program at the University of North Carolina), the Division for Early Childhood (1989) in the Council for Exceptional Children concluded that there are substantial differences across the 28 states studied in terms of which infants and toddlers are considered eligible for service. The reasons for this disparity among the states include

- Differing criteria: Different states will use different deviations from the norm to establish a cutoff of eligibility. The amount of delay used in assessment procedures may be as much as 50% or as little as 15% below the norm.
- Single versus multiple indicators: Some states will accept eligibility on the basis of a delay in a single developmental area, while others will require evidence of delay in two or more areas.
- Differing definitions of "at-risk": In terms of biological factors, the states have identified 53 different criteria (e.g., prematurity less than 32 weeks, ventilator dependency). In terms of environmental factors, the states have identified 36 criteria (e.g., parental substance abuse, poor nutrition).

Preterm Infants and Environmental Stimulation

One of the most critical periods in a child's life is the period preceding and immediately following birth. If the child is full-term, a "normal" period of fetal development has had a chance to occur. If the mother has been exercising self-restraint in terms of avoiding the use of drugs, alcohol, and smoking and has been eating in a nutritionally sound manner, the newborn has had a healthy, natural environment in which to develop.

When the child is premature, the intervention of a neonatal intensive care unit (NICU) replaces the normal development pattern with an environment in which the external environment can be manipulated to simulate (albeit imperfectly) the developmental stages through which the fetus progresses: vestibular, cutaneous, olfactory, auditory, and visual (Turkewitz & Kenney, 1985).

Heriza and Sweeney (1990) thoroughly and carefully reviewed the literature on theoretical models of infant development and clinical studies of neuromotor and developmental intervention for preterm infants in NICUs. Although extensive research has been carried out in recent years, it varied widely in the extent to which it conformed with rigorous experimental design. Appendices to the Heriza and Sweeney article review in detail 20 of these studies, grouped according to whether they were infant intervention studies, infant/mother intervention studies, or mother-training studies.

These studies include assessments of effects with unimodal stimulation, tactile kinesthetic stimulation, and multimodal stimulation. Most of the unimodal and multimodal studies appeared to enhance the infants' movement at least on a short-term basis, but several studies showed no difference at 6, 8, and 24 months. With respect to studies aimed at enhancing development, Heriza and Sweeney (1990) state that "the results relating to enhancing development seemed to be confirmed by the number and quality of the studies. In addition to having direct impact on the infant, these changes may also have enduring impact on the parents" (p. 2).

In reflecting on this research base, Heriza and Sweeney (1990) concluded that the interaction of environment and the infant is dynamic and central. They suggest that

1. the NICU environment must be assessed in terms of how it affects the infants
2. intervention programs should be made contingent on the infant's responses and tailored to reflect the infant's neuromotor, neurobehavioral, musculoskeletal, and physiological needs
3. parents and staff should be trained in perceiving infants' behavioral states and cues

Gottwald and Thurman (1990) reviewed the studies on parent-infant interaction in the NICU and noted that most studies have focused on the mother. Fathers tend to talk less and hang back from contact; their infants respond differently to them. Parents with a child in the NICU are understandably in a state of stress. If they receive family and social supports, they tend to participate more effectively in interventions. Importantly, it has been shown that parents can learn how to read the infant's subtle signals and act accordingly.

Substance Abuse

Medical evidence now shows that the effects of substance abuse are not only injurious to the person who is addicted and to the occasional user but will damage a fetus in a pregnant woman. Specifically, the effects of drugs on infants are many and varied, producing births where the child is at risk of disability or death. Van Dyke and Fox (1990) reviewed the effects of alcohol, cocaine, and phencyclidine hydrochloride (PCP) in a number of research studies:

1. Alcohol
   - In a study of 11 patients with fetal alcohol syndrome, a 10-year follow-up showed two dead, eight with growth deficiency and dysmorphic features, and one who could not be found.
   - Studies of the educational impact show relationships to learning disability (short attention span, distractibility, hyperactivity).

2. Cocaine
   - In a study of 40 infants, "the babies were smaller than most newborns, had abnormal brain wave patterns, and neurologic signs of irritability and poor caretaker interaction" (p. 161).
   - There was a reduction in birthweight and an increased stillbirth rate.
   - Combined exposure to narcotics and cocaine resulted in growth retardation and other growth abnormalities.
   - Eleven of 12 newborns showed abnormal visual evoked responses, with some showing them until 4 to 6 months of life.

3. PCP
   - Twelve infants were fearful; showed sensitivity to touch and environmental sounds, increased muscle tone, and abnormal eye movements; and at 9 months were uncoordinated in fine motor movements.
   - Jitteriness, hypertonicity, and vomiting were observed in exposed neonates.

According to Tyner (1989), staff at the National Institute on Drug Abuse and the drug abuse treatment unit of the District of Columbia General Hospital have compiled a list of these effects:

Cocaine abuse can produce
- fetal drug dependence
- fetal hyperactivity
- premature separation of the placenta from the uterine wall
- strokes
- neurobehavioral dysfunction in the newborn
- sudden infant death syndrome
- increased incidence of spontaneous abortion

Cannabis (marijuana) abuse can produce
- reduced blood flow to the fetus

- abnormally prolonged or shortened labor and delivery
- low birthweight
- small head circumference and body weight
- increased incidence of stillbirth
- meconium staining (fetal stool material escapes into the amniotic fluid surrounding the fetus)

Amphetamine/methamphetamine can produce
- congenital defects of the heart, eye, and central nervous system
- withdrawal syndrome
- increased preterm delivery and infant deaths

PCP and similar drugs can produce
- withdrawal symptoms
- agitation, rapid changes in consciousness, bizarre eye movements, sleeplessness (extending to age 1 or 2)
- meconium staining
- respiratory distress
- brain and head malformations
- increased risk of prematurity, low birthweights

Depressants (barbiturates, tranquilizers) can produce
- congenital malformation
- floppy infant syndrome (sucking difficulty, lethargy, defective muscle tone or tension)
- withdrawal syndrome
- decreased fetal movement
- breathing difficulties
- lethal drug overdose, independent of the mother's drug status*

In light of this evidence, the widespread national attention being given to prevention of disability is fully warranted. Quality of life is not an illusion to be gained through transitory, chemically induced "highs," nor is it to be gained at the expense of the next generation of children. They are not at fault, but they are unquestionably at risk both mentally and physically.

Source: Adapted with permission from Health Scene, a publication of Marshall Hospital, Placerville, CA.

Child Abuse

What constitutes child abuse? Punishment of a child and abuse of a child are not the same, yet the difference between them is mainly of degree and cultural standards. In Sweden, a parent who slaps a child can be imprisoned for a month (Zeigert, 1983), but in the United States it is more likely to be considered as one of the parents' options for controlling their children's behavior.

Although it can be argued that any child abuse is too much, it is reported that the incidence rate of severe abuse is decreasing, at least partly due to public education on the matter (Steinmetz, 1988a). It is a far cry from what was typical of the year 1646 in colonial America, when a child's persistent refusal to obey his or her parents was sufficient cause to be put to death under the direction of the court (Bremner, 1970). Nevertheless, where child abuse exists in today's society, it is not an isolated event but rather tends to be a pattern that the child must endure.

The ages at which child abuse seems to occur most frequently are early childhood and adolescence. Wittenberg (1971) found that physical punishment had been used with 41% of babies under 6 months and 87% of children under 2. The American Humane Association (1982) found that children between the ages of 10 and 18 constituted 36% of the reported abuse cases.

Child abuse has been widely recognized as a traumatizing influence on the child and a negative influence on social adjustment as the child matures. Steinmetz (1988b) has cited a body of literature linking violence toward children with later manifestations of violence by the child when he or she becomes an adult, such as murder (including assassinations and parental killings), rape, and assault. While the rate of abuse of their parents by adult children is 1 in 400 for the population as a whole, it is 200 in 400 in those cases where the parent abused the child as an adolescent. Violence toward children has also been linked to the development of a split personality (Schreiber, 1973).

Children can suffer from causes other than direct violence. McLeod (1990), in reporting on a study of the Select Committee on Youth and Families, put an international perspective on the plight of American children. Infant mortality rates in the United States are at 10 deaths per 1000 births (5 in Japan and 25 in the Soviet Union). The United States and Australia had the highest child poverty rates (17% in 1979, but almost 20% by 1988). Among developed nations, children in the United States are more likely to be in a family that breaks up due to divorce and are at highest risk for being reared in single-parent homes.

It is evident that much remains to be improved in the social environment for children. At the same time, we must start with each individual child's present status, however fragile his or her condition may be, and work from there.

IDENTIFYING NEEDS AND BUILDING ON STRENGTHS

A major task, which parents are often ill-equipped to perform, is the assessment of children's developmental needs. For some disabilities, the needs are obvious from birth (or even earlier). But if adults do not realize how the child's development differs from what is expected, it is easy for them to miss the signs that signal a need for intervention. Further, it is difficult to know what to do in the intervention if one lacks prior experience in similar situations.

A number of specialists have reviewed the medical aspects of 39 of the major disorders for children in the birth to 3 years age range (Blackman, 1989; Ensher & Clark, 1986). Curriculum materials for infants, toddlers, and preschoolers with special needs have been designed to span a number of domains of development. Curricula at the early childhood levels need to link assessment and intervention closely (Bagnato, Neisworth, & Munson, 1989). The Carolina Curriculum for Handicapped Infants and Infants at Risk (Johnson-Martin, Jens, & Attermeier, 1986) deals with 24 subdomains of development; the Carolina Curriculum for Preschoolers with Special Needs (Johnson-Martin, Attermeier, & Hacker, 1990) covers five traditional domains (cognition, communication, social adaptation, fine motor, gross motor) and over 20 subdomains.

The Washington State Department of Social Services Birth to Six Project, with a grant from the Office of Special Education and Rehabilitation Services, developed the Developmental Wheel, a tool for prescreening children for vision, hearing, and development problems, and made it widely available. The wheel is organized around observable actions of the child and is organized in nine time frames: birth to 3 months, 3 to 6 months, 6 to 12 months, 12 to 18 months, 18 months to 2 years, 2 to 3 years, 4 to 5 years, and 5 to 6 years. The activities to be observed typically occur at some point in the time frames. Designed as a tool for "anyone who works with children," it is expected that parents, child care providers, case workers, and preschool staff will all find it helpful in monitoring the child's development.

Neuromuscular Development

There is substantial agreement that a child whose movement and activity level are restricted will not develop normally. The reverse is also true—children who are not developing normally can benefit (albeit modestly in most cases) from a program of exercise and stimulation. Therapeutic intervention may begin in the neonatal intensive care unit with preterm infants, or it may be instituted during infancy or early childhood, depending on the individual case.

Heriza and Sweeney (1990) described neuromotor and developmental interventions in hospital and hospital-home studies. At the neonatal stage positive effects on vestibular development have been noted from interventions that mimic life in the womb—motorized hammocks or rocking waterbeds. Tactile-kinesthetic stimulation (stroking) has been shown to be related to better head control in pull-to-sit situations and greater hand-to-mouth ability. Visual and tactile stimulation during feeding had a significant effect on motor scale scores after 6 months. (A number of these interventions have shown a delay period before the positive effects of intervention are evident.)

An important element of neuromuscular intervention is timing it to fit with developmental stages. Heriza and Sweeney (1990) stated, "Even though cross-modal stimulation is important, the timing of such stimulation is crucial as the age and health of the infant influence the infant's ability to handle sensory information" (p. 37).

Building Awareness of Self and Others

Early in life, from infancy through childhood, the youngster with a disability needs to be exposed to social relationships both within and outside of the family unit. It is through these social relationships and attempts at skill development that the child will develop an awareness of self in relation to others. The core of social interaction is dependent on the family, and the outcome of this exposure depends on how the family frames the interaction.

Clearly, if social experiences are limited (usually by perceptions of the parents that there is no apparent benefit), minimal self-awareness will result. If social experiences are largely inward, such as direction giving, the child may form impressions of social interaction that cast him or her in a passive role. If social experiences are deliberately framed to encourage two-way interaction, the child can learn that his or her own communication influences the communication and actions of others. Awareness of self grows from repeated experiences, whether they are all successful or not. The child learns what works and what doesn't work, what he or she can and cannot do, and what receives positive or negative reactions from others.

As young children with disabilities enter the school years, their interaction with others may be constrained by the level of their disability, because that will often determine the setting in which they receive their education. The law calls for assignment to the least-restrictive environment, but that does not ensure that the social environment in the least-restrictive setting will lead to positive experiences. It should be kept in mind that the exhibited behaviors of persons with disabilities (like persons without them) are not simply a consequence of their own developmental level or skill level but are influenced by the way that others treat them or are perceived to treat them.

It is important to remember that in the early preschool years, it is extremely difficult for children with disabilities to build self esteem and gain competence if they are overprotected and never get the chance to try (and practice) new things.

Normalization of Contact with Others

According to Bailey and McWilliam (1990), the normalization of early intervention is something greater than "mainstreaming" or the integration of children that do not have disabilities with those that do. To them, normalization involves using the "least intrusive and most normal strategies" to achieve effective child development. This involves an examination of the environments in which learning takes place, the teaching strategies that are used, and the nature of services to families. They suggest that program quality in early childhood depends on dual criteria: effectiveness of service delivery and normalization.

Mainstreaming, however, is a more commonly used term and has been applied in the context of preschool environments where the child with disabilities is placed in a program in which the primary focus is on service to nondisabled children (Odom & McEvoy, 1990). There is no question under the law (PL 94-142 and PL 99-457) of entitlement to least restrictive services, though the interpretation of "appropriate" education intervention has sometimes varied substantially in different court decisions (Turnbull & Turnbull, 1990).

Very important to the concept of preschool mainstreaming is the way in which children with and without disabilities interact. Guralnick (1990b) stated that developing positive peer relations and friendships must be a central theme in the implementation of mainstreaming. A number of problems have been documented in achieving this interaction, such as difficulties in group play, atypical developmental patterns, and an inability to initiate friendship-related contacts with others. It remains to be learned how deficits shown by the child with a disability can best be accommodated in the context of preschool mainstreaming.

LEARNING HOW TO LEARN

Anyone closely observing a normally developing child is invariably fascinated by the aptitude for learning that it exhibits. For example, parents notice when the child begins to mimic speech and create intelligible communication—first a meaningful cry, then a sounded-out mumble, then a word, then several words. Parents usually take great pride in this accomplishment by the child but give themselves relatively little credit for having patiently repeated terms to the child for an indefinite period beforehand. In a contrasting example, no one intentionally "teaches" the child to exhibit behaviors that can be compared to a primitive form of psychological manipulation, such as baiting or badgering a parent until the parent responds (Pavlovian style) to the child's demand, but it is not too hard to observe these patterns of behavior developing in children. In yet another example, the child somehow learns the "looks" and behaviors of parents, siblings, and other frequently seen persons, to the extent necessary to be able to reliably "select" them in preference to a stranger even though they may have been staring at the stranger for some time.

What does the child do to develop in this way? How does he or she learn these things? A three-step sequence of events involving interaction with the child is central to early learning:

- Cues are present in the environment that attract the child's attention and help him or her to distinguish critical (functional) elements of the environment.
- The child initiates overt actions in response to those cues, which confirm the nature of the environmental stimulus or provoke a reciprocating response from the outside source.
- The cue-response reaction is repeated until patterning (early learning) is established.

Attention and Discrimination of Cues

Children notice things. They notice things they want, and they notice things they want to avoid. If they do not notice things (e.g., fail to reach for food, fail to turn in response to loud sounds from something out of their line of sight), they may have a sensory deficit. If the sensory system is functional (it may be malfunctioning in some ways, as in colorblindness, and still be functional for purposes of learning), attention should be given to developing the child's awareness of particular cues in the environment and the patterning of his or her skills of differentiation and discrimination.

An infant reacts involuntarily to a bath that is too hot or too cold. An infant automatically opens its mouth when it has been stimulated around the lips with an object—including its own hand or other object. A toddler "picks up" on the tones in voices. He or she learns to associate angry tones with physical punishment and soothing tones with caresses and feeding.

A child in a crib may find the immediate environment to be relatively barren of stimulation; mildly stimulating, inviting the child to reach for, observe, or hear stimuli; or a frantic place in which overstimulation and distraction interfere with the child's rest periods and meaningful play. How the child functions in the environment says something about the environment as well as about the child.

When children first begin to crawl or walk, they want to explore the environment. They don't automatically differentiate the things they can and cannot touch. They see them and they want to reach for them, without any inkling of what they will experience when they do touch them. They await an external cue to learn the difference—a candle will burn them, a parent will say no (or physically react) when a cherished or breakable item is approached. If the reaction is delayed until after the touching event, one chain of cause-effect learning takes place, but if the reaction is anticipatory, as when the parent says no before the touching takes place, a different cause-effect sequence occurs. Children are confused and do not learn well when cause-effect relationships are inconsistently applied.

As children move into the early childhood stages, they begin to associate cues at more complex levels. They learn, for example, that a certain storybook is present and used when a parent tells a bedtime story. They discover that listening to the story prolongs the time before the parent leaves the room and the light is turned out. They also learn that it is a time for touching, a time for concentrated parent attention, and, eventually, that certain words and pictures will be described or expressed in certain ways. They "read along" before they know the words. They learn to discriminate the words as they read along.

The importance of these natural learning opportunities is brought into focus when we place a child with disabilities in the situation. For example, it is clear that early language experiences of the type just described are not readily shared by children who are deaf. This does not mean that they won't learn to read but rather that this strategy and this context for reading are likely to be inappropriate. How the parent deals with this barrier depends to a very great extent on the timing and nature of early intervention assistance and training that the parent receives.

Self-Expression and Communication

As children normally develop, they first begin to move and "communicate" without conscious effort. They kick their legs and move their arms in reflex movements; they howl in response to constipation, discomfort, or hunger. As they begin to consciously reach for objects, such as the milk bottle or a soft toy, they are doing so in response to a need and an awareness of the presence of the object in the environment.

If the child feels the need, but the object is not in the environment, he or she may initiate an act of "reaching" by crying or other outward expression. If the need is basic, such as for hunger or sleep, the crying is unintentional at first but becomes intentional in subsequent years. If the need is not basic, the child will consciously and consistently initiate physical or oral reaching to the extent that a pattern has been established relating the need and the consequence in a cause-effect way.

The exception to this last statement is an important one. If there is no pattern established, child-initiated expression is exploratory or simply a matter of release. That is, it is a form of "looking around" or probing the environment, a kind of "taking stock," or it is done as a form of self-fulfillment, making sounds or singing just to hear them.

Overt child expression in an unpatterned situation can be thought of as an early form of curiosity. If it leads to something, and does so repeatedly, a cause-effect relationship is built, and a new "useful" behavior is learned.

Unfortunately, parent-child interaction is not always orderly and purposeful. Sometimes, with certain characteristics and disabilities of the child, the patterning process can be elusive.

Parents of hyperactive children can be overwhelmed with their children's expression and communication demands, while parents of autistic children can be desperate for this kind of interaction. In either case, the best chance for normalization is a pattern of prompting and response that is consistently applied in accordance with professional guidance.

We know that infancy and early childhood are critical times for children with disabilities. If their needs are recognized early and intervention takes place in consistent, professionally approved ways, children with disabilities may reasonably be expected to perform much better in school environments than if they are left to develop or "grow out of the behavior" on their own.

Appendix 2-A

Survey Findings from a
Government Accounting Office Study of
Early Childhood Education Programs*

- *Representation of handicapped children*: Almost 70% of the 208 centers en-rolled about 900 children. The number attending a given center ranged from 1 to 78. A variety of handicapping conditions were being served:

Handicapping Condition	Percent of Centers Serving
Developmentally delayed	54%
Speech impaired	50
Emotionally disturbed	31
Orthopedically impaired	17
Visually Impaired	16
Hearing impaired or deaf	16
Mental retardation	15
Multiple handicaps	11
Deafness and blindness	1
Other health impaired	1

- *Average annual cost per child*: With in-kind donations, the average was $4200; without them, it was $4800. Urban centers cost $1250 more than rural centers. Nonreligious centers cost $1365 more than religious centers. Centers serving no children of low-income families cost $500 to $900 more than centers that did serve them, primarily due to rent and salary differenc-es. Overall, the average monthly fee for a 4-year-old was $304. In centers where the fees were adjusted according to family size and income, the aver-age was much less (e.g., $34 per month for each child in families with four children and a maximum annual income of $8000).

Source: Early Childhood Education: What Are the Costs of High-Quality Programs? U.S. Gen-eral Accounting Office (GAA-HRD-90-43BR) January, 1990.

- *Average annual salary for directors of programs*: The average figure was $24,340. Their average number of years of experience was 14.6.
- *Salaries of teachers*: The average was $14,100, though urban centers were at $14,400 and rural centers were at $11,100. Regionally, the Northeast was at $15,500, the Midwest at $14,100, the South at $14,200, and the West at $12,900. Compared to public school teachers and private school teachers, the salaries of early childhood teachers lag substantially on an annualized basis (see Table 2-A1).
- *Years of teachers' experience*: The average was 6.3 years. Fifty-two percent had bachelor's degrees, 10% had an associate degree, 20% had some college, and 8% had high school diplomas or less.
- *Salaries of teacher aides*: The annual average was $10,219. They averaged 3.3 years of experience. Twelve percent had bachelor's degrees, 10% had an associate degree, 38% had some college, 30% had a high school diploma, and 8% had some high school. Overall, 48% had some college training.
- *Ages served by centers*: Infants were served in 33% of the centers, toddlers in 45%, 2-year-olds in 81%, 3- and 4-year-olds in 99%, 5-year-olds in 95%, and children over 5 in 55% of the centers.
- *Group size and staff-child ratio*: Average group size was 14 for all age groups and 17 for 4-year-olds. Overall, the average staff-child ratio was 8:1, with a slightly higher 9:1 for 4-year-olds.
- *Relationship between costs and changes in staff-child ratios*: A 10% increase in center size resulted in an 8% increase in costs. A reduction in the ratio (11:1 to 10:1) raised the operating costs by 4.6%.

Table 2-A1 Teacher Salaries in Early Childhood (EC) Education

Experience	EC Teacher	Public	Private
5 years or less	$14,460	$23,452	$16,267
6–10 years	$15,324	$27,617	$19,348
11–15 years	$17,582	$32,857	$21,904
16–20 years	$16,982	$36,961	$24,111
21–25 years	$18,448	$38,540	$22,078

Chapter 3

Educating the
Individual with Disabilities

1. Life Stage: The School Years
   - Federal Initiatives and Programs
   - Coordination of Educational Programming
   - Definitions of Disabilities
   - Parent Involvement and Advocacy
   - Attitude Barriers Presented by Others
2. Special Issues Concerning Children and Youth with Disabilities
   - Smoothing the Transition into Formal Education
   - Least Restrictive Environments and Mainstreaming
   - The Regular Education Initiative
   - Categorical and Noncategorical Programs
   - Youth at Risk
   - Multicultural and Language Problems
   - Accommodation in Assessment
     - ❏ Adaptive Testing and the Assessment of Educational Outcomes
   - Teacher Preparation for Social Skill Instruction
3. Developing Competence in Functional Skills
   - Establishing Readiness and Setting Goals
   - Basic Enabling Skills
   - Academic and Vocational Skills
   - Social-Employability Skills
     - ❏ Social Skills
     - ❏ Employability Skills
   - Responsibility and Independent Living Skills
4. Using Technology to Advantage
   - Computer-Based Instruction
   - Using Other Technologies

5. Identifying Vocational and Career Interests
   • Awareness of Career and Employment Alternatives
   • Intellectual and Physical Capacity
6. Preparation for Transition from the School Environment
   • Training and Placement Strategies
   • Community Living and Advocacy
     ❏ Community Living
     ❏ Advocacy
   • Predicting Needed Support for Persons with Disabilities
   • Postsecondary Education and Disability Services Offices
   • Gaining Experience in Competitive Employment
   • Follow-up

LIFE STAGE: THE SCHOOL YEARS

From a developmental point of view, children continuously learn, but at different rates. Society has accepted the responsibility for formal education for children, and their entry into a school environment is based largely on their chronological age and readiness. Traditionally, education is characterized as starting at kindergarten, but increasingly school districts are assuming responsibility for children at earlier points, not only because of the law but also because special attention *must* be given to children who are at risk or who clearly have some type of disability that will affect their performance in school.

Regardless of specific transitional points along the continuum of elementary-intermediate-secondary-postsecondary grade levels, formal education continues until each child drops out, ages out, or completes his or her educational program. In the context of this book, we are equally concerned with children with disabilities who are just beginning their education, passing through puberty, entering young adulthood, or with adults pursuing undergraduate or graduate education in order to pursue a professional career. They all have in common that the primary focus of their lives is directed toward learning as opposed to working, leisure, or other major life activities.

Figure 3-1, below, summarizes some of the inter-relationships and dependencies that are associated with the school years and the provision of services. Although each grade-to-grade transition is important, we emphasize three major transition points: from preschool into kindergarten/elementary schooling, into intermediate/secondary schooling, and into college or technical schooling.

Inasmuch as society has accepted responsibility for providing educational opportunities for children, young people, and adults, it is incumbent on society to make adequate provision for service delivery—not just for those who are in

Time Frame	Service Delivery Team	Services Delivered
Kindergarten, elementary grades	Educators and therapists, with parents and guardians	Instruction, remediation, socialization, and transition preparation
Intermediate, secondary grades	Educators and vocational rehabilitation specialists, with parents and guardians	Instruction, remediation, social skill development, vocational and transition preparation
Postsecondary schools	Faculty, disabled student services support staff, rehabilitation specialists	Instruction, remediation, career preparation and placement

Figure 3-1 The School Years: Interrelationships and Dependencies

the mainstream of society but also for those who need some type of special service in order to benefit from educational opportunities. As a concept, this seems like a simple proposition. In practice, there are many complications and considerations involved.

Federal Initiatives and Programs

The Education for All Handicapped Children Act, PL 94-142, was passed in November 1975. Together with Section 504 of the Vocational Rehabilitation Act Amendments of 1973, PL 93-112, these represent the two landmark pieces of legislation that have given rights and protections to persons with disabilities and have fundamentally influenced educational and rehabilitation practice (Ballard & Zettel, 1980).

PL 94-142 was the landmark legislation that assured children with disabilities aged 3 through 21 that they would receive "a free appropriate public education." Singer and Butler (1987), reporting on the implementation of the act in five major metropolitan school districts in their research project (The Collaborative Study of Children with Special Needs, discussed more fully later in this chapter), argued that the act placed schools in the position of becoming agents of social reform. Palfrey, Singer, Walker, and Butler (1986) reviewed the extent to which "related services" were being provided in accordance with the act and found that in the five metropolitan communities there was a need for improved collaboration between the health and education sectors.

The act specifies that specialists be called on to evaluate the children's special needs, determine the most appropriate environment for serving the child, develop an IEP for the child, notify the parents of the findings and involve them in decision making, and provide for appeals by parents that are dissatisfied. To the extent that it is in the child's best interest, each handicapped child is to be educated with nonhandicapped children.

Its implementation has not been without its problems. Early on, the challenge involved developing procedures for screening, testing, and identifying children who need special services, applying the definitions of handicapping categories correctly, assigning children to appropriate settings and services, designing meaningful interventions that could be stated in IEPs, and reviewing progress periodically. Positive and negative effects of PL 94-142 were weighed (Wright, Cooperstein, Renneker, & Padilla, 1982), and the positive effect of an increase in the scope and comprehensiveness of special education programs and services at the local level outweighed the negative effects, such as increased administrative burdens and paperwork.

Since then, additional concerns have arisen, some of which have led to litigation. Among the problems that have detracted from the high sense of purpose that characterized the original legislation were the following:

- continuing debates about the precision of definitions and the use of categorical labeling
- difficult-to-explain variations in child counts across the states
- questions about the appropriateness of IQ testing in the determination of disability
- excessive identification of minority children in certain categories
- IEP entries that too often tended to be automatic and predictable rather than sensitive to unique child needs
- indications that annual evaluations were not leading to less-restrictive environments for many students
- court decisions that increasingly placed education in a position of responsibility for services that it historically has not provided, such as health care
- social isolation of students with disabilities on a number of school campuses
- follow-up studies indicating that students with disabilities were ill prepared to function effectively in the community at large without further support services

A curious aspect of PL 94-142 is the perceptions of funding that are associated with the act. Generally, people familiar with the progress of special education in the schools have been much impressed with the resources that have been made available in terms of staffing, materials, and training. Regular educators have sometimes felt left out as they observe the allocation of resources. Yet the federal resources that were supposed to be made available under the law have never really been provided. Viadero (1990) noted that "when federal lawmakers passed the landmark law guaranteeing every handicapped child a public education, they promised to pay up to 40 percent of the average cost." However, Viadero pointed out, "the federal share of educating children with disabilities has never exceeded 12 percent. Federal dollars now pay only 7 percent of that cost" (p. 21). It has been left to the states to pick up the slack and provide the financial support required under the law. New York, for example, spent 16.6% of its 1988 state education budget for special education.

In recent years, new program emphases have been mounted at the federal, state, and local levels that offer great potential to fully implement the intent of PL 94-142. Among these improvements and innovations are

- the increased use of technology to overcome barriers of learning (of which more will be said later)
- the adaptation of "regular" education materials, such as textbooks, to better meet the needs of children with disabilities
- the greater involvement of parents in educational planning and service delivery
- the introduction of various types of work experience programs into the schools, to help students with disabilities prepare for employment, including special arrangements for students who are more severely disabled and new categories of personnel to serve them (e.g., job coaches)
- the introduction of cooperative interagency agreements that facilitate school-to-community transitions
- the increased attention to new approaches to testing (including curriculum-based assessment, repeated measure designs, and computer-based assessment)

In accordance with the Developmental Disabilities Assistance and Bill of Rights Act, the Administration on Developmental Disabilities allocates financial and advocacy support to the states and territories on a formula grant basis. The investment in advocacy is substantial. Anywhere from a quarter to half of the funds going to particular states are designated for advocacy activities on behalf of developmentally delayed citizens in the states. In New York, for example, the 1991 allocation was split about two thirds to one third: $3,744,205 for basic support and $1,121,593 for protection and advocacy (Office of Human Development Services, 1990).

Coordination of Educational Programming

The team of specialists meets to discuss and prepare an IEP each year, but its composition changes over time and across grades and schools. For a number of other reasons (not all child related), it is obvious that coordination among the members of the teams must occur with some frequency. Coordination is especially necessary at transition points–initially with preschool specialists, then between elementary and middle school staff, then middle school and high school staff; at exit from high school, coordination with higher education personnel or with community agency staff may be appropriate.

Definitions of Disabilities

Definitions of handicapping conditions are the responsibility of the states. However, since states must report statistics to the federal government on the numbers of children served with different disabilities, most states have used categories consistent with federal definitions.

In the traditional approach to classification, each condition is defined descriptively and labels and sublabels are attached to these definitions. Inconsistent terminology and categorical "rules" are applied in order to make distinctions within particular disability groups. For example, learning disability (a process-oriented label) is subtyped to reading disability or math disability (content-oriented labels). Mental retardation (an intellect-oriented label) is often subtyped to educable retarded, trainable retarded, or mildly or profoundly retarded (the first two are process-oriented labels, and the latter two are degree-oriented labels).

An example of the difficulties that arise with the use of labels is evident with students with behavioral or emotional disorders. According to a study conducted by the Bank Street College of Education, identification of these students varies greatly among the states. Some schools do not identify behaviorally or emotionally disordered students at all, and schools in some states "may be unwilling to saddle students with that label" (Report on Educational Research, 1990, p. 7).

The practice of labeling individuals according to a named disability has been resisted by a number of educators and parents on grounds that it stigmatizes the individuals who are so labeled. To some extent this is undoubtedly true. For instance, labels can hurt individuals when they are used by peers to ridicule them or isolate them from group activities. Similarly, an employer who is unfamiliar with the meaning of a disability, such as learning disability, could be expected to view the applicant less favorably if he or she is presented as "learning disabled" at the time of the interview than if it was not mentioned at all. What happens, quite simply, is that negative assumptions are made about the applicant that are based on the label. They do not necessarily reflect what will happen on the job.

One of the most injurious outcomes of the labeling process is the tendency to generate stereotypes about the capacities of the individuals who comprise the group. Clearly, some stereotypes have a basis in fact—for example, blind persons will not become pilots of commercial aircraft, but neither will most able-bodied people. Other stereotypes are likely to be more misleading than accurate—for example, blind persons can only read materials in Braille. Still other stereotypes stem from ignorance and are wrong—for example, that persons who are deaf and whose oral language is unintelligible to the hearing person lack intelligence.

On the other hand, the use of labels does make some sense from the standpoint of simplifying service delivery. For example, the needs of persons with vision loss are obviously different from those with hearing loss, and staffing and support services need to reflect the presence of these different populations within their service organizations. The aggregation of information about services at the district, state, and federal levels has always been expressed in terms of specific categories of disabilities. This is largely due to the difference in service needs and the resulting impact on financial and facility requirements associated with each type of disability. It also makes common sense to use terms such as "vision impaired" or "cerebral palsied" when they are simply meant to describe the nature of the physical problem with which the individual must cope.

Attitude Barriers Presented by Others

Students with disabilities are vulnerable to the negative thinking of others, including their peers in school (Stilladis & Weiner, 1989) and various insensitive adults they encounter in the community (Weisgerber, 1990). This is especially true for persons who are uninformed about the capacity that many persons with disabilities have to rise to a challenge and the natural variability that exists within any subgroup of persons with disabilities (just as variability exists in the nondisabled population). Far too often, assumptions are made by persons who are not disabled that lump persons with disabilities together in unfavorable, stereotypic ways.

The resulting attitude barriers and the actions that stem from those attitudes are often among the most frustrating experiences faced by persons with disabilities. Since attitudinal barriers stem from the predispositions of others, it is clear that negative attitudes can be encountered even when the disabled person is intellectually able, socially able, and capable of living independently in the community.

At the elementary, intermediate, and secondary levels, acceptance of the person with a disability within social groups is difficult to accomplish, but not impossible. Through teaming and other instructional techniques, teachers play a key role in encouraging these friendship-based relationships. Equally important, teachers should recognize their role in helping the young person with a disability deal with rejection when it occurs.

At the postsecondary level, compulsory education no longer applies, and students must be admitted to areas of specialization. In this context, students with disabilities may encounter some professors (but by no means all) who take the position that persons with certain disabilities (of a type that limits their functioning) do not "belong" in the field or profession. They take the view that "unless you can do it all, you shouldn't even apply for entry into our program." This attitude, not as uncommon as one would think, has prevented many persons with disabilities from pursuing the careers they have chosen. (Ironically, advances being made in adaptive technology, particularly adaptive computer equipment, provide an alternative way of accomplishing certain specific tasks in work settings, yet these types of technological solutions are infrequently available to college students.)

Similarly, faced with the prospect of having a person who is hearing impaired, vision impaired, or physically disabled in their class or laboratory, other professors may refuse to change their teaching or testing methods to accommodate the disability. They may claim that they are being "fair" because everyone in the room is being given the same information or assignment and is held to the same standard. However, by refusing to adjust their teaching and testing, they actually ensure that the person with a disability cannot gain the information or share his or her knowledge and thus "prove" that they were correct in their original assessment.

This type of uncompromising stance has caused many a person with a disability to change majors, caused others to enlist the help of readers, notetakers, or tutors to help them compensate, and caused still others to directly challenge the equity of the situation through administrative recourse or legal action. More often than not, these head-on approaches will work, but the confrontation process is neither easy nor pleasant, and despite the fact that the individual is attempting to right a wrong, can unjustly result in the labeling of the person with a disability as a "troublemaker."

Educators at all levels have a simple choice—they can become obstacles or they can be mentors, depending on the way they establish communication with the student with a disability. They must understand that the primary function of education is to prepare the individual for later life, and that in later life the person has many degrees of freedom in how he or she approaches the solution of a problem or the accomplishment of a task. Accordingly, it is important that educators adopt the mentor role, guiding and counseling, as well as teaching, their students with disabilities.

Parent Involvement and Advocacy

According to Goodall and Bruder (1986), parents play a central role in the school-to-work transition planning process. They can serve as members of the team planning the Individualized Transition Plan (ITP) and act in an advocacy role by reviewing the range of available work options open to the young adult with a disability who is preparing to enter the world of work. By so doing, they can constructively engage one of the four major stress periods that families (of children who are developmentally disabled) experience. Apart from the school-to-work transition, these include the child's (1) first awareness of disability; (2) realization of the extent of disability; (3) exit from a protected environment, when the child must function with a degree of self-sufficiency; and (4) the time when the aging parents can no longer provide for the individual's welfare.

SPECIAL ISSUES CONCERNING CHILDREN AND YOUTH WITH DISABILITIES

A number of issues surround the provision of appropriate education to children and youth with special needs. These issues relate to the way in which students' special needs are identified and how they can best be accommodated. Not surprisingly, given the wide range of disabilities encountered and variations in the level of severity, more than one kind of program needs to be put in place, and more than one kind of strategy used to provide services. From the outset, when children with disabilities first enter school, the nature of service delivery can be influenced by the extent to which they are ready and able to participate *effectively* in mainstream environments. There is presently a substantial difference of opinion about the extent to which special educational services can be delivered in regular education settings, especially when the disability (or disabilities) is accompanied by language barriers. Similarly, the estimation of effectiveness of instruction depends on various assessments of children's performance that are not easy to measure and may be difficult to administer in a truly fair and unbiased manner.

Although most people think of education as a place or program where subject matter is learned, educators (with the support of parents) are also responsible for developing "the whole child." By this we mean not only someone who absorbs and repeats knowledge but also a person who is able to interact with others in positive ways, problem solve and apply basic principles of self-management, and develop independence in performing activities of daily living.

Smoothing the Transition into Formal Education

A major objective in infant and early education is the facilitation of entry into the regular school environment. The perception of necessary "readiness" for transition seems to be different depending on the teaching level: preschool teachers emphasize academic and social characteristics more than do kindergarten teachers (Beckoff & Bender, 1989).

Conn-Powers, Ross-Allen, and Holburn (1990) pointed out that the transition process is difficult for children with disabilities because it means learning new procedures, making new friends, and functioning in a larger group with less teacher attention. It also presents challenges for the professional staff because "differences between ECSE [early childhood special education] programs and elementary school programs may interfere with good communication" (p. 92). Conn-Powers et al. described a transition model developed in Project TEEM (a five-district project in Vermont) that involves a five-step process for the school system that seeks to smooth this transition:

1. establish a planning team
2. develop goals and identify problems
3. develop written transition planning procedures
4. gain system-wide support and commitment
5. evaluate the transition process

Rule, Fiechtl, and Innocenti (1990) described a Survival Skills Curriculum developed to teach children to cope with nine commonly occurring mainstream activities. The curriculum is designed to introduce planned variation by varying cues, directions, task components, and performance criteria. This planned variation is designed to help the child respond independently in his or her new environment, rather than depend on set routines.

In a very real sense, the Project KIDS model (described in Chapter 2) prepares children for smooth transitioning into the regular K to 6 grades. Classroom-based instruction in the KIDS continuum takes place in early childhood classrooms located in elementary schools. Teachers in these programs consider themselves part of the regular faculty. They help to establish a working relationship with the family that ensures that fundamental needs are being met (e.g., the children are not coming to school hungry, bruised, ill, poorly clothed, or unbathed).

Project KIDS teachers also act as trainers for parents as the child moves through the public school system. For example, they introduce the family to the concept of the IEP and prepare them for participation in IEP meetings. This includes "establishing goals and priorities, knowing their rights, and developing the ability to question professionals regarding appropriate programming" (Wilson, Mulligan, & Turner, 1985, 137).

Teachers in the public schools need to be prepared to serve students with health care needs. Graff, Ault, Guess, Taylor, and Thompson (1989) developed a guidebook that explains the procedures to be used in different circumstances. These guidelines include preventive measures, such as identification of warning signs, specific steps, emergency actions, sources of training, and suggestions for maintaining the privacy and dignity of the student with disabilities.

Least Restrictive Environments and Mainstreaming

One of the important goals of education is to prepare youth to function in an adult world after their schooling ends. This is at least as true for individuals with disabilities as it is for students who are not disabled. The obligation of educators is to serve students both with and without disabilities, fairly evaluate their progress, and support those who need special help in their transitioning to adult life. Butler, Magliocca, Torres, and Lee (1984) proposed the use of a decision-making model for grading mainstreamed students. The model incorporates elements of the grading process, individual differences that may require modification of the grading system, and evaluations by the regular and special education teachers and the administrator.

It has been evident to many observers that socialization between students with and without disabilities can be beneficial to both—though not necessarily so. It can benefit persons with disabilities by helping them learn to cope and participate in interpersonal and social situations similar to those that they will encounter in later life, and benefit the nondisabled by breaking down their stereotypes about disabilities that otherwise might lead to bigoted and cruel behaviors in adult life.

"Mainstreaming" has become a widely used term in the context of formal education, employed whenever children with disabilities are placed together with regular students for classes where they were able to function reasonably effectively. For example, a student with a specific learning disability in reading or math might be expected to participate with other children in social studies, science, physical education, vocational education, or elective courses. There are substantial differences of opinion about how and when mainstreaming is best accomplished.

Mainstreaming is a concept that can be reduced to a simple notion that interaction between individuals with and without disabilities is helpful *in the long run*. Since we are all part of one society, and we want the student with a disability to feel a part of and ultimately participate in that society, the concept of mainstreaming deserves our attention, but only when it is executed properly.

When mainstreaming occurs very early in life, such as at the toddler and preschool ages, the level of acceptance of the child with a disability by those without disability is increased, though this is neither automatic nor easy to accomplish. Similarly, children with disabilities become more comfortable in associating with children without disabilities through the routineness of day-to-day contact.

Project PRIME (Programmed Re-entry into Mainstreamed Education) was a large-scale descriptive-correlational study conducted in Texas in the early 1970s to compare the conduct and outcomes of instruction for educable mentally retarded (EMR) students in regular, resource, and special self-contained settings. Kaufman, Agard, and Semmel (1985), reporting the extensive findings from this project, found that EMR students need to have controls to prevent negative outbursts, that they seem "not to prosper" when there is too much or too little structure in the classroom, or if there is too much emphasis on academics.

One of the major provisions of PL 94-142 is its specification that children should be taught in the least restrictive environment. The assumption follows that students who are assigned to special education for individualized services may benefit from those services and be terminated from special education services—or they may benefit from these services but still need them on an ongoing basis.

Walker, Singer, Palfrey, Orza, Wenger, & Butler (1988) conducted a Collaborative Study of Children with Special Needs by following, for a 2-year period, 1184 students in elementary schools in three cities (Charlotte Mecklenburg Schools, North Carolina; Milwaukee Public Schools, Wisconsin; and Rochester City Schools, New York) to determine the stability of special education students' mobility, status, and classification labels. They found that the prospect for termination from the special education program (and return to regular education) was most likely for speech-impaired children (33.1%), followed by learning-disabled children (14.9%), emotionally/behaviorally disturbed children (9.1%), and vision-impaired children (8.6%). Children were seldom terminated from special services if they were initially classified as hearing impaired, mentally retarded, or physically/multiply handicapped. Children with speech problems were more likely to be terminated if the services were "related" services, as in speech therapy, and if the children were in grades 4 to 6, or had no accompanying learning or emotional problem.

Recently, Rossi (1990) developed a computerized demographic accounting system (referred to as MAP) that allows the automatic tracking of students across service delivery levels across school years and after leaving school, and which projects student placements on a predictive basis, thereby giving administrators a planning tool that takes placement into account. The MAP procedure uses log-linear analyses to estimate the transition probabilities and to estimate the effects of age, sex, ethnicity, and disability on transition rates (Rossi & Wolman, 1988).

The Regular Education Initiative

The regular education initiative (REI) movement, sometimes referred to as the general education initiative, gained momentum and public attention in the late 1980s. REI is a current, controversial movement which seeks to sharply diminish the extent to which children with disabilities are educated in settings other than the regular classroom (Gartner & Lipsky, 1987; Stainback & Stainback, 1984). Others in the profession take a more balanced view, recognizing that while the special education system is not "perfect," neither is the present state of regular education, which comes under frequent attack as a result of falling achievement scores (Keough, 1988a, 1988b). In short, REI offers both promise and problems (Davis, 1989).

Algozzine, Maheady, Sacca, O'Shea, and O'Shea (1990) and Kauffman, Braaten, Nelson, Polsgrove, and Braaten (1990) have debated REI pro and con, using as a point of contention its characterization by Braaten, Kauffman, Braaten, Polsgrove, and Nelson (1988) as a "patent medicine" (defined as a drug or other medicinal preparation that can be bought without a prescription). Lieberman (1990) points out that the term "REI" is being misused and misinterpreted because it has not been clearly defined, because there is confusion about who it applies to (especially with respect to "mild" versus "severe" disabilities), and because it seems to imply that special education has failed–a premise he does not accept.

REI goes beyond the concept of mainstreaming, as that term is usually applied, since it presumes that a far greater proportion of students with disabilities should be placed in regular classrooms than is characteristic in typical mainstreaming situations.

In mainstreaming, the child with disabilities is in a regular class because a committee has considered his or her individual case and decided that the regular classroom is the least restrictive environment in which that child can be served "appropriately." Support and special assistance (tailored to the assignments and learning activities occurring in the regular classroom) are given by a special education teacher, who is typically located in another environment. Adaptation, then, is on the side of special education. In contrast, Stainback, Stainback, Courtnage, and Jaben (1985) have taken the position that changes needed to be made in regular education's traditional practices for mainstreaming to be successful. Among other adaptations, three are described below:

1. individualized programming, in which instruction is criterion based, using materials and pacing appropriate to the individual student
2. cooperative activities, where common goals are met by groups of students with differing ability levels

3. adaptive environments, involving diagnostic-prescriptive monitoring, description of learning needs in instructional rather than categorical terms, individualized plans, and teaching of self-management skills

In REI, pull-out programs are discouraged, as are services in environments other than the regular classroom. A "consultative relationship" is presumed to exist between the special education teacher and the regular teacher for *any* of the children in the class who are experiencing learning problems, including children not classified as special education students. In this context the adaptive instruction is to be provided by the regular educator in accord with strategies and techniques introduced by the special educator.

To put the REI movement in perspective, several historical facts must be considered. First, it has only been a matter of 3 decades since (1) children with mild disabilities were largely undiagnosed and unserved and (2) those with moderate disabilities, and especially severe disabilities, were frequently systematically excluded from participation in many public schools. Education for the latter was provided in special schools (often labeled by the type of disability being "served"), or, as frequently was the case, the child's educational needs were ignored altogether and he or she was left at home. If the child with disabilities was being served in the regular school system, it was typically because the parents actively pursued this type of school assignment, or because the disability was "hidden." It should be noted, however, that historically some of the early special schools for children with disabilities (such as Spalding High School, in Chicago's public school system) did a remarkable job of preparing talented youths with disabilities to become assertive, successful adults.

Second, prior to 1975 it was widely felt that students with disabilities being taught by regular teachers were not receiving the kind of individualized attention they needed, and that the regular teachers were ill trained or unwilling to provide appropriately tailored instruction. Pressure from dissatisfied parents and professionals in special education led to the passage of PL 94-142, which guaranteed that children with handicaps would be educated in "appropriate" instructional environments.

In consequence, educators established a hierarchy of educational settings ordered along a continuum of least to most restrictive instructional environments, often referred to as the cascade model. In this model the least restrictive environment is the regular education classroom; at the other end of the continuum is institutionalization.

The assumption was that following testing and other forms of assessment of students' capacity to benefit, they would be assigned to the most appropriate (least restrictive) setting. What developed in practice was the use of testing for (1) diagnostic purposes, to establish the nature and extent of disability, and (2) prescriptive purposes, to establish the current level of educational performance (e.g., reading level). Comparatively little attention was given to assessing interaction between the instructional environment and the special child—that is, the impact of different settings on the motivation and day-to-day performance of the individual.

It was also assumed, though relatively infrequently implemented, that students who had been assigned to one setting in the cascade model could progress upward to less restrictive environments as a result of reappraisals in the IEP process. Theoretically, students were presumed to be able to move in the direction of mainstreaming after they received appropriate instruction in settings that allowed more personalized attention. This readiness was hard to demonstrate because it meant that a student with disabilities who had been pulled out for special help was now placed in the position of trying to catch up to nondisabled peers (in fundamental skills such as reading and comprehension) in order to function effectively in the more competitive environment.

In practice, though not admitted because of conflict with the purposes of PL 94-142, administrative considerations have almost certainly had some influence on placement within the cascade model. Different teacher-student ratios at the different levels of the cascade model tend to reinforce the status quo because special education teachers want to give the maximum help possible (a lower child-to-teacher ratio is customary at the lower levels in the environmental hierarchy, and this means a child would presumably get more individual teacher attention than if he or she were moved upward in the hierarchy of service categories). Similarly, the need for committee action and approvals of parents probably makes for less inclination to change downward in the assignment of students because of reluctance to acknowledge failure or lack of benefit from the services.

The rapid growth of special education programs in the schools and substantial program funding for special education at federal, state, and local levels drew much attention to the outcomes of the use of the cascade model, its high per-student costs, and in some instances its misapplication. Nelson, Fischer, and Rubenstein (1985) stated that "there is little or no evidence that this approach by category is useful, indeed it often results in negative labels for students who then suffer problems of self-concept and peer relationships, especially during the adolescent period" (p. 136). Nelson and colleagues felt that a more productive approach would be to have noncategorical programming in which an emphasis was placed on access to job training programs, the development of students' self-advocacy skills, and greater coordination among service providers who have a role in students' career preparation.

The categorizations and service level assignments for learning-disabled students, a group that probably includes a number of mislabeled students, have been closely examined. Indeed, the inconsistencies that appear from state to state in the proportion of students labeled learning disabled (and the difficulties of measuring and applying the complex definition) have been a constant source of concern for those involved in serving learning-disabled children.

The impetus for REI came from several sources. Research by Algozzine and Ysseldyke (1981, 1983) failed to find support for distinguishing specific learning-disabled children from nondisabled children on a number of dimensions. To the extent that this was true, it could be argued that they were no more deserving of "extra services" than students who were simply slow learners for other reasons (e.g., low socioeconomic status, language barriers).

Wang and her colleagues (Wang, Gennari, & Waxman, 1985; Wang, Peverly, & Randolph, 1984) carried out studies to assess the effects of full-time mainstreaming and recommended a particular strategy called the Adaptive Learning Environments Model (ALEM), which is predicated on an individualized learning approach implemented in regular classroom settings. The ALEM conceptualizes a "partnership" and sharing of responsibilities between regular and special educators. It recommends that the government provide financial support to encourage "experimental trials" of the new approach.

Bryan and Bryan (1988) examined the literature reporting research in the ALEM strategy and found it less than convincing. Fuchs and Fuchs (1988) have been critical of the ALEM strategy and its large-scale implementation, arguing, among other things, that it demands a high level of teacher commitment and that there has been insufficient examination of the sites where it has been only partially implemented.

Wang and Walberg (1988), responding to this criticism, said the burden of proof of effectiveness should be on the side of those who argue for pull-out programming, citing a number of authors who failed to find evidence that the pull-out approach works. However, Keough (1988b) stated that "counter to these criticisms [of special education], there is also a body of evidence that demonstrates that special education programs can lead to important educational, personal, and social benefits" (p. 3).

The problem in this argument is in defining what constitutes proof that the dual system (mainstream plus pull-out) works to the advantage of the child with disabilities. It is unrealistic to expect that special education classrooms are designed to help students with disabilities catch up so that they may again be competitive in regular classrooms. Such an assumption means that the learner with a disability would have to learn faster than the regular education student. If that were true, it would cast doubt on the quality of the regular education program.

Reynolds, Wang, and Walberg (1987) compared special education with other compensatory programs and found the criteria for services to be similar. They concluded that there was "little research to justify present practices in the categorizing of children and programs in the domains represented here" (p. 392)—that is, in mildly handicapped children and other categorical programs serving economically disadvantaged children, migrant children, low-proficiency-English children, and the like. They did not, however, extend their criticism to include special education programs serving deaf, blind, retarded, or severely disturbed children.

Pressures toward REI also came from the administrative side of education and from policy makers, who were feeling the need for attention to the many students who were not performing up to standard but who were not classified as disabled. McKinney and Hocutt (1988) examined the policy issues involved in REI (and the ALEM studies). They noted that a number of assumptions that the proponents of REI have made cannot be supported by available evidence. For example, advocacy of the Direct Instruction Model in an REI environment overlooks the fact that the Direct Instruction Model is "very demanding to implement effectively" and that it is "seldom observed in regular classrooms."

Madeleine Will, then Assistant Secretary for the Office of Special Education and Rehabilitation Services (OSERS), argued strongly for integration of students with disabilities with their nondisabled peers and described it as "the fundamental issue confronting parents and professionals" (Will, 1985, p. 1). The thrust of her argument was that the least restrictive environment principle in PL 94-142 meant that students with disabilities should be taken out of the regular classroom only when "the nature of the severity of the handicap is such that education in regular classes, with the use of supplementary aids and services, cannot be achieved satisfactorily" (p. 1). Subsequently, Ms. Will came out strongly in favor of REI, as did some state directors of education and special education. (Ms. Will has since been succeeded by Robert Davila.)

In 1989 Judy Schrag, current director of the Office of Special Education Programs in OSERS, found herself newly appointed and already attempting to clarify what REI was all about. "I think if you got any 10 people in a room and asked them what is the Regular Education Initiative, everyone would have a different answer," she said. "I think that sometimes people view the Regular Education Initiative to mean that all kids are put back into the regular classroom without help. We want to emphasize the need for a full continuum of services and within that continuum certainly there is a need to explore the ways to serve the child in the general classroom, but there is room for a pull-out program as well" (Kirk, 1989, p. 1).

The stated rationale for REI has been that it would be better to restructure the way in which students with disabilities are taught. Instead of assigning them teachers who are not (and are not expected to be) experts in subject matter areas, and settings where there are low student-teacher ratios, the strategy would be to place them in regular classes along with "consulting" support staff who could help the regular teacher and the special education student. It was argued that this reallocation of staff effort would not only be less costly but would better accommodate the needs of at-risk students other than those who had been formally identified as disabled. However, research on the consultation model of teaching (as utilized by special educators) is less than encouraging.

Haight and Molitor (1983) surveyed special education teacher consultants and found that communication of basic information about their responsibilities was inadequate or nonexistent for most of them. Evans (1980) studied the amount of time that was devoted to the consulting role and found that the actual and ideal amounts of consultation differed substantially. The extent of consultation was half the amount all three groups of educators (classroom teachers, principals, and resource specialists) thought it should be. Sargent (1981) studied the amount of time that resource room teachers spent in direct instruction. It was found that the actual amount of time spent was considerably less than they estimated. One of the traditional arguments for resource rooms has been that there is more opportunity to work with the students who need special instruction, but the Sargent study seems to suggest that teachers may not be as aware of how their time is being allocated as one would hope.

Huefner (1988) described potential benefits and risks associated with the consulting teacher model. Potential benefits identified by Huefner include

- reduction of stigma for the students
- better understanding between regular and special teachers
- opportunity for on-the-job training of regular teachers in special skills
- reduction of mislabeling of nonhandicapped students
- spill-over of benefits of consulting teachers' skills to regular students
- suitability for the secondary school model of instruction in multiple content areas
- improved prospect for master teacher staffing in special education

Dangers of casual or premature implementation identified by Huefner include

- ineffective caseloads, which can vary for different disabilities
- converting the model to a tutoring or aide model
- unrealistic expectations, including seeing the consulting teacher as a panacea and undertraining the resource teacher
- inadequate support from regular educators
- inadequate funding mechanisms, especially as complying with PL 94-142
- faulty assumptions about program effectiveness
- faulty assumptions about cost savings*

---

*Source: From "The Consulting Teacher Model: Risks and Opportunities" by D.S. Huefner, 1988, *Exceptional Children, 54*(5), pp. 405-409. Copyright 1988 by The Council for Exceptional Children. Adapted by permission.

Only recently have the costs of special education program variations been studied in depth. The costs of providing special education in differing service delivery settings vary considerably (Moore, Strang, Schwartz, & Braddock, 1988). Studying a sample of 60 school districts across 18 states, an expenditures study was conducted under contract to the Office of Special Education. Moore and her colleagues found large variations in expenditures across school districts. Using an "ingredients" approach, they found that the average per-pupil expenditures for instructional programs and supplemental services were as follows:

Instructional Programs

Preschool	$3,437
Self-contained	$4,233
Resource program	$1,325
Home/hospital	$3,117
Residential	$28,324

Supplemental Services

Special vocational education	$1,444
Related services	$592
Adaptive physical education	$615
Assessment	$1,206
Transportation	$1,583

Figures from *Patterns in Special Education Service Delivery and Cost*, (p. C-34) by M.T. Moore et al., 1988, Washington, D.C.: Decision Resources Corporation, for the U.S. Department of Education.

These figures vary according to different subsets of children. For example, within the preschool subset, the infant and toddler programs cost about $3,461 per child, while the early childhood (ages 3 to 5) programs cost about $3,798 per child. In studying these figures, it is important to keep in mind that not all children receive all services; for example, only about 30% of special education students are provided transportation services. Overall, about 54% of the expenditures went toward instructional programs, 35% went toward support services, 8% went toward transportation, and 3% went toward pupil services.

To critics of the REI movement, the new approach is questionable. Some educators and parents who worked hard to support the passage of PL 94-142 see the initiative as a sellout. They know from personal experience how difficult it is to accelerate the learning rate of students with disabilities so that they can compete in a regular classroom (under even the most ideal instructional conditions). They know that it was the inability to perform in this environment that first brought these students to the attention of special education. They argue that it is an "end run" to divert special education funds for other purposes, such as having the consulting teacher work with nondiagnosed but "slow" children in the classroom. They also point out that there is little evidence to support the contention that the new approach will be more cost-effective or produce better results.

Kronick (1989) pointed to the greater risk for the student from special education in terms of scapegoating and increased social stress in the REI setting. She also questioned the validity of the research on which some of the REI arguments are founded. She went so far as to say that "in that educational change is fickle, I have no doubt that the REI will eventually be discarded" (p. 5).

Fox (1989) investigated the nature of the social contact between learning-disabled children and nonhandicapped peers in regular classrooms. Fox noted that "previous research has shown that mainstreaming will not automatically help handicapped children become more socially accepted by their handicapped peers. In fact, there is sufficient evidence to demonstrate that handicapped children are more often socially rejected by their peers than are nonhandicapped children" (p. 50). Fox noted the mixed results of various approaches to improving the social interaction.

A key to effective implementation of the regular education initiative is collaboration between general and special education. Pugach and Johnson (1989a) indicated that although collaborative arrangements are gaining favor, achieving real collaboration in consultative relationships between special education teachers and regular education teachers is a much greater challenge than is often realized. One such area of collaboration is in prereferral interventions, where the process of informal problem solving is attempted before time-consuming formal referrals are made (Pugach & Johnson, 1989b). In this situation two assumptions are being made: dependence on the special educator for appropriate problem solutions and the transfer of problem ownership from the initiating teacher.

Vergason and Anderegg (1990) stated that

> To endorse the REI a person must believe labeling is not necessary, that special education as a system is nonfunctional, that special education does injurious "things" to children, that all students with handicaps are better off in total mainstreaming, that pull-out programs are ineffective, that regular classroom teachers can handle a much wider range of abilities and problems than previously believed, that waiving the current rules and regulations would usher in a new age, and that the REI is more cost-effective than other models of service. (p. 9)

Those are major assumptions, and most have not been empirically demonstrated one way or the other, so it is not surprising that the worth of REI continues to be debated (Byrnes, 1990; Carnine and Kameenui, 1990; Davis, 1990; Jenkins, Pious, & Jewell, 1990).

Lieberman (1990) stated, "The regular education initiative (REI) is an ongoing professional discussion that must continue in every educational forum for many years to come" (p. 56).

While this may turn out to be true, to debate these issues endlessly does not help children. Rather, in the American tradition of preferring local options over central direction, *we should encourage those who are committed to one or another of the viewpoints about REI to pursue their beliefs in pragmatic rather than rhetorical ways, and we should evaluate the effects of their different interventions along common dimensions.*

We should evaluate REI not in terms of how policy makers, administrators, and teachers embrace or reject it, but rather on clear evidence of how students respond to it in matched conditions. In particular, we need to systematically judge the effects of education (REI or other programming) in terms of both near–and long-term outcomes for students.

Categorical and Noncategorical Programs

One of the difficulties that has faced students and educators alike is the use of categorical labels for children. For many years, society has been upgrading the terminology used to refer to persons with disabilities. No longer are terms like "imbecile" or "moron" used in educational environments, but "mentally retarded" and "developmentally delayed" are, and neither is flattering. We no longer hear the word "cripple" used to describe someone in a wheelchair, but we do hear terms like "paraplegic" and "quadriplegic" being used to describe (not always accurately) the extent of the disabling condition.

Difficulties in labeling are not restricted to severe disabilities, either. "Learning disability" is a term that has caused great confusion, largely because the functional characteristics associated with it are neither obvious (as are deafness or paralysis), defined consistently and agreed on among experts, nor simple to measure.

The use of labels has often led nondisabled persons to think in false, stereotyped ways (e.g., the deaf are "unable" to speak intelligibly) and act in wrong, stereotyped ways (e.g., speaking to a third party as though the blind person present cannot hear). In schools labeling has sometimes led to grouping children according to the labeled disability, even though the range of severity may be greater within a particular disability group than across several. About all one can say in favor of labeling is that it carries diagnostic meaning, much as does the naming of a disease or illness, and that it implies possible areas of difficulty that need to be addressed.

On a social level, it is a difficult, somewhat denigrating experience for children to be labeled "handicapped" by their peers, regardless of the fact that the label may be technically correct under the law, entitling the child to receive special services.

Because of these and other arguments, noncategorical programs have been implemented in some states. Teacher certification becomes a special consideration in noncategorical programming, as does the teacher-child ratio. Lilly (1977), advocating a special education delivery system that is noncategorical, stated that a teacher could deliver both direct (resource room) instruction and indirect (consulting) services to a maximum of 15 students.

Youth at Risk

Chapter 2 discussed the devastating impact of drug abuse on infant and child development. It is also a serious problem as children move upward from grade to grade in the schools. Botvin (1983) summed up the situation this way:

> Experimentation with a wide variety of substances for many adolescents appears to have become an integral part of the coming of age in America. Unfortunately, early experimentation often leads to regular use and for all too many individuals, this may result in compulsive patterns of uses characterized in many cases by both psychological and physiological dependence. (p. 115)

Students with disabilities are not exempt from this frightening trend.

To address this problem, drug abuse education programs aimed at prevention are necessarily shifting toward younger students. The need for this is shown by the 1988 National Household Survey on Drug Abuse, which showed that among 12-year-olds and older youth, 37% had tried marijuana, cocaine, or other illicit drugs at least once, and 14% had taken an illicit drug in the past year. Since 1985 there has been a 33% rise among those who use cocaine frequently (one or more times a week) (Research Triangle Institute, 1990).

Children and youth who are dependent on drugs are at risk both in their health and in their schooling and preparation for the future. Once "hooked," their school performance suffers, and they are more likely to drop out. At the same time, there is increasing awareness, prompted by the reactions of students, that intervention programs may not be taken seriously by students. For example, most programs in the schools have been almost completely informational, yet "evaluations of programs that focus on factual information clearly indicate that increased knowledge has virtually no impact on drug use or on intentions to use drugs" (Botvin, 1983, p. 119). Similarly, intervention programs that take an affective approach have frequently neglected specific skill training.

Botvin (1983) convincingly argued that the development of personal and social competence by adolescents is a key to effective drug abuse programs in the schools. Recognizing that substance abuse is socially learned, purposive behavior in response to environmental and personal factors, he advocated a life skills training (LST) approach derived from Bandura's social learning theory and Jessor's problem behavior theory. Evaluations in New York schools have shown LST to be effective. Elements of the life skills approach, which seeks to develop critical thinking and decision making in social situations, involve

- cognitive strategies for enhancing self-esteem, such as goal setting, behavior change techniques, and the use of positive self-statements
- assertiveness skills, such as the use of "no" statements and expression of rights
- self-management skills, such as stress reduction techniques and mental rehearsal
- social skills, such as conversational skills and dating skills
- skills in resisting persuasive appeals, including formulating counterarguments
- communication skills, both verbal and nonverbal

Multicultural and Language Problems

Students with disabilities may or may not be from the mainstream of white, middle-class American culture. If they are not from such a background, then a number of special considerations can come into play. Language differences compound the problem of diagnosis and instruction.

Whether they are Asian, Hispanic, or Afro-American in origin, cultural differences may present special problems. Children with disabilities who have different cultural backgrounds sometimes display communication and social strategies that are misconstrued or missed altogether by instructional staff. For example, the staff might consider the child's behavior to be uncooperative if he or she reacts negatively in a test-taking situation, when the child may be showing justifiable resistance to an inappropriate procedure or test content (Bennett, 1987).

Fradd and Correa (1989) cited the growing number of Hispanic minority students in the United States and the issues of nonbiased assessment, second language acquisition, and bilingual education that are critical in understanding the needs of these students. Figueroa (1989) described the psychological testing of linguistic minority children as being like "random chaos." He cited 47 different "knowledge gaps" reported by bilingual school psychologists regarding tests, language issues, cultural issues, schooling issues, professional issues, and affect or emotional impact.

Baca and Amato (1989) indicated the importance of teacher training in connection with service delivery to language minority children. They described a school district with high Hispanic representation in the student body, in which the general education program for limited-English students was strong and the teachers were not referring students to special education, to the extent that Hispanic students were under-represented in the special education program.

Rueda (1989) related the problems of language minority students with disabilities to the larger question of providing services to all students with language-related problems in learning. He suggested that a major restructuring of the education system (as in the REI initiative) may be necessary.

Accommodation in Assessment

Assessment takes many forms and has many purposes in education. Most commonly, assessment is used to evaluate current student ability through tests or systematic observation. Tests are also used to sample students' knowledge and skills for selection purposes. Typically, they are paper and pencil tests (printed, as in qualifying examinations for college entry). They can also be performance based, in which particular skills are measured against a particular standard, for instance, to qualify the individual for participation on an athletic team.

Assessment serves an important diagnostic function for children whose academic (or other life skill) performance is less than expected. It is used to pinpoint the problem in a way that can lead to some form of alternative instruction or remediation.

Assessment is a useful adjunct of learning when it is used to show progress or identify areas in which progress is needed. In this application, assessment is closely aligned with curriculum (i.e., it is curriculum based) and can be embedded in instructional materials and classroom activities.

Assessing the educational attainments of students with disabilities is not a simple matter. Setting aside the complexities of language barriers as discussed previously, there remains the difficulty of ensuring that the test itself is not a barrier and thus responsible for lowering the true assessment of ability for the individual with disabilities. Some of the common problems with tests that can interfere with an accurate appraisal of individual knowledge and ability are

- inability to see the printed matter—a problem for the blind and visually impaired

- inability to read the printed matter at a rapid rate without visual error—a problem with timed tests for persons who are learning disabled
- inability to perform handwriting requirements—a problem for some persons who are physically disabled
- inability to manipulate objects, as in a laboratory situation—a problem for persons who are blind or physically disabled
- inability to hear orally administered directions or questions—a problem for the hearing impaired
- inability to express oneself in responding to oral questions—a problem for any individual with speech impairment
- inability to access the location at which tests will be administered—a problem for persons who are physically disabled
- inability to understand and act upon complex oral or written instructions—a problem for learning disabled and mentally retarded persons

For some persons, such as a person with severe cerebral palsy, a combination of these problems exist. Additionally, other less common problems (e.g., seizures, limited stamina) can exist for certain individuals. Given these many potential problem areas, it is clear that if fairness is to be applied, then accommodations are required.

When testing involves standardized assessment, the student is being challenged to match up to the nondisabled population on which the test norms were developed. The kind of accommodation in test taking necessary is then left up to local judgment. It is far from consistently implemented (even for the same individual) by different test administrators. Further, since the development of norms for different disabilities (and different levels of severity within the disability categories) is not a practical consideration for test developers, the interpretation of measured knowledge or ability becomes arguable.

Sherman and Robinson (1982) summarized findings of the Panel on Testing of Handicapped People, National Research Council. The Panel found numerous problems associated with ability testing of people with disabilities for selection purposes, particularly with tests that are used (1) for college admission and entry into most professional and technical training programs and (2) for entry and advancement in jobs.

Special education teachers and school psychologists generally share in the administration of diagnostic instruments. Additionally, for achievement testing, the special education teacher sometimes becomes the "designated test administrator" for teachers of students in mainstreamed environments. At the college level, where proctors are used heavily by the teaching faculty, a special proctor should be assigned who is knowledgeable about the disability; a faculty-administered, one-on-one administration of the test would also be appropriate. In many instances, extra time needs to be allowed, an adaptation provided, or assistive technology utilized.

Adaptive Testing and the Assessment of Educational Outcomes

Diagnostic tests and checklists are numerous and extremely diverse in purpose and in format. The assessment of children for diagnostic purposes is a complex undertaking. The selection of appropriate measures is sometimes controversial, as in the case of IQ tests. The appropriateness of the measure to the variable being assessed is an important consideration; thus skills and abilities may be tested in more than one way, depending to a large extent on whether relevant behavior or relevant knowledge is being assessed. Moreover, the extreme variability in behaviors and knowledge (referred to as level of functioning) among individuals with very different disabilities only adds to the complexity of interpretation after the assessment has been carried out. Barnett (1983) made the case for multifactored assessment in separate, but overlapping, assessment domains and has reviewed various measures in these seven domains:

1. personal and social functioning
2. cognitive and intellectual functioning
3. language and communication skills
4. academic skills
5. adaptive behavior
6. vocational assessment
7. visual-motor and gross-motor skills

A number of rating scales address "adaptive" behaviors and social competence of children with presumed disabilities. Two examples of measures published by the Psychological Corporation will suffice to illustrate this range of instruments:

- *The Kohn Social Competence Scale,* developed by Martin Kohn and published in 1986, is a bipolar rating scale used to assess social-emotional functioning in preschool children. It is used by two teachers observing the child in day care and kindergarten contexts. Analysis is aided by the use of a microcomputer program.
- *The Normative Adaptive Behavior Checklist,* developed by Gary Adams and published in 1984, contains 120 items that are said to measure the behavior of individuals, birth to 21 years of age, in six skill areas: (1) self-help skills, (2) home living skills, (3) independent living skills, (4) social skills, (5) sensory and motor skills, and (6) language concepts and academic skills.

Items are dichotomous, and a rating of "no" on an item indicates that the individual does not perform or needs prompting to perform the behavior.

Amos (1980) questioned the application of minimum competency testing for learning-disabled students. In light of the trend toward minimum competency testing as a requirement for school completion, Amos called for test modifications that are appropriate to the individual case. As a classroom teacher, Amos suggested three procedures that can be used to facilitate the testing of basic competencies. All three alternatives involve the child's IEP committee:

1. Submit the test to the IEP committee so they can select appropriate test items that can be used to evaluate the attainment of the educational objective.
2. Let the committee choose a different, appropriate test.
3. Allow the committee to develop an alternate test.

The State of Florida adopted a minimum competency testing program as a requirement of graduation from high school, but statutes allow adjustments to be made for students with disabilities. Research was supported by the U.S. Department of Education to address two questions: how students with learning disabilities compared with nondisabled students and how well the tests measured skills of interest to employers (Algozzine, Crews, & Stoddard, 1986). Learning-disabled students demonstrated fewer competencies than the nondisabled comparison group in communications and math skills. This is not altogether surprising, but it takes on added significance because the employer valuations of competencies placed a high emphasis on basic skills and functional literacy. Reading, writing, and number problems were named as important to entry level jobs by 92% of the employers.

Whether developed for national use or developed by teachers for their own use, norm-referenced tests present difficulties in selection, administration, and interpretation. Other forms of testing have been tried with some success, including curriculum-based assessment, repeated measure designs, and computer-based assessment. Gaylord-Ross, Forte, Storey, Gaylord-Ross, and Jameson (1987) have used criterion-referenced instruction and testing effectively with individuals with severe disabilities. More is said about this approach subsequently in this chapter.

As stated previously, repeated measurement and curriculum-based assessment have become increasingly accepted over the last 6 years (Blankenship, 1985; Deno, 1985; Germann & Tindal, 1985; Marston & Magnusson, 1985). Instead of the limited amount of sampling that typically occurs in standardized testing, curriculum-based assessment develops a "history" of measurement of the child's behaviors within the context of the learning tasks and course content under study. Typically, these trials are charted over time, revealing a growth pattern that can be directly interpreted either as error reduction or as acquisition of learned skills. When it is properly applied, there is evidence that curriculum-based assessment can lead to greater student achievement (ERIC/OSEP Special Project on Interagency Information Dissemination, 1988a).

A promising new approach to testing that may help to bridge the assessment gap between persons with and without disabilities is in the area of adaptive testing with the use of computers. One advantage of the computer over human-administered testing is the "patience" of a computer, for it will wait for an answer indefinitely and nonjudgmentally, unless programmed for a timed response. Among the benefits of using computerized testing (over paper and pencil assessment) are (1) flexibility in being able to present item content in the form of graphic design, (2) testees do not have to take the test at the same time, and (3) additional information can be gathered about each testee's behavior, such as time taken, sequence of changes in answers, and branching to alternative items of varying difficulty (Bracey, 1990; Wise & Plake, 1989). In prototype software being developed at the Educational Testing Service, computer assessment is performance based and involves problem solving and the conduct of science experiments (Anrig, in press).

Unlike paper and pencil tests, the selection of items for a computer-based test does not have to be done on an a priori basis. That is, instead of deciding what subset of items will sample the universe and then requiring that all students take that sample, computer testing can include decision rules in the programming of the software that permit the presentation of new items in a sequence that is sensitive to the responses students have given to previous items. For example, using a hypothetical test situation, suppose an assessment is to be made of a learning-disabled student's vocabulary acquisition. Since the *rate* of test taking may be a factor for this student, a computer-monitored adjustable rate of presentation could be used, in which the speed of presentation is accelerated or decelerated automatically by the computer according to error rates. This is fair to the student because vocabulary, not rate, is being assessed, and lacking the speed adjustment the student's knowledge would be masked by the interference of the disability.

Similarly, the *pattern* of responses within a content domain could be matched by the computer against a set of criteria and values preassigned by experts who are knowledgeable about the subject matter domain. Using a large pool of items, which could be accessed randomly or in a scaled order of difficulty, the computer would present an item, record the student's response, and immediately and concurrently take note of the attributes of the item and of the response selection. The selection of succeeding items (by the computer) can then be influenced by the response pattern that develops and the decision rules that have been built into the program by the subject matter experts.

The assessment of student outcomes entails much more than the administration of tests or informally developed instruments to sample knowledge and behavior. The term "outcomes" refers to evidence that the educational activities in which the student with a disability participated during his or her schooling did, in fact, make some observable difference. Basic mathematics represents subject matter that is learned in school and tested as an area of competence. However, the ability to carry out banking activities, such as writing checks and balancing checks against bank statements, is an *outcome*. It provides observable evidence that at least certain mathematics skills were both learned and *transferred* to real-life situations.

Although outcomes can be (and are) assessed at any stage of life, we are naturally especially concerned with outcomes of the educational system, both because education is society's way of ensuring its future in the hands of the next generation and because education becomes the focus of much popular criticism when literacy falls and dependence on welfare increases. Intervention on behalf of persons with disabilities also can (and should) be evaluated in terms of the outcomes produced. Follow-up studies, such as the Scuccimarra and Speece (1990) research on the lives of persons with disabilities two years after high school, described later in this chapter, are examples of outcome assessment.

Attention to outcome assessment is increasing as a part of "accountability" movements that call for an examination of productivity in teacher/administrator/school performance. If we view the outcomes of schooling in terms of standardized scores of achievement, we have limited our assessment of outcomes to the topics that schools *do* teach, not necessarily what they *should* teach, if students are to be well prepared for adult life.

Because the needs of students with disabilities are like those of nondisabled students in many ways, it is fair to consider both groups in making outcome assessments. However, students with disabilities are, by definition, different from typical nondisabled students. Most have a greater need for living, employment, and social skills (as differentiated from academic skills) than do regular students. For that reason, outcome assessment needs to be on a broader basis for this special needs group.

The development of indicators of effectiveness for special education is still in its initial stages. Indicators of student performance, competencies, behaviors, and attitudes have been suggested on a preliminary basis (National Regional Resource Center Panel on Indicators of Effectiveness in Special Education, 1986). Included are such indicators as attendance, graduation, dropout, and suspension rates of students with disabilities, along with vocational competencies, academic competencies, positive behaviors, expression of creative interests, self-help abilities, and independent living.

Presently, through contracting mechanisms, the Office of Special Education Programs in the Department of Education is supporting the development of a comprehensive model of outcome indicator assessment that will, it is hoped, be adopted by most or all of the states as a regular and integral part of state-level assessment of educational impact for special needs students.

Teacher Preparation for Social Skill Instruction

The provision of appropriate educational services to students with disabilities is directly related to the knowledge, skill, and adaptability of the instructional staff. While this seems an obvious statement, it is unfortunately true that the amount of training teachers receive in preparation for serving students with disabilities varies considerably. For special education teachers it is substantial, but for regular classroom teachers it is minimal.

Regular teachers lack the in-depth preparation about disability that special educators receive, while the latter lack the specialized instruction in academic disciplines that the former receive. The former are thus well prepared to present subject matter, and the latter are equipped to adapt that instruction to meet the unique needs of individual students with disabilities.

There is sometimes a mismatch between the instructional preparation that special education teachers receive and the realities of the job market (McLaughlin, Valdiviseo, Spence, & Fuller, 1988). This mismatch arises when state education agency policy changes and teacher training institutions find it difficult to comply with the changes quickly, or when the change conflicts with their own view about what is desirable in the way of teacher competence. McLaughlin et al. point out that special education teachers' competence tends to be rated critically by state education staff in areas of implementation of PL 94-142, understanding of "due process," and the consultation skills necessary in dealing with regular teachers.

Typically, neither regular educators nor special educators receive substantial amounts of specialized training in the area of social skills, either in preservice or in inservice training programs. Given the primary emphasis schools give to mastery of subject matter as compared to socialization skills, this is hardly surprising. But special education students often have socialization problems that (1) prevent or delay their integration into the mainstream (including the classroom and the community), (2) affect interpersonal relationships with peers, (3) interfere with the development of close friendships, (4) interfere with their ability to focus on academic or other tasks in group settings, and (5) detract from their attractiveness as prospective employees.

Teacher training in social skill instruction can be facilitated by video cassettes such as "Skillstreaming," a demonstration of effective social skills training techniques, available from Research Press. Instructional strategies that have been used for developing social skills in students with disabilities include the following:

- modeling: exposing the child to role play or other displays of appropriate behavior on the part of others
- strategic placement: placing the child in situations where he or she will come into contact with children who display prosocial behaviors
- correspondence training: building positive correlations between verbal reports of behaviors and the actual behavior
- positive reinforcement/shaping: use of tokens or other contingencies, such as differential adult attention, to reinforce positive actions
- prompting and coaching: giving hints, providing assistance in discriminating among cues, or highlighting antecedent conditions to encourage the student in appropriate behaviors
- positive practice: following a wrong behavior in a situation with the rehearsal of positive behaviors
- multimethod training packages: commercial materials using combinations of instructional strategies (Carter & Sugai, 1988)

Carter and Sugai (1988) cite a variety of instructional materials on the market at the present time, and more enter the marketplace each year to help teachers impart social skills to students who are deficient in them.

DEVELOPING COMPETENCE IN FUNCTIONAL SKILLS

In Chapter 1, reference was made to a basic model for growth in self-sufficiency (Weisgerber et al., 1981) that generalizes across skill dimensions and applies to everyone, with or without disabilities. With respect to any particular enabling skill, the model recognizes three stages of personal growth: dependence, semi-independence, and independence.

The change from dependence to semi-independence to independence is not accidental—it is learned. For many persons with disabilities (but by no means for all), learning enabling skills to a point of self-reliance is a major undertaking. It is the knowledge that this is so that leads special educators to be especially aware of (and pleased with) small gains in a student's performance that others, less sensitive to the underlying behavioral change, would be likely to miss.

Educators (both regular and special) together with counselors and parents all provide support to students as they develop functional skills. Figure 3-2 below illustrates the idea that the individual's awareness of his or her skill affects decisions and performance in the different contexts of school, work setting, residence, and the community at large.

During the school years, many students are discouraged by the extra time it takes them to work out effective strategies for analyzing critical course content, taking notes, doing homework, studying longer hours, taking tests, or even moving about the campus. Nevertheless, it is the factor of individual determination that plays a major part in determining whether competence is developed or not, and whether the individual perseveres to overcome the attitudinal and physical barriers that are encountered.

Establishing Readiness and Setting Goals

Students with disabilities are not unlike regular students in that they need to be guided into developing the kinds of skills that will be needed in later life. Deciding what skills are needed and when it is appropriate to develop them is a highly individual matter. Because those who lack skills may be the poorest prepared to judge whether they need to develop them, it is typically the case that someone who is aware of the individual's strengths and weaknesses needs to be involved as a guiding influence.

It is important to note, however, that the involvement of the significant other should be in a *guiding* mode. That is, the individual who is in need of skill development should feel involved in the decision to develop the skill and in goal setting with respect to the level or type of skill to be developed.

This strategy takes advantage of two principles of skill-based learning:

1. People *learn best* what they *want* to learn and *see a reason* to learn.
2. People *remember what they learn* if they are able to *practice* the skill at appropriate times or places and their *performance is acknowledged* in a positive way.

Everyone has skills that he or she has not fully developed and will never develop. That doesn't mean that we are less human or less deserving of understanding than anyone else. This diversity in skill is what makes society so varied and interesting. At the same time, most people have a core set of skills that allows them to function effectively in day-to-day life. These skills are the minimum set necessary to enjoy a reasonable quality of life. They are skills toward which students with disabilities need to be guided.

Basic Enabling Skills

Basic enabling skills can be defined as those skills necessary for functioning at an "adequate" level of self-sufficiency and within the bounds of socially "acceptable" behavior. The absence of enabling skills means that activities of daily

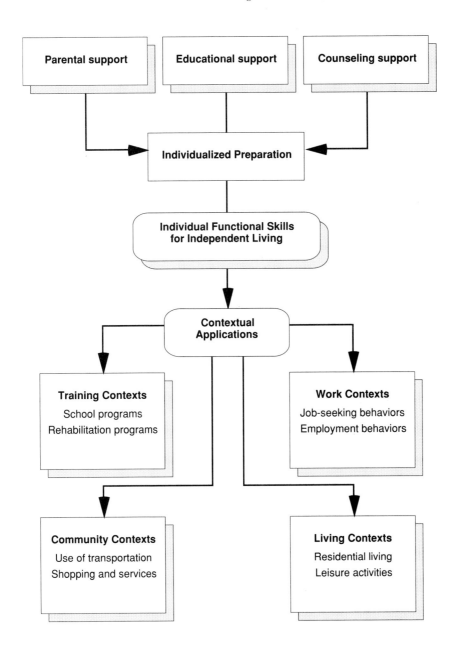

Figure 3-2 Individual Functioning and Awareness of Skills Needed in Various Environmental Contexts

living for the individual are likely to occur only if externally initiated and carried out. For example, a baby lacks the enabling skill of being able to feed himself or herself and depends on others for help at each feeding. Normally, the child learns quickly, passing through a stage of needing occasional help and becoming self-sufficient. Some children with disabilities may not quickly achieve self-sufficiency in feeding, others may never reach it.

However, the operational definition of self-sufficiency should not be taken too literally. For example, a quadriplegic individual whose physical condition is such that he or she is prevented from attending to his or her own bodily needs can still exhibit command and control through the act of directing an attendant to take certain actions to address those needs. In other words, the individual with quadriplegia is consciously directing the execution of the enabling skills by someone else and can be said to have the requisite enabling skill.

Enabling skills can be thought of as underlying skills, essential to individual performance. It is easy to see that perception is a prerequisite to the athletic skill of shooting baskets and must be combined with neuromuscular skills. Memory skills are necessary to learning rules and carrying out duties. Memory and cue recognition/discrimination (automaticity) are enabling skills that are antecedent to the academic performance of reading. Both perception and cue discrimination are necessary for the social skill of being able to recognize and interpret body language "messages." In their absence, interpersonal "closeness" and under-standing can be very superficial. Attentional skills are necessary as a precondi-tion to developing travel and mobility skills. In these and other examples, it is clear that enabling skills must be put in place during the school years if a person is to achieve independence and self-sufficiency as an adult living in a social world.

Academic and Vocational Skills

We use the terms "academic" and "vocational" to refer to all the content-related courses that form the core of instruction in schools and colleges. Of course, the basic education skills of reading, writing, and mathematics are fundamental. They represent a floor of academic performance for persons with disabilities who are intellectually intact, while they may represent a terminal goal for others with mental retardation. For those who have the potential to succeed in academic coursework, "mainstreaming" in competitive educational environments helps to prepare them for postsecondary education.

Madden and Slavin (1982) reported findings on the self-perception and behavioral benefits of mainstreaming for students who are mildly disabled. They state that mainstreaming can be "more effective" in building these students' self-esteem. However, they add that this finding "should not be construed to mean that special education can be abandoned or that mildly academically handicapped students should simply be moved back into regular classes and forgotten" (p. 26). They point out that mainstream teachers often resist students with academic handicaps who are placed in their classrooms and add, "It is not uncommon to see a classroom in which a teacher is teaching 29 students a unit on verb tenses while one 'mainstreamed' student is sitting in the back corner coloring or doing nothing at all" (p. 4).

One of the more promising approaches to the integration of mainstreamed children with disabilities into regular classes involves cooperative learning (ERIC/OSEP Special Project on Interagency Information Dissemination, 1988b; Madden & Slavin, 1982). Cooperative learning changes the competitive structure of the classroom, with students working in small, heterogeneous learning teams. Team Assisted Individualization (TAI) is a variant of cooperative learning in which dramatic gains in social acceptance for the student with a disability have been found between pre- and post-test assessments under experimental conditions (Slavin, Madden, & Leavy, 1982). In the TAI approach, teams are formed on the basis of pretests. The individuals then work on individualized learning packets at their own level; their teammates check their answers and help with problems. Evaluation is based on team averages.

Hayward and Wirt (1990) reviewed the access to vocational education of handicapped and disadvantaged students. Interestingly, they found that students with disabilities earned an average of 5.2 credits in vocational education as compared with an average of 4.02 credits for nondisabled students. Of those students with disabilities who took vocational education classes, 81.7% took them in regular classes as opposed to self-contained classrooms. However, it appears that gender, combined with disability, does tend to prevent female students from participating fully in vocational education classes. Hayward and Wirt recommended that greater emphasis should be given to placement services as students leave school and the provision of structured "follow-on" services to gather information on their progress.

Social-Employability Skills

Everyone has to learn the boundaries of acceptable behavior. Those boundaries are established either by rule or by custom, and they may change from setting to setting. For example, students must conform to certain social standards that characterize the conduct of formal instruction in school settings. In contrast, when one enters the world of work, things are different—though work rules may have much in common, such as getting to work on time, they are also unique and specific in different business organizations.

When boundaries are set by convention, such as in social situations, it is frequently harder for the low-functioning individual with a disability to know what is permissible and what is not. Nevertheless, if the disabled individual is to live independently in the community and enjoy the company of others, it is very important to learn what is "off limits" and what is not. For example, hugging can be an appropriate act in particular circumstances (e.g., celebrations) or when greeting someone to whom one feels personally close, but it is inappropriate as a way of showing friendliness unless those criteria are met, and rarely is it appropriate in places of business.

Social Skills

Gresham (1981) reviewed the status of social skills training and concluded that it is a potentially effective approach to successful mainstreaming of handicapped children. Kelley (1982) applied time-series analysis to the measurement of learned social skills in applied settings. Hoier and Foster (1985) discussed ways of assessing children's social skill status and needs. They differentiated three kinds of criteria used in social skill assessment: (1) direct, short-term outcomes produced by the behavior, (2) comparisons of the behavior to a standard or norm, and (3) subjective judgments of peers and adults.

More recently, Gresham and Elliott (1990) developed the Social Skills Rating System (SSRS) to provide educators with a tool for assessing the current status of children's social skills and for linking evaluation to intervention. Rating scales are provided for the preschool level (ages 3 to 5; 40 behaviors rated), the elementary level (48 behaviors rated), and the secondary level (42 behaviors rated). The rating system involves a three-point scale on each item, asking "how often" for each social skill (never, sometimes, very often), either observed or estimated. A separate three-point scale of importance (not important, important, critical) establishes the teacher's feelings about the skill in relation to "success" in his or her classroom.

Rusch and Schutz (1981), addressing the vocational and social behavior of the mentally retarded, studied social survival skills, which they defined as the behaviors of workers that influence the behavior of other workers. They noted that one of the most critical social skills is being able to follow directions, and they cited research that indicated that techniques designed to increase attention were helpful in making instructions understood. Rusch and Schutz argued that it is especially important that social skill training should address maintenance and transfer of learned skills. One of the maintenance strategies that appears to be helpful involves training individuals who are severely disabled in self-management and self-reinforcement of appropriate behaviors (Lovitt & Ballew, 1988).

Weisgerber (1984b) and his colleagues at the American Institutes for Research conducted a multiyear study aimed at the development of a curriculum for building self-reliance in the domain of social skills. In this study, the essential social skill needs were identified by a survey of service providers in educational institutions and community agencies across the country. These questions were put to the providers: Based on the persons with disabilities that you serve, what social skills do these individuals lack that are likely to interfere with their functioning in school, community, or workplace environments? Of these, which are they unlikely to develop on their own to an adequate or self-sufficient level?

Analysis of the hundreds of named social skills led to a classification system that then became the basis for curriculum development. Eleven areas of need and 85 topics or "learning points" were identified. In descending order of frequency of their nomination by service providers in the field, the eleven areas were

1. handling stress and conflict (involving 18 topics)
2. taking responsibility for actions and decisions (12 topics)
3. communicating effectively (11 topics)
4. naming and expressing feelings (10 topics)
5. responding to suggestions and directions (6 topics)
6. developing close, caring relationships (7 topics)
7. contributing to groups (6 topics)
8. caring for yourself (4 topics)
9. touching in the right way (5 topics)
10. respecting the rights of others (3 topics)
11. showing honesty and fairness (3 topics)

Inspection of the topics reveals functional skills that should be developed during the school years for application throughout the balance of the school years and into the adult years, when the students will be given the opportunity to exhibit self-reliance in society at large. In the first area listed above, topics included handling personal failure, embarrassment, rejection, fear, frustration, criticism, pressure, complaints, arguments, teasing, anger, and conflicting messages. It also addressed the need to negotiate compromises, find solutions to problems, be helpful to others, do difficult but necessary things, accept fair punishment, and respond to emergencies.

The behaviors above are representative of a large variety of skills that self-reliant adults utilize more or less routinely as they mature and gain experience. To the extent that emotional-behavioral disorders are present, these social skills are not likely to occur as a result of maturation. Realistically, some skills may never be learned beyond the level of semi-independence. Nevertheless, they deserve attention in programs of rehabilitation, including programs that prepare students for independent living.

Stowitschek and Salzberg (1987) developed a social protocol curriculum in which three dimensions of training affect the transfer of learned skills: (1) ecological analysis of key social skills, (2) identifying the interactions of these skills with different work environments, and (3) the generalization of effects to contexts where training did not take place. Ratings of skill development were along a five-point scale, with the midpoint representing use of a particular skill about 50% of the time. The 22 competencies and 102 subcompetencies in the curriculum were distributed across three main areas—daily living skills, personal social skills, and occupational guidance and preparation.

Adolescents and young adults have a special need for social communication skills, such as are required in job interviews (Schmitt, Cartledge, & Growick, 1988). The kinds of social skill instruction that students with disabilities are taught in the elementary school, therefore, will not suffice as the students approach the time when they will be leaving school and will be "on their own." Secondary students with disabilities need to be taught skills that will be expected in community-oriented social settings, especially work settings.

Too often, social and interpersonal skills are infrequently considered as a basis for choosing one occupational area over another, and this can be a costly oversight. Typically, employers value employees who have social and interpersonal skills (O'Neil, 1976). If social skills are not displayed and the productivity of the work team is disturbed, the employer may (and frequently does) terminate the individual. Consequently, the selection of an appropriate job or career should reflect the extent of social interaction, both directly (interpersonal relations) and indirectly (performing a fair share of the work), that will be encountered on the job. These can be called employability skills.

Employability Skills

Weisgerber, Dalldorf, Jabara, Feichtner, and Blake (1989) pointed out one way to differentiate jobs along social-employability dimensions. The key is to classify them according to whether the job requires interaction in settings that involve three levels:

1. Level 1: independent, supervised work, where interactions are mostly with the immediate supervisor
2. Level 2: group or crew-type work situations, where coworkers are a critical factor
3. Level 3: customer-oriented work situations, where strangers are encountered

The expected level of sophistication in social and interpersonal skills is clearly different in these three categories of work situations. In the first level, the emphasis is on being able to take directions, ask questions if necessary, and follow through reliably. In the second level, these are still necessary, but in addition the employee must be able to work as part of a team, sharing in the work at an acceptable rate and with consistency and not disrupting coworkers as they perform any specialized duties. At the third level, the worker needs an array of social skills with strangers. To the extent that customers represent the lifeblood of businesses, it is critical that persons with disabilities be prepared for the unpredictable behaviors that "outsiders" can exhibit, such as making unreasonable demands. If the individual is weak in work-related social skills at this highest and most complex level, he or she must either be trained in them or a job must be selected that is commensurate with the actual level of skill.

The Social Competence and Employability Skills Curriculum (Weisgerber, Armstrong, Sacks, & Steele, 1989) is designed to provide a system of instruction for secondary students with disabilities who are transitioning out of school and into the workplace. The curriculum, which addresses the three different levels of social demand on the job, provides separate guides for administrators, teachers, counselors in community agencies, and employers.

Administrators of transition programs are being called upon to organize and supervise transition programs that are partly school based and partly community based. They must show leadership in

- determining the scope of the program
- organizing the service delivery team
- building support for the program in the community
- setting goals for the program
- recruiting students to the program
- maintaining records and assessing program outcomes

Instructors in transition programs and counselors in community agencies should collaborate closely as they prepare the students. A careful, individual evaluation of each student's needs and interests should *precede* instruction. They should assess students' job readiness *after* appropriate training and *during* work-relevant tasks. This assessment can take place initially in students' completion of assigned duties and "jobs" within the educational framework but must also occur during work experience in the community at large. The former can be accomplished by the teaching staff, but the latter is best accomplished by a placement specialist or job coach from the school, or by a counselor from rehabilitation services or other community agency.

Employers who agree to be involved in the provisional placement of students with disabilities often have apprehensions at first. They need to be informed about the positive aspects of the experience, and they appreciate knowing that if help is needed with the student, it will be forthcoming (Weisgerber et al., 1989). This is especially true of the more severely disabled students, who ordinarily need supported employment services on a prolonged basis.

Responsibility and Independent Living Skills

School-based training is, in and of itself, somehow inconsistent with the development of individual resourcefulness and independence, personal characteristics that are desirable in adult living. Some, but not all, students with disabilities do receive community-based training, such as mobility training in the use of public transportation for blind persons. However, there is less than widespread agreement on the extent to which skills needed by all special students in order to meet the demands of their community environments is a major school concern. There is greater agreement when the individuals are moderately or severely disabled.

Wiggins and Behrmann (1988) presented the case for increasing independence of moderately and severely disabled youth through community learning. By this they meant providing instruction in the community in a structured program, beginning at age 10 and continuing throughout the balance of schooling. Instructional settings, or extended classrooms as they are sometimes called, include restaurants, grocery stores, banks, and drugstores. Safety instruction is an important part of this functional training, as are many of the elements of social interaction. Among the latter are how to make eye contact, how to ask for help when lost, how to order and eat a meal, and so forth. Money skills play a part in this instruction and, perhaps not too surprisingly, participating students in the community-based program in the Fairfax County, Virginia, schools described by Wiggins and Behrmann have improved in functional academics as well.

Sheldon, Sherman, Schumaker, and Hazel (1984) developed the *Social Skills Curriculum* with the intention that instruction would take place in both school and community settings. Many of the 30 skills in the curriculum lend themselves to instruction in multiple settings, and many of the skills are essential in building personal responsibility and the behaviors that are necessary for independent living. Instruction takes place in three sequenced activities: awareness, practice, and application. In the awareness phase, learners interact with written booklets and workbooks. In the practice phase they are involved in role playing. The application phase involves assignments out of the classroom.

USING TECHNOLOGY TO ADVANTAGE

Technology has been the source of tremendous breakthroughs for students and adults with disabilities. Not all problems can be overcome with technology, of course, but it is nonetheless true that the opportunity to function fully in society is aided considerably to the extent that people who are disabled in some way can afford to acquire and learn to use technology that is appropriate to their needs and ambitions.

Computer-Based Instruction

Computerization has changed the face of American society. It has also had a major impact on the ability of persons with disabilities to function more effectively. The question naturally arises, how can computer technology be exploited for the benefit of persons with disabilities? The answer is, in more ways than one can imagine. Reller and Weisgerber (1987) reviewed some of the "breakthroughs" that have been accomplished by persons with disabilities as a result of using computer technology. McDermott and Watkins (1983) pointed out that there are numerous parallels between teaching techniques recommended by special educators and the attributes of computer-assisted instruction (CAI):

- frequent and immediate feedback
- individualized pacing and programming
- modularized and hierarchical curriculum
- outcomes stated as performance objectives
- a mastery learning paradigm
- clarity of presentation
- motivation
- a multisensory learning format
- personalized instruction

In planning for a comprehensive study of the application of computer technology to the problems of students who are learning disabled, Project CRE-ATE, supported by the Office of Special Education Programs (Weisgerber, 1984a, 1987), examined the implications of research and theory for computer use. He established that there was evidence to support the use of computers in a hierarchical learning paradigm. As shown in Figure 3-3, research was formulated at four hierarchical levels. From low to high, these include neuro-muscular vision skills, enabling visual-perception skills, cognitive processing skills, and academic performance skills. Academic performance skills, dealing with subject matter content, were not researched in Project CREATE since they were the focus of studies in related research at other institutions.

In Figure 3-3, we see examples of the major skills that are associated with each functional level. Separately, we see some of the indices that are commonly used to draw inferences about the level of performance that each person exhibits. Thus at the academic performance level, educators base their judgments about students' knowledge acquisition skills (e.g., learning style and study skills), language skills (e.g., expressive and receptive skills), and test taking skills (e.g., problem solving and recall) on how well they read (orally or silently), handle vocabulary (definitions and contextual applications), and spell (other than phonetically). These indices may be discrete or combined. They definitely tend to be additive; that is, reading is directly linked to all three of the skills indicated in the figure in the academic performance area.

The rationale for this hierarchy is straightforward and can be illustrated by a hypothetical example. Suppose that Student A is having difficulty in reading. Assume that it has been determined that intelligence, family support, and other factors are not at fault and that Student A has shown high performance in other scholastic endeavors. Assume also that the school has computer software, mostly of the drill and practice type, and that Student A has used it but still experiences difficulty in reading. Why?

Of course, we don't know why, but we do have evidence that the form of educational support offered so far has not worked. There is no reason to believe that "more of the same" will lead to any important change in the academic performance skill of reading (or grammar, or spelling) until the barrier that Student A is encountering is addressed directly.

If the performance skills are low, and the use of performance training (i.e., direct practice in reading, spelling, etc.) isn't working, then the key to the problem might be in deficient cognitive processing skills. If this is the case, then appropriately designed computer software might help in such processing skills as literal comprehension (e.g. identifying facts and details), sequencing (e.g., forming time-based logical relationships), or concept formation (e.g., finding the main idea in textual material).

Similarly, cognitive processing skills must be built on a solid foundation of perceptual enabling skills. Perceptual enabling skills involve differentiating letter shapes and features (singly and in combination), word shapes and features, line tracking, and other fundamental elements in the reading process. It is reasonable to expect that Student A's visual discrimination abilities had to be in place before he or she could begin to manipulate textual meanings at the cognitive level. Furthermore, these discrimination skills had to be at a near-automatic level if higher-level cognitive processing was to be accomplished efficiently.

Academic Performance Level:

Effective, efficient reading
in school contexts

Skills	Indices
Knowledge acquisition	Oral and silent reading
Language skills	Vocabulary mastery
Test taking	Spelling accuracy

Cognitive Processing Level:

Rapid, accurate acquisition
and comprehension of text

Skills	Indices
Note facts and details	Organized relationships
Follow sequence of events	Comprehension
Draw inference	Reasoning
Grasp main ideas	Problem solving

Perceptual Enabling Level:

Rapid, accurate visual discrimination
of symbols and words

Skills	Indices
Perceive character features	Differentiate letter shapes
Perceive sets of characters	Recognize letter combinations
Identify words by length, shape and letter combinations	Recognize words on sight
	Identify target words in a field

Neuromuscular Vision Level:

Efficient binocular vision at
near and far distances

Skills	Indices
Muscle balance	Phoria and eye alignment
Depth perception	Stereopsis discrimination
Accommodation	Adjusting focus far and near
Sensory and motor fusion	Fusion speed and endurance
Ocular motility	Tracking eye movements

Figure 3-3 A Conceptual Hierarchy of Skills Contributing to Effective Reading

Again, if it is apparent that Student A is experiencing difficulty in the perceptual area, there might be an underlying problem in the neuromuscular vision skill level. Difficulty encountered at the visual-neuromuscular level due to deficiencies in the focusing and converging systems of the eyes will quickly fatigue the student; his or her attention will wander, and reading becomes a chore to be avoided. Some students improperly fuse images appearing on the retinas, have poor binocular vision at "near" (the usual reading distance with a textbook), or have difficulty in accommodation of far to near (as in adjusting between the chalkboard and the printed matter on their desks).

With the support of the Office of Special Education Programs, Weisgerber and Rubin (1985) and Grisham (1985) conducted interlocking research studies using computer technology with learning-disabled students. Prototype software was developed at each hierarchical level (except the academic performance level) that took advantage of the nature of computer technology.

For example, the research on neuromuscular vision skills by Grisham (1985) involved assessing 221 students in special education and special reading programs in the intermediate and secondary grades. Of these, 51 (23%) were referred to vision specialists for disorders of acuity, refractive error, eye alignment, convergence, ocular health, and color vision. Students who passed the visual screening were then given a comprehensive binocular vision assessment to establish their visual efficiency. The incidence of visual efficiency disorders in 180 students was unexpectedly high, as shown in Table 3-1.

A comparison of deficiencies with students randomly chosen from normally achieving students at the same schools showed a difference in incidence, summarized in Table 3-2.

Students with visual efficiency disorders were then challenged to develop these skills through specially designed software that presented a series of two- and three-dimensional computer "games" (resolved with special glasses); a number of the students showed significant improvement (Grisham, McLaughlin, Rubin, Bacon, Silverman, & Joers, 1986).

Table 3-1 Incidence of Visual Efficiency Disorders for Students in Special Education or Reading Programs

	Intermediate Grades (N=113)		Secondary Grades (N=67)	
	N	Percent	N	Percent
Focusing deficiency	47	42	18	27
Vergence deficiency	38	34	19	28
Gross convergence	24	21	25	37

Table 3-2 Incidence Rates for Readers with and without a Disability

	Incidence				Chi Square Probability
	Without Disability		*With a Disability*		
Fusion deficiency	3/34	9%	38/112	34%	*p*<.005
Focusing deficiency	7/37	19%	47/113	41%	*p*<.02
Gross convergence deficiency	2/36	6%	24/113	21%	*p*<.03

For students who had difficulty in discriminating characters (e.g., letter confusion and reversals) and who labored at decoding words rather than automatically recognizing their critical features, experimental prototype software, called Turboscan, was developed to build automaticity into these enabling skills. Because automaticity and correct discriminations were both goals, it was essential that no other distracting variables impede skill acquisition. Consequently, the software was designed so that the interface between the child and the screen display required neither a fine motor skill nor a set of learned operating rules any more complex than "Press any key." Additionally, the software had features that

1. allowed the setting of the rate of presentation (either at some specific rate or at a variable rate that was speeded or slowed by the error rate of the student)
2. provided motivation in a gamelike context where students' correct answers earned them "gold bars" that were "collected" on screen by a sprite (either a duck or a robot)
3. provided corrective feedback in a nonthreatening way
4. displayed the student's progress toward a discrimination goal on the screen and recorded and printed out the student's progress so that teachers could assess for themselves whether particular problems were being overcome
5. provided a means for changing the program material through a built-in editing program that allowed teachers to easily modify the content, including the ability to invert and reverse letters or present them in either normal or much-enlarged format.

In controlled experiments, significant gains were achieved in cue discrimination and automaticity by elementary and secondary students with learning disabilities.

For students who needed to develop their comprehension skills, prototype software was developed in the CREATE (Center for Research and Evaluation in the Application of Technology to Education) project that initially focused on recognition of facts and moved progressively toward the higher skill of inferring from facts. The software consisted of a series of detective stories that built these skills. It became clear that these skills can be developed through software that places a premium on attention to detail but also encourages thinking that integrates information to higher levels of abstraction.

Using Other Technologies

Technology has made an impressive contribution to the education of persons with disabilities when its use has been thoughtfully planned, the materials carefully designed, and the application of the technology clearly tied to instructional goals or improvements in functional performance in general living. Technology is very much a contributor to the quality of life of persons with disabilities. As such, technology needs to be made available to young people with disabilities as early in their lives as is practicable. They need to grow comfortable with its use and apply it effectively in the solution of everyday challenges.

Illustrative of the application of technology to both learning and day-to-day functioning are the different devices that have been developed for the blind and visually impaired. The Optacon, an optical-to-tactile converter, was developed to enable blind persons to "read" ink print text through the fingertip. Researched almost 20 years ago by Weisgerber, Everett, Puzarne, and Shanner (1973) to establish its potential for use in education, this pioneering device (developed by Telesensory Systems, Inc.) has been instrumental in allowing totally blind persons to gain access to print materials of all kinds and even to computer screens. Both Braille and speech output are now available on microcomputers, and another computer-based device, the Kurzweil Reading Machine, directly converts printed text material into "spoken words." There are even "talking" calculators. For persons with low vision, devices have been developed that use video technology to dramatically enlarge images, increase contrast, or provide reversed field (white on black) displays.

There are also a number of special purpose devices for sensing the environment and thereby enabling greater mobility and functional awareness of the environment (de Haas & Weisgerber, 1978; Weisgerber & de Haas, 1978). All of these technologies offer a significant measure of independence to the blind individual. In turn, this independence allows the blind individual to be more active in the community in general.

Without attempting to elaborate on the extensive advances in technology that have benefited persons with disabilities (far too many to be recited here), it is important to add that breakthroughs in the design of components used in technology are becoming more and more common. Frequently, these advances result from interdisciplinary efforts among medical, scientific, and engineering professionals.

Special purpose equipment can greatly extend the existing physical capacity of individuals with disabilities. For example, rehabilitation equipment vendors offer a variety of manual controllers that allow gross motor skills to supplant fine motor skills. In addition, "sip-and-puff" controllers can replace manual control altogether in a number of applications, including telephone operation and environmental control in the home.

Some technological developments are natural extensions of work that has been evolving over many years, such as the technology involved in wheelchairs. According to its manufacturer, the Permobil wheelchair has been designed for use in rough terrain (e.g., a 20-degree incline out of doors) and still be workable for a long time (87% of chairs 13 or more years old are still in use) (Permobil, 1990). In a recent innovation, an electric wheelchair has been designed by staff at the Rehabilitation Research and Development Center at the Veterans Administration Hospital in Palo Alto, California, for use by quadriplegics; infrared sensors "read" the head motions of the individual and translate that movement into directional commands for the wheelchair (Jaffe, 1988).

Among the more exotic and exciting developments in technology are those involved in applying new knowledge in neural sciences to the direct stimulation of paralyzed limbs and to the control of artificial limbs worn by limbless persons. This technology is so sophisticated and elegant that it begins to approximate the way our mind, nerves, and muscles work naturally to allow the accomplishment of simple and complex tasks. Evidence of the range of work being undertaken in this area can be seen in the fact that 29 different research projects were reported on in the Proceedings of the 10th Annual Conference on Rehabilitation Technology (Steele & Gerrey, 1987).

In some instances, technology has been adapted for leisure purposes (e.g., hand-powered bicycles, noise-emitting balls). In other cases, such as the many variations of communication boards, technology enables persons without speech to express their thoughts, feelings, and needs, certainly one of the most fundamental functions in life. Recent federal legislation encourages the development of technology for persons with disabilities, both through specialized engineering research centers and through increased technology transfer from space science and other "high-tech" fields. It is a safe bet that the rate of technological development will only accelerate in the years ahead, and persons with disabilities will assuredly benefit in ways we cannot yet imagine.

IDENTIFYING VOCATIONAL AND CAREER INTERESTS

Students commonly are concerned with the here and now. Most of them are less concerned with planning for the future than with getting through the immediate problems encountered each day. Long-range thinking, like relating experiences and coursework to possible career choices, is relatively unusual. Some students simply assume they will follow in the footsteps of their parents or someone else who is close to them. All too frequently, students with disabilities postpone career decision making until close to graduation, or they neglect it altogether. Unless the school takes the initiative in having students think in terms of their vocational future, they are unlikely to make good decisions and begin planning for the time that they exit school.

Fairweather (1989) surveyed a nationally representative sample of 1549 secondary-level local education agencies to determine the availability of vocational programs and transition services for students with disabilities. There were 1450 respondents for a response rate of 93.6%. Findings from this survey indicated that

- traditional forms of school support are fairly widely available in the local education agencies (LEAs) (counseling, 86%; special education students participation in vocational education, 71.9%; occupational therapy or physical therapy, 57.1%; assignment of a local vocational rehabilitation counselor to the school, 52.3%)
- nontraditional programs are somewhat less available to special education students (transition programs, 44.6%; staff to find jobs for the students, 36.5%)

Eagle (1989) suggested a model for successful programming of students with disabilities in vocational programs and identified 20 practices that are "most essential to making exemplary programs work" (p. 2).

Awareness of Career and Employment Alternatives

In 1960 the American Institutes for Research undertook a major study aimed at showing the relationship of patterns of interest and ability to career entry and satisfaction. In Project Talent, extensive baseline data were gathered from a representative sample of 400,000 high school students in grades 9 through 12. Eleven years later a follow-up was conducted with 38,000 job-holders who had been in the 11th and 12th grades in 1960. Based on the findings of this study, a handbook was prepared (American Institutes for Research, 1976) covering 151 ability and interest profiles for different jobs in 12 career groups:

1. engineering, physical sciences, mathematics, and architecture
2. medical and biological sciences
3. business administration
4. general teaching and social service
5. humanities, law, social and behavioral sciences
6. fine arts and performing arts
7. technical jobs
8. proprietors and sales workers
9. mechanics and industrial trades
10. construction trades
11. secretarial, clerical, and office workers
12. general labor, public and community service

It is worth noting that six of the career groups typically require college degrees, while six do not necessarily require degrees.

Intellectual and Physical Capacity

As one might expect, the range of career alternatives open to persons with disabilities increases in accordance with their level of functioning in skills that make them desirable as employees. Given the opportunity, higher intellectual capacity will ordinarily lend itself to career goals in technical and professional fields. Conversely, low intellectual functioning tends to lead toward jobs in service (especially food service, gardening, and janitorial) and, to some extent, manufacturing (assembly).

Distinctions in occupational choice may arise from physical capacity. Apart from the obvious job-specific requirements that may exist regarding mobility and agility, strength and endurance, or dexterity and eye-hand coordination, there may exist hidden problems. For example, quadriplegics' employment options do not include labor-intensive jobs, but more than that, their paralysis may affect the elimination of bodily waste, which means that they must factor this problem into their choice of work sites. Similarly, their disability is likely to affect the ability of the body to adjust to temperature extremes, limiting the kinds of environments in which they can work.

One approach to the assessment of physical and intellectual demands associated with particular occupations is to refer to the *Dictionary of Occupational Titles* (*DOT*), which details this information. However, matching the physical and intellectual demands of the job to individual capacity is not straightforward, and many considerations come into play (Weisgerber, 1980).

Increasingly, temporary work placements while the young person with disabilities is still in school are valuable in testing whether interests and abilities are well suited to particular jobs. At the secondary level, it is important to keep in mind the youthfulness of the persons being placed—most of them are simply getting some type of work experience that teaches them what is expected of them on the job (e.g., punctuality, reliability), and the first job seldom blossoms into a career. At the college level, job placement is far more critical; here the significance of getting placed within the career field that one has chosen is often related to opportunities for advancement.

PREPARATION FOR TRANSITION FROM THE SCHOOL ENVIRONMENT

Certainly the most well-known transitional model for school-to-work transition is the one advanced by OSERS (Will, 1984b). Sometimes called the "bridges from school to working life" model, this simple model, which is shown in adapted form below, has been the basis for most of the comprehensive transition programming in the secondary schools.

As can be seen in Figure 3-4, the essence of the model is that three levels of service provision are assumed during the transition period. The first transition level assumes that no special vocational placement services are needed. That is, services that are made available are essentially the same for exiting students both with and without disabilities, and they are provided in the context of general school programming. Although not shown, the possibility of postsecondary education as an intervening stage between secondary school and work is accounted for within the first level.

Some students who received special services in secondary school and are admitted to higher education prefer to remain "unlabeled." However, assuming that they were receiving services in secondary school as a result of an appropriate diagnosis of disability, the opportunity to enter higher education does not necessarily mean that their need for assistance is gone. Some students are determined to do as much as they can on their own. Others see services as a path to becoming more competitive in what is certainly a highly competitive environment.

The second transition level in Figure 3-4 assumes that the transition will be successful if "time-limited services" are made available. The individuals following this transitional bridge may be assisted for a time-limited period. Services may take the form of vocational rehabilitation, postsecondary vocational education, or other job training programs. The over-riding assumption about persons with disabilities at the second level is that once they have been job trained, helped with transportation or other special needs, and have been placed on the job for an initial period, they will no longer need special assistance to perform satisfactorily.

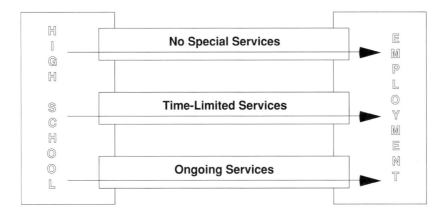

Figure 3-4 Major Components of the Transition Process. *Source:* Adapted from "An Advocate for the Handicapped" by M.C. Will, 1984, *American Education*, January-February, pp. 4-6. Published 1984 by the U.S. Department of Education.

This time-limited transitional service strategy applies to most of the transitional programs undertaken by regular high schools in which students have been mainstreamed. There are substantial limitations, however, in how long most schools feel an obligation to follow up with on-the-job support once transition (dropout or graduation) occurs.

The third level of transition in Figure 3-4 assumes that ongoing services will be needed. The term that has been used for this ongoing service is "supported employment." Supported employment has been defined in the *Federal Register* as consisting of competitive work in an integrated setting for individuals who, because of their handicaps, need ongoing support services to perform that work. The status of the supported employment initiative in the field has recently been reported in the literature (Wehman, Kregel, & Shafer, 1989).

Not considered acceptable (to OSERS) is providing lifelong custodial care or preparing individuals for later vocational services by means of make-work activities. Practically, this distinction means that many sheltered workshops for more severely disabled individuals are not viewed as valid work placements by OSERS. Rather, OSERS argues for work placements within competitive work environments. In this situation ongoing services are typically provided by agencies in the form of an assigned supervisor or coordinator.

It is appropriate to note, however, that all sheltered workshops are not the same, and that the label is not necessarily a good indicator of what takes place in each such setting. Some do function effectively as transitional vehicles to prepare severely disabled persons for "regular" work placement. Schill, McMartin, and Matthews (1988) pointed out that while some sheltered workshops pay as little as 10 cents an hour because there is little or nothing for the subjects to do, there are others that involve productive activity and pay minimum wage and above.

Access to rehabilitation services is not age-dependent, but it is often overlooked by parents and school personnel. If students with disabilities leave school without either being admitted to college or having a job prospect, they can still approach vocational rehabilitation services for assistance. (For most students, we take the view that this linkage should be made before leaving school.)

Recently, the demonstration transition programs in two school districts (Santa Barbara, California, and Grays Harbor, Washington) have been examined as case studies. Both were reaching the end of their funding periods. Carried out in ethnographic style, these case studies provide a sense of how service providers and parents who were involved in the programs viewed them, and what they thought were program strengths and weaknesses (Stake, Denny, & DeStefano, 1989). Interagency cooperation was found to be quite important in the evolution of the two projects and played a central part in making the transition programs work smoothly.

For a number of reasons, the interface between special education and rehabilitation services has often been uncoordinated, though coordination would obviously be advantageous to both. This lack of coordination stems, in part, from different federal (and state) regulations, definitions, priorities, methods, and criteria for judging performance of professionals (Szymanski, King, Parker, & Jenkins, 1989). In recent years, jointly issued memoranda from the state commissioners of education and rehabilitation services have begun to have some effect, though at the field level smooth coordination is still more infrequent than common. Nevertheless, for those students with disabilities who make the transition into the community and require the assistance of agency staff in some manner (and who are eligible for vocational rehabilitation services under existing criteria), the transition can be greatly facilitated by sharing information and collaborating in service delivery.

Special education and vocational rehabilitation counselors share similar concerns—both are charged with preparing persons with disabilities to function in a competitive adult world to the maximum extent possible. For many persons with disabilities, this includes employment in the mainstream of competitive employment. Further, it means preparation for a variety of occupations, with the possibility that the person can advance within the career path that he or she chooses.

Both special educators and rehabilitation counselors are expected to help individuals with disabilities decide on appropriate employment goals (both immediate and long range). They are also expected to provide opportunities that will lead to attainment of the goal(s) and to provide reasonable, meaningful support in preparing the individual for entry into a job leading to advancement in the chosen career.

Persons with disabilities need to be involved, early and frequently, in the determination of vocational and career goals. Perhaps more than nondisabled persons, individuals who have been disabled from birth or early childhood may be unaware of the vocational alternatives open to them, and of what it takes to qualify. To the extent that they remain unaware and uninformed, they will take themselves out of consideration for many viable options.

Students with disabilities frequently do not understand the relationship between occupational demands and intellectual and physical capacity. They may not appreciate the importance of social and interpersonal skills in the choice of career goals. They are likely to be unaware of the ways in which technology, particularly computers, can open careers that otherwise might have been closed to them.

Training and Placement Strategies

Training strategies are numerous and varied in their effectiveness. Any attempt to comprehensively review all of them is beyond the scope of this book, but attention can be paid to selected strategies that are supported by a theoretical framework, are innovative, and have been shown to be effective. Agran, Martin, and Mithaug (1989) have emphasized "adaptability instruction" in the schools as a way of preparing students to deal with the numerous changes that they will encounter on the job, such as different work environments and task assignments.

Wehman, Kregel, and Barcus, (1985) developed a model for school-to-work transitioning by students with disabilities that has several distinctive characteristics. First, during the transition process, the model calls for input from the parent and the student. They are included, not excluded, from the goal-setting process. Second, there is an emphasis on interagency cooperation among the school, rehabilitation, adult day program, and vocational-technical center staff. Third, there is a formalized individual transition plan, which specifies the responsibilities of all who are involved. Fourth, alternative vocational outcomes are anticipated, including competitive placement, work crews and enclaves, and specialized sheltered work arrangements. Fifth, there is a follow-up 1 to 2 years later to determine the effectiveness of the transition programming.

The Specialized Training Program at the University of Oregon considers work and community integration to be essential to the quality of life of individuals with severe disabilities. They have identified several models of training and employment that can enhance social integration in community settings:

1. The enclave model: A group of 6 to 8 severely disabled individuals work in an integrated employment setting (biomedical equipment assembly) and receive training and support in that setting. They worked a 40-hour week and earned an average of $400 monthly (in 1984).
2. The supported jobs model: Individual placements are made by a not-for-profit organization in community settings. Each moderately or severely disabled individual receives support and training on an ongoing basis as required to maintain employment. The average monthly pay was $250.
3. The mobile crew model: A company employs several crews of workers with disabilities, each with five severely or moderately retarded individuals and a supervisor. Work is done from a mobile van rather than a permanent facility. Workers' earnings averaged $80 to $150 per month.
4. The benchwork model: About 15 to 28 workers with disabilities (IQ below 45) are at each employment location. The staff ratio is 1:5. The settings are segregated, but the program emphasizes community-oriented training in areas such as travel to and from work. Wages varied from $45 to $90 per month.

The Rehabilitation Research and Training Center at Virginia Commonwealth University has as its purpose the improvement of employability for persons who are severely disabled. According to a recent newsletter from the Center (Rehabilitation Research and Training Center, 1990), the number of persons placed in supported employment on an individual basis has risen in the 1986 to 1988 period from less than 4000 to about 10,000. The enclave approach is the next most often used method of placement, increasing from about 1000 placements to a little less than 4000 in the same period, followed closely by mobile crews, where placements increased from 1000 to a little more than 3000. In 25 states, the proportions of disabilities served in supported employment environments were 70.2% mental retardation, 14.8% mental illness, 2.7% sensory impairment, 2.1% cerebral palsy, 0.8% traumatic brain injury, and 9.3% other disabilities.

Community Living and Advocacy

Just as it is important (for many people) to get a job and earn an income, it is also very important that they be able to participate in the community. Many young people with disabilities have problems once they leave the protective environment of the school and try to live on their own. Advocates and group living arrangements can help ameliorate these problems to some extent.

Community Living

Minskoff, Sautter, Sheldon, Steidle, and Baker (1988) reported on a comparative study of the self-perceived "problem areas" of high school students with learning disability (N=114, average age 17.7) and adult applicants for vocational rehabilitation services (N=381, average age 23.2). In addition, 114 high school teachers identified six major problems faced by learning-disabled adults (the adults were not the same as those who self-reported): health, learning, daily living skills, personal adjustment, social skills, and vocational adjustment.

The three samples differed significantly in many areas in terms of their perception of problems. The numerous specific problems that were perceived differently by the samples at least at a .05 level of significance are listed below:

1. health: ear problems, sleep (teachers not included in this comparison)
2. learning: reading, coordination, listening, talking, thinking, visual perception, arithmetic, remembering, auditory perception, written composition, handwriting
3. daily living: shopping, handling money and banking, grooming, using public transportation, keeping track of time, housekeeping, using restaurants, driving
4. social skills: making and keeping friends, dating, making conversation, using free time, dependence on others, shyness, talking or acting before thinking
5. personal problems: control of emotions and temper, control of actions, depression, feeling angry often, feeling frustrated, lacking self-confidence
6. problems in getting and keeping jobs: knowing where to find a job, knowing how to get job training, filling out a job application, reading want ads, interviewing, having to be told each step in doing a job, making the same mistakes repeatedly, following directions, having inadequate time to learn job skills, taking criticism, finishing work on time, paying attention to job, working carefully, needing praise all the time

Adults with learning disabilities consistently characterized themselves as having more problems than did the high school students. The evaluations of the teachers of the learning disabled were closely aligned with the self-perceptions of the adults with learning disabilities. Minskoff and her associates (1988) attempted to explain these differences by suggesting that the high school students are sheltered from a number of these problems by the protection offered them within the education environment and that they therefore show a "lack of understanding of the reality of their situation" (p. 121).

In looking ahead from school to life in the community, these learning-disabled students, who would generally be considered high functioning in comparison with other special education students, seem to have underestimated their needs for assistance as adults. It is highly likely that students who are low functioning in school would also underestimate their needs, perhaps to a greater extent. As will be discussed in the next chapter, various group living arrangements in the community can help to address these practical problems.

Advocacy

Advocacy is a proven mechanism for affecting change. It is arguably an essential element in the quality of life of some lesser-abled persons, particularly the mentally retarded. It focuses energy and attention in areas where energy and attention should be directed and provides a basis for monitoring progress toward needs. Advocacy is the result of voluntary action based on conviction and experience.

An example of this self-help principle is shown by the deaf and hearing impaired community in San Leandro, California, where the Deaf Counseling, Advocacy, and Referral Agency (DCARA) publishes the *DCARA News*, a newspaper addressing issues and information "of, by and for the deaf." A recent edition of the newspaper provided a forum for discussion of policy issues at the federal and local levels, information on employment training opportunities, an article on computer networking, and information about pending legislation and current and coming lectures and other events of interest to members of the deaf and hearing-impaired community.

Advocacy is often used quite successfully by individuals with disabilities in situations when they find it necessary to speak out for their rights or demonstrate in the face of some inequity of opportunity. It can take the form of either self-advocacy or group advocacy. Since self-advocacy requires some form of public expression, knowledge of the alternatives in a given situation, and commitment to a principle, it has been more successfully practiced by persons with physical or sensory impairments than by persons with mental impairments.

Consider an actual experience of a college student with a disability who was overtly discriminated against by a faculty member who expressed the view that "a person with your handicap should not be entering the field which this course is designed to prepare qualified students to enter." In the absence of evidence, the faculty member made the assumption that the student with a disability was not going to be able to succeed in the chosen field and that he or she was not "qualified." However, three possibilities exist:

1. The individual with a disability has erroneously, even foolishly, selected a career that is totally inappropriate (e.g., vision is a criterion for control tower operators, pilots, and the like).
2. The individual is pioneering in a field where there is limited existing participation by persons with a similar disability (this can be a reflection

of past biases by professionals in the field more than an indication of a general inability to perform).

3. The individual is willing to work in the field in a specific role that does not require the capacity to perform *all* the functions that are "normally" associated with the job.

In either of the last two situations, which have been shared by many youths with disabilities entering "unlikely" professions, there is a need for the individual to stand up for himself or for herself. Rather than yielding to a prejudicial view about disability, the individual affected should be aware of his or her rights and seek remedies with authorities on the campus. Just how the individual takes action can make all the difference, both in the short term and the long term. Tact, persistence, and properly assembled evidence are the first steps to take; if necessary, recourse to legal action may be pursued.

The experiences reported by a number of successfully employed scientists, engineers, and mathematicians with disabilities suggests several effective strategies that may be used by undergraduates:

- meeting privately with the instructor at the beginning of a course to discuss possible problem areas and work out necessary adjustments (an example might be laboratory work, where specific techniques may not be readily accomplished due to the disability)

- enlisting the help of a third party (such as a notetaker among the other students) to accomplish specific tasks (for a blind student, for example, this might consist of taking down information written on the chalkboard)

- requesting third party intervention (in the case of an infringement of rights or unreasonable demands on the part of the faculty member) by the dean of the school or, more often, by the office serving students with disabilities

Effective advocacy requires strategic planning. When individuals and groups are irrational, irresponsible, or coercive in their advocacy actions, they run the risk of alienating the support of society as a whole and may even cause a backlash, to the ultimate disservice of their constituency. When advocates are persistent, logical, and "smart" in using the system, they tend to bring about many positive changes.

As stated previously, advocacy is a way of helping people with disabilities to reach their personal goals and maximize their functional potential in society. It can be used effectively in the community, on the campus, or within any organized group. But in the long run, advocacy that influences federal policy may be the most effective of all strategies. It has been instrumental in most of the major legislation passed in the last 15 years and the development and 1990 passage by Congress of the Americans with Disabilities Act (ADA).

Predicting Needed Support for Persons with Disabilities

The business of education is to develop in students *all* the tools they need to function effectively as adults and contribute to society in productive ways. Educators have increasingly come to realize that their role with students with disabilities consists of far more than seeing that subject matter mastery is achieved.

Everson, Barcus, Moon, and Morton (1987) indicated that interagency coordination is essential to the transitioning of students who are not self sufficient and who will need support in finding employment. They targeted the following areas as important for interagency training:

1. employment or postsecondary needs
2. residential needs
3. financial/income needs
4. recreation/leisure needs
5. medical needs
6. social/sexual needs
7. transportation needs
8. advocacy/legal needs
9. personal/home/money management needs

Campeau and Ananda (1989) identified functional performance indicators in four domains that are important in adult life: (1) self-help skills of daily living, (2) interpersonal skills used in social situations, (3) functional literacy and basic skills, and (4) skills for competitive employment. A student performance instrument called PASS (Performance Assessment for Self-Sufficiency) has been developed by Campeau and her colleagues at the American Institutes for Research to assess the readiness of students to make the transition from school to adult life and to estimate their need for adult services. The functional areas assessed with the instrument are as follows:

1. daily living
   - personal hygiene and grooming skills
   - health and safety skills
   - food skills
   - money management skills
   - mobility and transportation skills
   - housekeeping skills
2. personal and social development
   - communication skills
   - acting responsibly

- coping skills
- relationships with others
3. employment
  - job-seeking skills
  - work performance skills
  - working with others
4. educational performance
  - reading (including graphic displays, Braille, or other symbols)
  - writing (by hand, typewriter, computer, or other device)
  - mathematics (including the use of assistive devices)
  - academic work habits and skills

Following a national field test (expected to begin in federal fiscal year 1991) a refined version of the instrument will be introduced as a tool for local, state, and federal policy makers to use to estimate the level of demand for service delivery in adult service programs.

Students with disabilities vary considerably in their capacity to benefit from subject matter instruction. It is true that the basic skills need to be addressed in the educational plans of both low- and high-functioning students, and it is also true that high-functioning students need appropriate coursework to prepare them for college-level study. However, entitlement to the "provision of appropriate education" does not equate to or dictate a concentration on academic subject matter for *all* students with disabilities in public and private school programs. For example, students who are low functioning will need training in activities of daily living if they are to live in the community and share responsibility for their own well-being.

High-functioning students who can benefit from academic instruction should not overlook "extracurricular" activities and nonacademic studies. For example, such students may find that in addition to learning the traditional core content taught in educational programs, if they can gain hands-on experience in the use of computers, it will be much to their advantage. Whether in programming computers or simply using commercial programs, these students will be better able to find a competitive job or find it easier to compete in a college, university, or technical school.

Postsecondary Education and Disability Services Offices

Although many students with disabilities lack the intellectual capacity to be considered "college material," a number of students do (and should) enter higher education. Smith (1988) points out that "as a result of Section 504 of the

Vocational Rehabilitation Act, colleges receiving federal assistance can no longer discriminate against individuals in their recruitment or admissions procedures and must make reasonable accommodations for the LD (learning disability) student" (p. 54). Smith argues that professionals who serve students who are learning disabled "need to address the problems of the learning disabled throughout the life span" (p. 53).

In recognition of the special needs of students with disabilities at the post-secondary level, a national clearinghouse has been established. The Higher Education and Adult Training for People with Handicaps (HEATH) Resource Center has a wide variety of materials available (HEATH, 1989). For example, its 1989 resource directory was a compendium of 150 annotated references and resources for postsecondary education and disability.

HEATH staff are frequently asked about the importance of standardized tests for college admission (usually the SAT [Scholastic Aptitude Test] or the ACT assessment from the American College Testing Service). They point out that college admission is usually based on more than test scores (it is a range and not an absolute score that matters), including such things as prior grades, class standing, the rigor of high school courses, letters, interviews, and essays (HEATH, 1988).

The Pennsylvania State University, the University of Wisconsin at Whitewater, Wright State University, and Southern Illinois University have been identified as having outstanding broad-based postsecondary support programs. Other examples of university-based support programs include California State University at Northridge, where there is a strong program in support of learning-disabled, deaf, and orthopedically disabled students, and the University of California at Berkeley, where the support services for learning-disabled students include an admissions specialist and a learning disabilities specialist who acts as a resource person (Association for Children and Adults with Learning Disabilities 1990). An extensive list of postsecondary disabled student service offices is available through the Association of Handicapped Student Service Programs in Postsecondary Education (AHSSPPE).

Gaining Experience in Competitive Employment

Phelps and Lutz (1977) were among the early exponents of career exploration for special needs learners. They described procedures for cooperative work experience that were the forerunners for much of the training that occurs today.

Wehman and his associates (Wehman, Moon, Everson, Wood, & Barcus, 1988; Wehman, Wood, Everson, Goodwyn, & Conley, 1988) have been in the forefront of planning for the transition from school to work of severely disabled young people. They developed a step-by-step methodology for pre-employment training while the student is still in school that ensures a clear path from school to employment. The thrust of their approach involves community-based training and supported employment.

Gaylord-Ross et al. (1987) demonstrated community-referenced instruction with severely disabled students in technological work settings. The disabilities represented among their 12 students included mental retardation (7), learning handicaps (3), deafness (1), and communication handicaps (1). Training of tasks occurred over a three-semester period in the chemical laboratory of a major oil company. Learned tasks included a centrifuge test, flashpoint test, viscosity test, aeration test, foam test, pH test, making a saturated solution, calibration, pretreater/attachment, pretreater/assembly, and aniline point test. Most students learned three of these tasks. Training also included generic work skills such as grooming, use of public transportation, and worktime behavior. The median number of trials to criterion was 27, and the range was 9 to 97 trials. The median number of training hours for learned tasks was 2 hours and 37 minutes, and the range was from 45 minutes to 23 hours and 25 minutes.

In a separate study carried out by Gaylord-Ross and his associates (1987), three of these students were videotaped as they learned tasks in the chemical laboratory setting. In addition, three students were videotaped as they were trained to handle long distance calls in a community branch office of the phone company. These videotapes were then shown to groups of college and high school students to evaluate whether the subjects (six students) had developed vocational competence. Results were affirmative at the .001 level of confidence. Gaylord-Ross observes that community-referenced instruction

- should consist of a series of community training experiences during the secondary school years
- should involve variation in the types of work settings
- should span a range of difficulty in the job tasks performed

In the State of Washington, the Division of Developmental Disabilities has established supported employment guidelines as (1) working at least 20 hours per week, (2) wages based at least on a minimum wage/ productivity formula, and (3) integration of no more than eight persons with developmental disabilities working in proximity to one another (Nelson & Stowitschek, 1988).

Follow-up

Levine, Allen, and Wysocki (1986) compiled an annotated bibliography of follow-up studies, organized into four time periods: 1900 to 1939, 1940 to 1959, 1960 to 1974, and 1975 to 1986. The latter time period included 41 papers.

Fourteen papers related to developmentally delayed/mentally retarded persons; eight to learning-disabled persons; six to handicapped/special education students in general; four to emotionally or behavior disordered persons; three to language disordered persons, two to physically disabled persons; two to "mildly handi-capped" persons; one to mentally retarded, hearing-impaired, vision-impaired persons; and one to language-impaired, articulation-impaired persons.

Neubert, Tilson, and Ianacone (1989) reminded us that although a great a-mount of attention in the literature has been given to persons who are severely disabled and to their need for supported employment, the fact remains that a larger population of mildly handicapped students also needs attention to their postsecondary needs. In a postsecondary study of 64 mildly handicapped individuals who participated in a time-limited transition program called Job Training and Tryout, interesting employment patterns were revealed:

- The amount of staff time in support of the new workers decreased dramatically over the first 4 weeks on the job (week 1, a mean of 4.7 hours per person; week 2, a mean of 2.7 hours; week 3, a mean of 1.2 hours; and week 4, 47 minutes).

- About 74% of the students had some form of difficulty on the job in the first month, while 26% had no problems. In order of frequency, the difficulties were task related (inability to do the work, inadequate production rate, difficulty following directions), work adjustment related (attendance and punctuality, hygiene and grooming, social-interpersonal problems), or health related (seizures, low stamina).

- About 52% of the participants requested intervention by staff and made some kind of job change.

- Some 45 of the 64 individuals had the opportunity to be employed for a year. The fall-off in their employment at 2-, 6-, and 12-month periods was 84% employed, 76% employed, and 64% employed, respectively. Reasons included going to college (1), repeated seizures (1), staying home with child (1), entering a therapeutic counseling program (3), choosing not to work (4), and electing to enter an alternative day program with less emphasis on com-petitive employment (6).

This study does not indicate failure or success but rather a need for continued attention to the needs of individuals with disabilities after they have left the educational environment and made the transition into community life.

Scuccimarra and Speece (1990) examined the quality of life of mildly handicapped students two years after leaving high school. In particular, they examined the employment outcomes and social adjustment outcomes for 44 males and 21 females with disabilities who were part of a randomly drawn sample of members of the 12th grade class in a Washington, DC, school system consisting of 19 high schools. Of the original sample of 70, 60 were learning disabled, 6 were mentally retarded, 2 were emotionally impaired, and 2 were physically handicapped.

Although this is a small sample, and generalizations to the larger population of school-exiting youths with disabilities across the country must be done with caution, it is nevertheless informative to note the following findings regarding their employment and social status two years after leaving school:

- Some 90.9% of the males and 52.4% of the females were employed. Of these, 87.5% of the males and 54.5% of the females were employed full-time. Some 60% of the males and 63.6% of the females who were working had begun working over a year earlier.
- The wages for 62.5% of the males and 72.7% of the females were in the $3.36 to $5.00 per hour range.
- Most of the work was unskilled (60% of the males, 63.6% of the females). Most jobs for males were evenly distributed across structural occupations, clerical/sales occupations, and service occupations, with fewer in the professional/managerial, machines and trades, processing, and miscellaneous occupations. For females, jobs were largely distributed across professional/managerial, clerical/sales, and service occupations.
- About 83.1% of the respondents lived with parents or a guardian, 71.4% of them for economic reasons, but 76.6% of them had a preference for independent residence.
- By far the largest number (96.9%) were unmarried. However, 13.8% had children.
- Their social activities consisted of television (100%), movies (90.6%), church (63.1%), recreation center (45.3%), sports (43.1%), hanging out (41.5%), and hobbies (39.1%).
- Participation in these activities was largely with family for church and television activities, alone for hobbies, and with friends for sports, recreation center, movies, and hanging out.
- Those who were working expressed satisfaction with their social lives more often than those who were not working. More than a quarter of the respondents indicated some dissatisfaction with their social life, lack of friends, or limited social activities.*

*Data from "Employment Outcomes and Social Integration of Students with Mild Handicaps: The Quality of Life Two Years After High School" by D.J. Scuccimarra and D.L. Speece, 1990, *Journal of Learning Disabilities, 23*(4), pp. 213-219.

Taken at face value, these data appear to suggest that the schools had prepared these students reasonably well for entry into work but that their financial circumstances prevented them from attaining the independence they would like. The findings also suggested that most of their social activity was passive (television and movies) and that a substantial number of these young people with disabilities felt that their social life was not altogether fulfilling. Nevertheless, many of them were well on their way to living productive adult lives.

Although learning is a lifelong process, formal education takes place in highly structured environments over approximately 2 to 3 decades. In those years, students with disabilities have to be taught how to (1) maximize their potential, (2) overcome barriers and communicate their needs and desires, and (3) develop persistence and independence. They have to do this in addition to gaining knowledge and exhibiting that knowledge in their academic studies.

There is ample evidence to suggest that educational professionals best serve their students with disabilities when they play the part of mentors and friends. Educators should de-emphasize the making of judgments of a normative nature (contrasting the student with a disability to persons who have none) and substitute in place of those judgments a guiding, encouraging, and future-planning mode of interaction. If they do, they will be favorably remembered by these young people once they leave the school and enter their productive years.

Chapter 4

Entering and Advancing in the Working World

LIFE STAGE: THE PRODUCTIVE YEARS

It is the thesis of this book that each life stage calls for a different priority in skills from the one before it. The traditional model of formal education is a protective environment in which order is provided and tasks are decided in conjunction with instructional goals, influencing and shaping the behavior of students with disabilities. A question that is receiving more and more attention as far as students with disabilities are concerned is how well formal education has prepared them to function in the next life stage, the productive adult years.

As is true with nondisabled youth who exit secondary school, some students with disabilities will go to college, and others will not. Some will "age out" of the benefits provided under PL 94-142, while others will leave school as soon as the law allows and simply become individual citizens. To the extent that these ex-students hope to be self-sufficient in a competitive society, they must become productive to the extent that their disability allows.

Many young people get their first exposure to personal productivity with part-time jobs during their schooling. These youthful workers tend to have jobs in food service, retail sales, cashier work, clerical positions, manual and semi-skilled labor, and other entry-level work. Hall (1986) defined the transition from young worker to adult worker as the time at which the individual attempts to enter the full-time labor force. He pointed out that this time of entry can vary widely, depending on the delays that occur as a consequence of higher education or military service.

A number of persons with disabilities do not go on to higher education. And due to the presence of a disability, military service is not likely (except for persons with a learning disability). Nevertheless, their entrance to the full-time labor force may be long delayed or never take place. For these nonpostsecondary and nonmilitary individuals, entry into the labor force is very much dependent on

- whether they have been well prepared by educators in the schools
- whether they have been served by counselors in community agencies
- whether employers have been educated to the potential benefits of having persons with disabilities in their work force and are assisted in making appropriate accommodations in work setting or job duties

Post–high school adjustment also has a social component that parallels the employment component. Where one lives, who one lives with, and what social activities are engaged in are just some of the more obvious social adjustments that will be faced during the productive years.

As shown in Figure 4-1, this chapter explores many of the issues involved in employment and socialization that affect productivity. Generally speaking, the productive years can be thought of in terms of three time frames: a period of initial employment and adjustment in independent living, a period of career change and growth, and the later productive years, in which individual skills are fully developed and, it is hoped, acknowledged.

As is discussed in this chapter, the productive years can and should be the best years for persons with disabilities in the sense that they provide the opportunity to get a job, live independently, develop new friends, and engage in social and leisure activities. For many persons with disabilities, who have sought recognition and acceptance in their formative years, the productive years provide them with their best chance to develop a sense of self-worth and dignity. For example, building a family of one's own leads to a sense of accomplishment and pride.

While this prospect exists, various factors coming into play affect the outcome. Some of these factors are indicated in Figure 4-1; they include the process of preparing for and finding jobs, acceptance into the work force, availability of support systems, social integration, and advancement. Curiously, there are also disincentives to independence, particularly in the area of social security and health coverage, simply because independence and entrepreneurship involve risk taking that does not provide the security inherent in social welfare.

Time Frame	Service Delivery Team	Services Delivered
Initial employment	Placement/rehabilitation/ independent living specialists, employers and coworkers, family and friends	Job finding, integration into work force, social skills
Career change and growth	Job referral services, support specialists, employers and coworkers, family and friends	Job training, raises and promotion, increased responsibility, social integration
Later productive years	Employers and coworkers, support specialists, family and friends	Acknowledgement of developed skills, mentoring, social integration

Figure 4-1 The Productive Years: Inter-Relationships and Dependencies

During the productive years, when the individual with a disability functions in a community or working environment, the frequency and nature of services needed are likely to change from what they were during the school years. Similarly, there is likely to be a change in the extent of coordination that is required among service providers. For example, with severely disabled individuals, coordinated support may be required among an employer, rehabilitation personnel, social services, and the family or significant others (such as other persons with disabilities in a group living setting).

Federal Initiatives and Programs

The Rehabilitation Act of 1973 was a major piece of legislation affecting individuals with disabilities who seek employment and meet the criteria for service eligibility. Amendments provided for assistance related to independent living. Sections 501 and 503 of the act required affirmative action by federal agencies, contractors, and grant recipients. Section 502(B) of the act set up the Architectural and Transportation Barriers Compliance Board, which sets standards and establishes minimum guidelines. Section 504 of the act required that "otherwise qualified" handicapped individuals not be excluded from participation in a federally funded program "solely by reason of handicap."

The Rehabilitation Act was revised and extended with the passage of the Rehabilitation Amendments of 1984, PL 98-221. Opportunities for severely disabled persons were improved when the phrase "beyond any reasonable doubt" was struck from the requirements for eligibility. Section 114 of PL 98-221 calls for an expansion of services to those clients "with the most severe handicaps," directs special services and programs for those "individuals who have unusual or difficult problems in connection with their rehabilitation," and directs that programs be carried out to "maximize the use of technological innovations in meeting employment training needs."

The Social Security Disability Insurance (SSDI) program was initiated in 1956 to provide support for people who were unable to work due to illness that could be expected to last into the future. In 1958 it was expanded to include dependents; in 1960 the age requirement (originally 50 years of age) was lifted; in 1972 beneficiaries became eligible for Medicare benefits. Supplemental Security Income (SSI) was initiated in the mid-1970s to replace separate programs for the blind, disabled, and elderly poor and is the principal income support for those persons who do not qualify under the criteria of SSDI (Yelin, 1989). SSDI was predicated on a medical model; that is, it had to be medically certified that the disability was not temporary. However, the application of the medical model is inconsistent and not straightforward. Many persons with severe disabilities work, and others with seemingly minor disabilities do not. Political maneuvering (during the Carter and Reagan administrations) had the effect of cutting back the numbers of eligible persons, a trend that has sub-se-quently been reversed (Yelin, 1989).

Recent legislation—the Technology-Related Assistance for Individuals with Disabilities Act of 1988 (PL 100-407)—should prove to be of great value to those persons with disabilities who need assistive devices in order to function effectively. Administered at the national level by the National Institute on Dis-ability and Rehabilitation Research, the act puts in place a system of grants for consumer-responsive statewide programs of technology-related assistance. Without regard to the age of persons with disabilities, the act is intended to "en-able persons with disabilities to have greater control of their lives, to enhance their participation in education, employment, family, and community activities, and to otherwise benefit from opportunities that are commonly available to indi-viduals who do not have disabilities" (Department of Education, 1989). Several models for delivery of technology are possible under this legislation. They include a centralized state provider model, a consultative model, and a decen-tralized model (Office of Special Education and Rehabilitative Services, 1989).

In 1990 the Americans with Disabilities Act, sometimes referred to as the Disabled Rights Bill, or simply ADA, enjoyed the strong support of Congress (Holmes, 1990). This bill became law with President Bush's signature on July 26, 1990. It did not come about by accident, but as the result of long and concerted effort by many individuals with and without disabilities, and it was not unopposed. Its opponents expressed concern over the costs of its implemen-tation in three areas—small businesses, telephone companies, and organizations involved in public transportation (Karr, 1990) .

The major provisions in this legislation will have an extraordinary impact in terms of giving people with disabilities needed leverage in getting jobs, access to the workplace, access to public facilities, access to communication, and access to transportation. President Bush termed this "the freedom they could glimpse but not grasp." Some of the important provisions of the legislation in-clude the following:

1. *Employers* (with 15 or more people employed)
   - may not discriminate in hiring, limit advancement opportunity, use tests that tend to screen out individuals with disabilities, or ask about disabi-lities
   - are to make reasonable accommodation in existing facilities (except as exempted due to excessive cost), provide special equipment and training as needed, and modify work schedules
2. *Transportation*
   - must ensure that new buses, trains, and subways are accessible to wheel-chairs

3. *Establishments* (hotels, restaurants, doctors' offices, theaters, retail shops)
  - may not refuse to serve people with disabilities or deny them the opportunity to participate
  - are to remove barriers affecting access (except where this would constitute an undue burden)
  - make new and renovated facilities accessible
  - otherwise make services available

The new law will take effect in 2 years for employers of 25 or more people and in 4 years for employers of 15 or more people. Large bus companies would have 6 years and small companies 7 years in which to conform. Establishments would have 18 to 30 months to conform.

As important as it is, the ADA legislation does not solve all the problems that persons with disabilities face as they try to lead "normal" lives. More legislation is needed. Next on the agenda for disability advocates are health protection and insurance coverage, areas that all too often still involve inequities.

Apart from its operation of organizational units that are dedicated to the needs of persons with disabilities, the executive branch of the federal government has promulgated a number of directives to agencies and departments concerning persons with disabilities. These directives address the need for nondiscrimination on the basis of disability.

Illustrative of this trend are rules issued by the Department of Transportation (1990a, 1990b) concerning access to commercial aircraft. Similarly, the Information Resources Management Service of the General Services Administration has taken the lead in suggesting computer accommodation for federal employees with disabilities who are actual or potential users of computers. The Department of Defense has issued directives that have the effect of accelerating the hiring of persons with targeted disabilities (nine categories of disabilities that are traditionally hard to place in employment) in a wide range of white-collar and blue-collar occupations.

Federal and State Advocacy

In terms of advocacy at the federal level, there is no higher level of influence than presidentially appointed committees whose roles involve advocacy. Originally established in 1978 as an advisory board with the Department of Education, the National Council on Disability (previously called the National Council on the Handicapped) was established in 1984, under Part D of PL 98-22, as an independent federal agency to "advise the President, the Congress, the Commissioner, the appropriate Assistant Secretary of the Department of Education, and the Director of the National Institute of Handicapped Research on the development of programs to be carried out under this Act." The chairperson of the council, Sandra Parrino, is the mother of a severely disabled son. She played a major role in the inception of the council's comprehensive equal opportunity proposal, which promotes independence and equality for people with disabilities. Other council members are either disabled in some way, the parents of children with disabilities, or professionals with experience in serving persons with disabilities in a leadership capacity.

Another advisory group at the highest level is the President's Committee on Employment of Persons with Disabilities. By presidential order (Executive Order 12640 of May 10, 1988), implementing the Rehabilitation Act of 1973, PL 93-112, as amended, the committee members serve without compensation (though their transportation and per diem costs are paid). Through their chairman, they are to "report annually to the President, who may apprise the Congress, and other interested organizations and individuals on the progress and problems of maximizing employment opportunities for people with disabilities."

It can be said with assurance that the committee is an outstanding source of information on disability matters in the United States. For example, a recent publication, *Out of the Job Market: A National Crisis*, available from the President's Committee on Employment of the Handicapped (no date), gives statistics that make clear the special needs of persons with disabilities and sub-groups—women, ethnic minorities, veterans, and the 55 to 64 age group. They also provide information that is directly useful in alleviating the problem of unemployment. In another example, the Job Accommodation Network, which was originated by the committee, provides a continuing source of information to employers who seek information from other employers concerning how job accommodation can be accomplished for persons with disabilities.

Within the executive branch of the government, a number of individuals with disabilities provide leadership by example in departments and offices. For example, Justin Dart's disability has not prevented him from engaging in 30 years of advocacy for persons with disabilities, during which time he served as commissioner of the Rehabilitation Services Administration and as chairperson of the Congressional Task Force on the Rights and Empowerment of Americans with Disabilities; currently he leads the President's Committee on Employment of People with Disabilities.

It has been recognized that the relationship between agencies and individuals often puts the individuals at a practical disadvantage. This is likely to be a forgone conclusion for mentally retarded persons, who are often unaware of possibilities for influence within the larger social system. In acknowledgement of this problem, advocacy has been formalized as a service offered to mentally retarded individuals by agency staff in regional Developmental Disabilities Services Offices.

Rehabilitation and Rehabilitation Engineering

Whether individuals acquire disabilities adventitiously or have them from birth, it is important that they be helped to function effectively as adults. *Rehabilitation*, defined here as systematic evaluation, training, and support antecedent to functional performance in competitive work environments and independent living settings, and *rehabilitation engineering*, defined here as the application of science and technology to improve the human condition and increase the options for self-sufficiency for persons with disabilities, are both important to the improvement of service delivery. Either can make a critical difference in helping the individual with a disability to become a functioning, adjusted, and fulfilled member of society.

Rehabilitation

Rehabilitation-oriented services take many forms and involve a variety of organizations with different missions and different clients. The first that comes to mind is the State Office of Vocational Rehabilitation (VR) (the actual name may differ from state to state), because it plays a central role in financing the services needed to evaluate, retrain, and place in competitive employment persons who qualify for services. In addition, following changes in the authorizing legislation, VR also has been assigned responsibilities in the area of providing support related to independent living. Among the services VR provides or purchases from vendors are diagnostic and evaluation services, transportation, restoration services, supplemental allowances, and a variety of training-related activities. These include personal and social adjustment training, on-the-job training, business school, vocational school, and academic education.

Unlike many other federal programs, budgeting in support of the states' VR programs has been kept lean in recent years. Inevitably, this has a limiting effect on the numbers of counselors and other staff in the program and constrains the numbers of clients who can be served. The consequence of this is that not all deserving persons with disabilities get served through VR, and those who do get served may not receive certain types of support that they feel they most need. This is especially true when the comparatively high cost of a particular item, such as a specially equipped van, may be well justified for the individual but at the same time represents funds that might be spread across more people with less costly interventions.

When VR programs are aimed at employment, the criterion for successful case closure is whether the client re-enters the labor force and gets a job. Because the performance of counselors, district offices, and even states is monitored in terms of successful case closures, there is a natural inclination to "cream" the ideal applicants for VR services, accepting as clients only individuals who have an exceptionally high chance of being employed. Early in the history of VR services, this resulted in an uneven and unfair service delivery system from the perspective of those truly needing help. Eventually, partly in response to criticism, special directives were issued that caused priority to be given to severely disabled individuals.

Nevertheless, successful case closures (in terms of employment or independent living) continue to be a basis for judging the performance of VR units at the local level. The administrative response to the challenge of providing full, appropriate service with budgetary restrictions varies from VR office to VR office. Although all are guided by the same regulations and directives, some counselors are given more latitude in making decisions than others. In addition, we are beginning to see a shift from overdependence on a full range of "evaluation" (including psychological evaluation, work-readiness evaluation, etc.) toward more tailored services that streamline interactions with clients.

One of the more promising changes in VR policy in recent years began when the Office of Special Education and Rehabilitative Services was created in the Department of Education, and vocational rehabilitation and special education programs became organizationally related. Cooperation between the two programs has been a relatively recent, growing, and most welcome phenomenon. At the state and local levels, jointly written statements by special education directors and VR directors have promoted collaboration between the two agencies such that students with disabilities have less chance of falling through the cracks as they make the transition from high school. However, being served in special education does not automatically equate to eligibility for VR services, nor do all special education students need such services.

In addition to the VR and special education programs, the Office of Special Education and Rehabilitative Services also includes the National Institute on Disability and Rehabilitation Research (NIDRR). Established under the 1978 amendments to the Rehabilitation Act, NIDRR has a broad mandate of applied research and training and also has responsibilities for information transfer. An example of the latter is ABLEDATA, a central computerized database with on-line search capability in the area of assistive technology (appliances, adaptive or special-purpose equipment) for people with disabilities. Recently, NIDRR supported applied research at Trace Research and Development Center, a nationally known leader in development of assistive technology, located at the University of Wisconsin, to devise a means for making the ABLEDATA system more easily accessible at local levels without incurring connect-time charges or requiring the use of modems (Vanderheiden, Berliss, Borden, & Kelso, 1989). As a result of this research, Hyper-ABLEDATA has been developed, a version of the central on-line database designed for use with Macintosh microcomputers.

NIDRR supports a number of rehabilitation research and training centers around the country. The centers have two main purposes: (1) the production of new knowledge about rehabilitation methodology and service delivery based on research and (2) the conduct of training programs to disseminate and promote the transfer of research findings into practice. A study of new models for delivery of personal assistance services carried out by Nosek and Fuhrer (1989) at the Research and Training Center on Independent Living, is illustrative of the type of project that the rehabilitation research and training centers conduct. This project seeks to inform policy makers about the consumer perspective on the need for and availability of personal assistance or attendant services.

A list of the current centers and their missions, as reported by the National Rehabilitation Information Center, is found in Appendix A.

Rehabilitation Engineering

A major activity in the United States, and in other developed countries, is the application of engineering and research of a technical nature to the needs of the chronically ill and persons with disabilities. This has resulted in the formation of a number of Rehabilitation Engineering Centers supported by NIDRR. (See Appendix B for a listing.)

As just one example of how customized solutions can be found to individual problems through rehabilitation engineering, one need look no farther than the case of Tim Mason (Popovich, 1989). Eleven-year-old Tim was born with no limbs. Without arms and legs, his mobility was reduced to rolling around on the floor. However, as the beneficiary of intervention by the team of the Prosthetic Clinic of the Rehabilitation Engineering Center, Children's Hospital at Stanford, Tim is now able to move about either with a swivel walker (in which he ambulates independently in an upright position) or in a motorized wheelchair that he operates with an above-elbow prosthesis, fitted with a hook. Tim also has a fabricated seat that has "legs" to allow him to ride a horse. His interests are musical, and thanks to the technological aid that he has gotten, he's learning to play the drums.

Basic research has led to an understanding of how the human body functions, and applied research has led to understanding of how technology can supplant some of its abilities. An example of this understanding is the study of functional electrical stimulation (FES) as a way of energizing nerves and muscles that are no longer useful due to paralysis. Research along this line holds promise for improving the health, physical fitness, and rehabilitation potential of patients with spinal cord injury (Granat, Smith, Keating, Andrews, & Dalargy, 1989; Yamaguchi & Zajac, 1989).

Robotic aids are under investigation as a means for assisting persons to live more independently in the home and function better at work, and both tabletop and mobile units have been successfully demonstrated (Cheatham, Regalbuto,

Krouskop, & Winningham, 1987; Horowitz & Hausdorff, 1989; Van der Loos et al., 1989).

Over the years, a considerable amount of research has been carried out to evaluate the effectiveness of new technology in relation to its intended use. For example, in the 1970s a national evaluation of the Optacon, a device allowing blind persons to read inkprint materials, established the utility of the device for young children and adults (Weisgerber, et al., 1973). Since that time it has been widely used in educational, work, and leisure activities and has gone through a number of technological improvements.

In a subsequent project, Weisgerber and de Haas (1978) developed a systematic procedure for matching blind persons with one of several alternative electronic travel aids. The foundation of this work was a comprehensive analysis of what environmental sensing consists of, since travel is so inextricably linked with that ability. They developed a reference compendium that analyzed the knowledge and behaviors involved in gaining awareness of one's environment so that blind persons could begin to develop greater independence. Definitions and explicit rationales were developed, effective and ineffective behaviors illustrated, and requisite skills listed for eight incremental levels of environmental sensing:

1. relating body image and surrounding space
2. perceiving and defining the environment
3. relating personal movement to environmental factors
4. relating personal movement to distance, time, and rate
5. compiling a cognitive map
6. planning, executing, and assessing travel routes
7. optimizing travel performance
8. analyzing personal attributes for greater independence

Similarly, and much more recently, research has been focused on helping consumers make wise choices among the assistive devices that already exist. For example, Batavia and Hammer (1989) have identified and prioritized consumer criteria for evaluating assistive devices. The priority order, which is instructive to those who design and manufacture equipment, is listed below:

1. Effectiveness—how well the device really improves the functional performance of the individual
2. Affordability—the cost of purchase, maintenance, and repair of the device
3. Operability—ease of use and control over the device
4. Dependability—repeatable, predictable use in a range of environmental situations
5. Portability—choices in location of use, size and weight of device, and length of charge on batteries

6. Durability—useful life of the device
7. Compatibility—extent to which the device will be useful in conjunction with other devices in the future
8. Flexibility—availability of options for consumer choice
9. Ease of maintenance—extent to which normal cleaning and service can be performed easily
10. Securability—the extent to which the device can be secured against theft or vandalism
11. Learnability—how quickly operation of the device can be learned and then put to use
12. Personal acceptability—psychological comfort level associated with the use of the device in public due to its cosmetic qualities
13. Physical comfort—whether use causes pain or discomfort
14. Supplier repairability—access to a repair shop, parts, and quick turnaround for repair service
15. Physical security—extent to which the consumer is at risk of harm, either injury or infection
16. Consumer repairability—feasibility of the consumer fixing the device if it is broken
17. Ease of assembly—how simply it can be assembled upon receipt*

Information describing the devices and systems that have been developed to assist people with disabilities in independent living, communication, seating mobility, vocational applications, transportation, recreation, and rehabilitation assessment has been organized in a resource handbook by Smith and Leslie (1990).

As implied above, a tremendous amount of research has been conducted through ongoing rehabilitation engineering centers and through individual projects supported by one or another of the funding sources that have a disability-related mission. One problem that persists, however, is bridging the gap between the research laboratory and clinical settings so that the benefits of the research are enjoyed by those on whose behalf the research was conducted. With a view toward improving the track record of rehabilitation research laboratories in implementing their research, the Veterans Administration supported a study of technology transfer, supporting a project aimed at developing a guidebook for researchers to aid in the dissemination of rehabilitation technologies. (Weisgerber, Armstrong, Sacks, & Steele, 1989).

Source: From "Consumer Criteria for Evaluating Assistive Devices: Implications for Technology Transfer" by A. Batavia and G. Hammer, Proceedings of the 12th Annual Conference of the Rehabilitation Engineering Society of North America, June 1989.

During the period in which this VA study was conducted, a major policy change came about at the federal level. It was recognized that government/business collaboration in Japan and Germany had produced substantial technological productivity, while in America the arms-length relationship between federally subsidized research centers and private enterprise was counterproductive to technology transfer. Passage of the Technology Transfer Act of 1986 reversed this pattern, and incentives now encourage research scientists and engineers to move their inventions through to a marketable stage. Hopefully, this will spur more rehabilitation researchers to do the same.

Private Sector Involvement

American disability policy has differed substantially from that of other industrial countries. In comparing our policy with that of Germany and Sweden (Burkhauser & Hirvonen, 1989) and of Holland, Great Britain, Germany, and Sweden (Berkowitz, 1989), it is clear that the United States places much more dependence on private sector, voluntary employment of persons with disabilities than is true in the other countries.

Sweden's social policy is built on the premise that government intervention should assure persons with disabilities that they will have work (if necessary, through government-supported public works), scaled to their ability to work productively. This policy is rooted in two assumptions: that gainful employment is essential to personal dignity and a sense of self-worth and that there should be a "reasonable" income for all citizens, whether or not they have disabilities.

Germany's social policy provides for quotas directed toward employers, specifying the proportion of their work force that should be filled by persons with disabilities. This has the effect of causing employers to look for, rather than reject, applicants with disabilities. Great emphasis is put on health rehabilitation and also on vocational rehabilitation. In addition, Germany also has a liberal policy toward early retirement for persons with work disabilities.

Holland, not unlike Sweden, has no difficulty in conceptualizing a social program in which work income and disability support are treated compatibly and are combined to assure workers a decent income. This is quite unlike the United States, where work income and disability support are put in direct opposition, engendering bitterness among persons with disabilities who want to work but fear the prospect of losing benefits that they feel they need due to their disability.

Britain utilizes a quota approach to employment but has been reluctant to enforce it; Berkowitz (1989) states that only nine prosecutions of employers have been brought since 1947. Berkowitz, citing McCrostie and Peacock (1984), states that some 60% of British companies had failed to reach their quotas in

1978. However, at the same time, the registry of persons with disabilities was smaller than the number of vacancies that had to be filled to meet the quota.

Berkowitz (1989) rather neatly contrasts the Swedish and American approaches by using a hypothetical example of two 30-year-old workers with disabilities, one residing in the United States and one in Sweden. His comparison is paraphrased below: Upon becoming disabled, the Swedish worker receives social assistance (if his income is low enough), and gets cash sickness benefits and medical care. He receives medical and vocational rehabilitation unless the disability is so severe that he cannot be rehabilitated, in which case he receives a permanent disability pension. He has access to a wide variety of training programs and, as necessary, can be employed in public works projects, subsidized jobs, or sheltered workshops. In contrast, the 30-year-old worker in the United States will not get a cash sickness benefit from the government, nor would the federal or state governments necessarily pay for her medical care. She would not be guaranteed a program of rehabilitation, and retraining programs would be more limited. Social Security disability insurance would be available unless the disability arose in the course of employment. In that circumstance, the company policy on disability becomes paramount. Ultimately, the benefits due the employee would be a matter that depended on "the creativity of the worker's lawyer, who might very well discover a means of recovering damages from a deep pocket" (p. 223).

In the United States, job creation on behalf of persons with disabilities is left largely to the private sector. A number of business firms have excellent track records in hiring persons with disabilities (of which more will be said later) and agree with the slogan, "It's good business to hire the handicapped." They typically find that employees with disabilities are not liabilities (as they had expected) but instead are as good or better than their regular employees on a variety of criteria (Weisgerber et al., 1981). Nevertheless, in comparison with persons with disabilities in the countries mentioned above, our citizens with disabilities find it much more difficult to seek employment. Many feel that our present social support system is structured poorly and contains more disadvantages than advantages for helping them get jobs.

Private Sector Advocacy

Professional organizations, especially those that are concerned with specific disabilities, play an important supporting role. The Council for Exceptional Children (CEC) and other professional organizations closely monitor the political scene. When any issue arises that promises to have substantial impact on services, such as access to enabling technology by persons with disabilities, these professional organizations inform their constituents and solicit their involvement in the form of petitions, letters, and the like.

The Learning Disabilities Association of America (LDA), formerly known as the Association for Children and Adults with Learning Disabilities (ACLD), is typical of associations that have substantial numbers of members who are either parents or persons with disabilities. The leadership of LDA (and other specific disability organizations) often takes the form of information dissemination. As a consequence of the composition of its membership, LDA newsletters sometimes focus on parents' feelings and frustrations in trying to get appropriate services or jobs for their children. They serve to remind us that there is much remaining to be done before the needs of persons with disabilities are fully met.

Sensitivity and awareness are revealed not only by the spoken or written word but also in terms of concrete action. The news media graphically remind us that persons with disabilities will actively and publicly campaign for their rights when they feel those rights are being systematically denied. But public advocacy by people with disabilities is not restricted to complaints against injustice. Increasingly, we see television and newspaper coverage devoted to the accomplishments of individuals with disabilities who set out on near-heroic undertakings designed to draw attention to the *abilities*, rather than the disabilities, of their peer group. Their motto is "can-do," not "cannot do."

On a voluntary basis, advocacy has been increasingly displayed by nondisabled people whose professional skills can be used to benefit persons with disabilities. For example, an increasing number of volunteer groups within engineering-oriented businesses have begun to apply their skills to the solution of equipment-related problems that are either unique to an individual with a disability or so infrequent as to discourage commercial development of marketable solutions. These company-backed volunteer programs typically involve the cooperation of technical and nontechnical staff, as well as management, in a team effort. Working on their own, during off-duty time, usually with space and facilities supplied by the company, these volunteer groups are having a positive impact on the quality of life of persons with disabilities in their communities.

Volunteers for Medical Engineering, Inc. (VME), located in Lutherville, Maryland, is a good example of the contribution that can be made through the voluntary efforts of private citizens and businesses (Staehlin, 1985). The organization is essentially a network of volunteers. They include company presidents, aerospace engineers, rehabilitation engineers, accountants, secretaries and many other concerned citizens. Beginning with a small group of concerned engineers, and enjoying the good will and cooperation of Westinghouse Electric Corporation, the volunteer program has been expanding and has chapters operating in other areas of the country.

The VME model is a simple one: Volunteers with technical expertise apply their knowledge about materials and engineering design to the solution of biomedical problems of individuals with disabilities. They work with individuals whose needs are not readily met by existing technology or equipment in the marketplace. Some of the products that they have developed to meet individual needs include

- a servo-driven orthosis that allows quadriplegics to grasp objects with their hands
- a "blinkwriter" computer cursor controller operated by blinking an eye
- microwave treatment of brain tumors
- tractor modification to allow its operation by a quadriplegic
- a "computalk" portable computer with a talking keyboard and message storage on each key
- a spinal clamp modification to correct curvature and add stability
- a computer program to assist an aphasic individual in recognizing various words, phrases, and objects
- a mobile standing frame for a paraplegic
- a binary input keyboard to a computer, requiring minimal finger movement
- an infrared controller unit operated with buttons on a wristwatch to activate/deactivate four separate devices in the home, such as a light switch

SPECIAL ISSUES CONCERNING ADULTS WITH DISABILITIES

Adults with disabilities encounter special problems that are similar to, but often more complex than, those encountered by nondisabled adults. This is particularly true in the areas of health care, independent or group living, and relationships with parents and other family members. Special issues also arise when there is a necessity for retraining, when existing learned skills can no longer be applied in an occupation following the onset of a disability.

Health Needs of Working-Age Persons with Disabilities

In recent years, considerable attention has been given to the health care needs of disadvantaged persons and ethnic minorities. Much less attention has been given to the unique health care needs of persons with disabilities. They warrant special attention because the disability often serves to complicate (sometimes needlessly) the provision of appropriate medical care by the health provider team.

Using Delphi research methodology, which involves reaching consensus by repetitive cycles of information gathering from sets of "knowers," Weisgerber (1976) studied the health care needs of three categories of persons with disabilities—the orthopedically disabled, the deaf, and the blind. The study was aimed at identifying and prioritizing health care needs in several complementary areas: (1) emergency situations, (2) routine health care and treatments, and (3) preventative health care activities. A second purpose was to identify areas of health care in which there was substantial dissatisfaction with federal and state services in the health care area.

The Delphi panels consisted of the following groups:

1. 28 orthopedically disabled panelists (20 in diverse occupations, 4 unemployed, 2 students, and 2 who did not indicate an occupation)
2. 29 deaf panelists (25 in diverse occupations, 2 unemployed, 1 retired, and 1 who did not indicate an occupation)
3. 22 blind panelists (20 in diverse occupations, 1 unemployed, and 1 student)

Although there were similarities across the priorities for the three panels, there were a number of differences in perceived needs. Each of the three Delphi panels agreed that emergency situations were of greater concern for them than receiving regular health care or preventing health problems.

The expressed difficulty of self-care in emergency, regular, and preventative situations was compared with the panelists' degree of dissatisfaction with the federal- or state-level provision of services. Table 4-1 shows the ranked order of difficulty and the ranked order of dissatisfaction among orthopaedically disabled, blind, and deaf persons that were revealed by the analysis.

Finally, each of the panels was asked to name areas that they felt were special problems but that were not specifically listed in the Delphi survey. They named the following as particularly important problems:

1. *Orthopedically disabled panelists pointed to*
   • inadequacies in design of public transportation
   • mechanical failures (e.g., elevators, aids)
   • inadequacies in the design of buildings
2. *Deaf panelists pointed to*
   • inability to receive warnings about hazardous situations
   • high cost of aids and appliances
   • lack of proper screening for hearing loss, especially among very young children
3. *Blind panelists pointed to*
   • high initial cost of aids and appliances
   • safety in environmental crises (e.g., fires)
   • need for transportation in an emergency

It is unfortunate that in the years that have passed since this study was conducted, most of the needs identified still remain unsatisfied.

DeJong, Batavia, and Griss (1989) characterized working-aged persons with disabilities as "America's neglected health minority" (p. 311). Differentiating among different subgroups of disabilities on the basis of presence or absence of physically disabling conditions, DeJong maintains that national health care data do not properly and fully reflect the true situation. For example, exclusions by private health insurers tend to minimize risk by not covering persons with pre-existing medical conditions.

Table 4-1 Priority Areas of Health Care Need, by Disability

Problem Area	Ranked Difficulty for Disability Group			Ranked Dissatisfaction with Services		
	Orthopedic	Deaf	Blind	Orthopedic	Deaf	Blind
Dealing with emergency situations						
Dealing with fire and other environmental hazards	1.0	3.0	2.0	1.0	2.0	9.0
Dealing with severe reactions and seizures	2.0	1.0	1.0	4.0	3.5	10.0
Dealing with physical injury	3.0	5.0	3.0	9.0	10.0	11.0
Obtaining help in emergency situations	4.0	2.0	5.0	3.0	1.0	13.0
Obtaining regular health care						
Administering or receiving therapy	5.5	7.5	6.0	6.5	9.0	3.5
Using aids and appliances to overcome disabilities	8.5	7.5	7.5	10.5	3.5	8.0
Obtaining routine medical/nursing consultation	12.0	6.0	11.0	5.0	6.5	6.0
Administering or receiving medication	14.0	10.5	7.5	14.0	13.0	6.0
Preventing health problems						
Maintaining personal safety outside the home	5.5	10.0	4.0	2.0	6.5	2.0
Obtaining health counseling	11.0	4.0	11.0	8.0	5.0	1.0
Maintaining proper diet and nutrition	10.0	11.0	11.0	10.5	11.0	3.5
Accomplishing routine body care	8.5	12.5	13.5	13.0	14.0	6.0
Maintaining personal safety inside the home	13.0	9.0	13.5	6.5	8.0	14.0
Maintaining sanitary conditions	7.0	12.5	9.0	12.0	12.0	12.0

In terms of personal assistance, which is central to independent living for many persons with disabilities, including those in the work force, DeJong (1989) points to the 50-state survey of in-home service programs conducted by the World Institute on Disability in 1987. This study showed that among publicly funded, in-home service programs,

- 67% do not allow attendants to assist in personal care involving medications, catheters, suppositories, or menstrual needs.
- 50% do not serve persons with incomes above the poverty level.
- 44% exclude certain disabling conditions.
- 42% do not cover both domestic and personal services.
- 22% do not cover services 7 days a week.

In sum, DeJong paints a picture of difficulty concerning access to services by persons with disabilities. The picture directly contradicts the concept of quality of life that people with disabilities are seeking when they work. Clearly, there must be a solution to the health care needs of these people, and it should be accomplished within the larger context of health reform for the mainstream of our population.

Fox (D. Fox, 1989) has reviewed the problem of chronic illness and disability broadly, both in terms of its evolution and in terms of its impact on entitlements under various medical care programs, Medicaid and Medicare in particular. Advocating reform, he takes the view that Medicaid makes a significant contribution to the well-being of persons with chronic health problems, but it is not the only locus for improving the health care entitlements of people with disabilities. Reasonable expansion of the coverage provided in Medicare and Medicaid is needed, and it should be made uniform across the states.

Burnett (1989) reported on a comprehensive study by the California Alcohol, Drug, and Disability Study on the tendencies of the disabled members of the community to use drugs and alcohol. Staff were interviewed in 212 disability service agencies throughout the state, as were clients with disabilities at a number of those agencies. Almost 30% of the people with disabilities used alcohol and drugs to deal with depression, and just under 33% reported using marijuana. Even more troubling than these high percentages was the fact that 54% of those who had sought treatment for alcohol or drug problems had encountered accessibility problems. Moreover, 64% of the agency staff thought that they needed training and other help in identifying alcohol and drug problems, 46% didn't question clients with disabilities about chemical problems, and 65.5% felt that community-based services for these problems were not readily available.

Verbrugge (1989) extensively studied the effects of health on individual physical and social functioning. Referencing the World Health Organization's (1980) conceptual scheme for disease impact, Verbrugge stated that health surveys have focused primarily on social disability (defined as personal care tasks [activities of daily living], household management tasks [instrumental activities of daily living] and major productive role (job, housework), and argued that less is known about basic physical disabilities, such as cardiopulmonary or musculoskeletal capabilities in the population. While skeletal and sensory impairments are included in the National Health Interview Survey, disfigurement and intellectual and psychological impairments have been studied less.

Independent Living and Group Living

A key indicator of quality of life is the ability to live as independently as possible. For many persons with disabilities, living on their own is a viable goal, much preferred to living in the protective care of their family or in an institutional setting, where their needs are "taken care of." Figure 4-2 describes important, but not exclusive, contributing factors (social skill training, contextual practice, support systems) that play a part in developing the functional skills that are involved in living as a self-reliant adult in the community. Implicit in the model shown in Figure 4-2 is the assumption that social skills, if they are truly learned and habituated, are applicable (transferable) across different contexts.

Increasingly, society is discovering that given sufficient intellectual capacity, training, occasional assistance (as in transportation), and advance planning for emergency care and other contingencies, people with mild and moderate disabilities can function reasonably effectively. The sense of self-worth and accomplishment that this independence generates is substantial. Independent living centers across the country testify to the ability of persons with a wide variety of disabilities not only to live on their own, but also to help one another in cooperative situations.

For persons with disabilities whose condition is severe, a community-based, group-oriented living environment is often a viable goal. Over the last decade many pilot projects aimed at deinstitutionalization have grown into full-fledged community-centered programs. These group-living situations characteristically involve a small number of persons with moderate to severe disabilities living in homes that are shared with (and sometimes owned by) a nondisabled person. While these are not truly independent living environments, they do allow considerable individual initiative, and they involve participation in the duties and leisure activities that take place there and in the nearby community. Personal

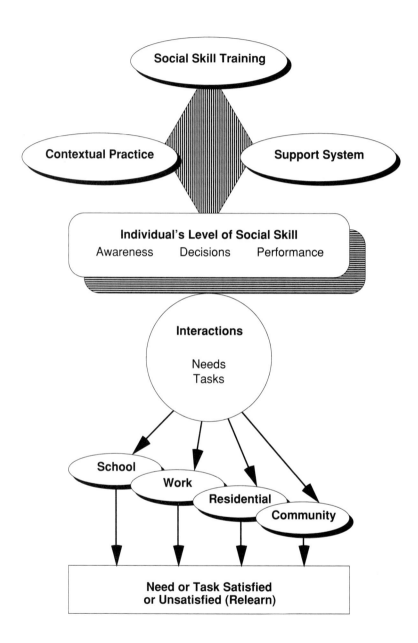

Figure 4-2 Process Model for Interpersonal Skill Development and Application in Social Situations

and social living skills are essential for successful participation in independent and group settings. Meyer and Evans (1989) have suggested specific procedures for implementing nonaversive intervention when excessive behavior problems jeopardize appropriate adjustment by adults and children in nonschool settings.

Self-Advocacy

Growing into adulthood as a person with a disability is not easy and is often filled with frustration (Jones, 1983), but many of these individuals learn that there is strength in linked effort. Estimates made by Scotch (1989) place the number of persons with disabilities who belong to advocacy organizations at around 100,000, with a somewhat larger number of members being people who are not themselves disabled, including parents of persons with disabilities. Of these members, it is likely that only a few thousand are active participants on a regular, ongoing basis. Nevertheless, the impact on policy that these small numbers have made by joining forces and becoming visible is hard to overestimate.

In community contexts, action through advocacy has been a hallmark of the independent living centers movement. While these centers have many purposes, the one for which they are perhaps best known to fight to get public support for private housing in which teams of persons with disabilities can share in the work and responsibility of operating a shared or group home. Their advocacy has been characterized not by claim alone but by proof through demonstration, providing participants in the independent living movement with a sense of purpose and dignity that would be hard for them to obtain in any other way.

Persons with disabilities have shown repeatedly that singleness of purpose (whether the disabilities are the same or different) is effective for affecting change. For example, disability groups have recently demonstrated a real talent for attracting political support for their cause by direct lobbying of legislators or officials.

Legal representation is an important aspect of the disability rights movement. Herr (1989) stated that legal representation of persons with developmental disabilities presents special challenges for the lawyer. The federal definition, which is functionally oriented, considers a person to be developmentally disabled if the condition is a severe, chronic impairment that substantially limits three or more areas of major life activity: independent living, language, self-direction, self-care, capacity for learning, and economic self-sufficiency. In terms of specific disabilities, "developmentally disabled" covers mental retardation, autism, cerebral palsy, epilepsy, and other developmentally linked neurological impairments.

For such individuals, exercising decision-making control over legal counsel is not practical. In such circumstances, self-advocacy groups can be supportive.

The Association for Retarded Citizens is one organization that regularly uses the tools of law reform. Case managers also provide an important function by drawing infringements on the rights of an individual (or classes of individuals) to the attention of legal counsel. Class actions represent one of the most powerful ways to change policy and also to spur legislative action.

One area that generates advocacy from many quarters is the problem of public transportation for persons with disabilities. This has been a repeated problem and sometimes leads to heated dispute. Advocacy has ranged from public protests and boycotts by persons with and without disabilities, to the carrot-and-stick strategy of the President's Committee on Employment of Persons with Disabilities. The latter group shifted its annual meeting from San Antonio to Dallas in protest of restrictive policies by city transportation authorities. This action had much to do with the retention of the transportation provisions in the language of the Americans with Disabilities Act recently legislated by Congress and signed into law by President Bush.

Family Support and the Support of Mentors

Previously, the point has been made that parents who are overly protective of their children with disabilities may inadvertently limit their children's capacity to deal with situations encountered as adults. Similarly, parents who fail to recognize the changed status of young adults with handicaps are likely to be reluctant to see them move out from under their direct supervision. Most experts agree, however, that prolonging this dependency is counterproductive, and in any case, the advanced age of the parents eventually becomes a factor pushing children's independence.

While parents have a useful advocacy role to play, their responsibility should stop short of interference. For example, parents should not repeatedly call a place of business and ask to speak to the person with disabilities in order to check up on him or her. By doing so, they interfere with the natural conduct of business, and they have imposed themselves in a setting where they do not belong.

What, then, is the best role for parents and other family members? Quite simply, it is one of encouragement and understanding, coupled with a transfer of responsibility to others who are not so deeply and personally involved. Parents have been found to be the most commonly used source of support in the making of postsecondary plans (Dowdy, Carter, & Smith, 1990). If the young person is not functioning at a level where college is an option, he or she still may want to live and work independently. Parents can be a real asset in this process of separation through their supportive participation in the vocational placement process and the selection of a group home or other independent living arrangement, and in the nature of the reinforcement they supply the young person.

As youths with disabilities form ideas about their own future (and many have difficulty doing so), they tend to form those ideas on the basis of what they see or what others tell them. Young adults with disabilities that do not impair their intellectual functioning can benefit from encountering a mentor, an older, experienced person who can guide them in decision making by the nature of the advice that is given or the skills exhibited. In many instances, where interactions take place at critical decision points, such as when the individual decides whether to go to college or seek employment, a mentor can be instrumental in helping with the decision.

It follows, then, that the exposure of the person with disabilities to persons who might become mentors is a potentially productive activity. When the mentor (or potential mentor) is disabled in a way that is similar to the young adult, the processes of interpersonal identification, understanding, and credibility are nearly instantly established. Emulation often follows and lifetime friendships can develop even though the mentor may be located far away and communication is infrequent.

Not surprisingly, employers who hire persons with disabilities and find them to be good workers are more likely to hire other persons with disabilities. When this happens, the first "successful" employee with disabilities typically is looked to as the exemplar or model to be followed. In this way, a mentoring relationship can develop between one "leader" and several "followers," all with disabilities. In such a situation, other benefits accrue, such as lessened isolation for the person with a disability and an opportunity for increased socialization with others, both with and without disabilities.

Work-Related Disability

"Work-related disability" is a term that is used quite frequently, but it and associated terms are not universally understood. Operational definitions associated with work-relevant disability used by the U.S. Bureau of the Census are:

- impairment: a physiological, anatomical, or mental loss or abnormality
- functional limitation: a restriction in a physical activity (e.g., walking, reaching, hearing), an emotional activity (e.g., maintaining satisfactory personal relationships), or a mental activity (e.g., solving problems)

Altogether, 8.6% of our population between the ages of 16 and 64 are persons with work disabilities. The definition of "disability," as used by the U.S. Census Bureau, is based on a concept advanced by Saad Nagi of Ohio State University: A person has a disability if he or she has a limitation in the ability to perform one or more of the life activities expected of an individual within a social environment (Bennefield & McNeil, 1989). The 1980 census asked whether any household members had a health problem or disability that prevented them from working or limited the kind or amount of work they could do. Thus the counts reflected in the census only reflect frequencies in work environments and not other environments.

As of March 1988 there were 13,420,000 people (8.6% of the general population) with a work disability. Of these, 7,457,000 (4.8%) had "severe" work disability, because they

- had a long-term mental or physical illness that prevents the performance of work
- did not work at all in the previous year because of illness or disability
- were under 65 years old and covered by Medicare
- were under 65 years old and receiving SSI

When sex is considered, the data show percentages of the general population with a work disability as follows:

Men	8.7%
Women	8.4%

When education is considered, we find that the percentage of persons with a disability is inversely related to the amount of education completed:

Less than 8 years	29.7%
8 years	24.6%
9 to 11	17.7%
12	8.8%
13 to 15	7.5%
16 or more	3.8%

When age is considered, we find that the percentage of persons with a work disability is positively correlated with increased age:

16 to 24 years	3.8%
25 to 34 years	5.6%
35 to 44 years	7.1%
45 to 54 years	10.3%
55 to 64 years	22.3%

When race is considered in combination with disability, we find these percentages:

White	7.9%
Black	13.7%
Hispanic origin	8.2%

Emphasis is added to this latter statistic by Jay Rochlin, executive director of the President's Committee on Employment of People with Disabilities, who has stated that 82% of black persons with disabilities in America are unemployed, and of the 18% that are employed, 65% earn $4000 or less a year (Rochlin, 1989).

Data on the employment status of persons with disabilities indicate that their unemployment rate is much higher than that of the nondisabled. Census information as of the Current Population Survey (CPS) in March 1988 (Bennefield & McNeil, 1989) relating to percentages of employed persons who have work disabilities and rates of unemployment is summarized in Table 4-2.

Table 4-2 Employment Status for People with and without Disabilities

Group	Employed		Unemployment Rate*	
	With Disability	Nondisabled	With Disability	Nondisabled
Men	35.7%	88.9%	14.2%	6.2%
16 to 24	40.4	69.5	22.6	12.8
25 to 34	49.5	96.2	15.9	6.1
35 to 44	43.7	98.0	14.0	4.3
45 to 54	38.6	97.3	12.4	3.4
55 to 64	20.7	80.5	9.2	4.1
Women	27.5%	69.5%	14.2%	5.2%
16 to 24	43.9	62.4	28.0	10.6
25 to 34	41.9	74.5	13.9	5.1
35 to 44	40.9	77.6	14.7	3.9
45 to 54	22.9	73.3	13.0	2.6
55 to 64	13.1	35.6	3.9	2.3

* Unemployment rate includes those persons who want to enter the labor market and have actively sought work but are unable to find employment.

Source: Labor Force Status and Other Characteristics of Persons with a Work Disability, by R. Bennefield and J. McNeil, 1989, Current Population Reports, Series P-23, No. 16, Washington, D.C.: U.S. Department of Commerce, Bureau of the Census.

In examining the data in Table 4-2, we see that the percentage of work-disabled men who are seeking work but are unable to find it is 14.2%, more than twice the figure for the non-work-disabled. Among the work-disabled women, the percentage is the same as for men (14.2%), but non-work-disabled women are more successful than men in finding work if they want it.

In examining the age data in Table 4-2, we see that at the prime working ages of 25 to 34, men with work disabilities are only about half as likely to be employed as nondisabled men. Similarly, nondisabled men in the 25 to 34 age bracket are able to find work more than twice as often as is the case with those who have a work disability. Large disparities also exist for the women.

In a state-by-state analysis by Haber (1987) using 1980 census data, the states with percentages of persons with work disabilities above 10% were as follows:

Alabama	11.3%
Arkansas	13.5
District of Columbia	10.3
Florida	10.5
Georgia	11.0
Kentucky	12.1
Louisiana	10.1
Maine	10.3
Mississippi	12.6
North Carolina	10.4
Oklahoma	11.4
Oregon	10.3
South Carolina	10.6
Tennessee	10.9
West Virginia	12.9

The presence of a number of southern and eastern states in the list is worth noting. So is the presence of rural, low socioeconomic status, and minority populations in most of these states. In addition, job opportunities are limited in most of these states. It becomes clear that trying to find employment for persons with work disabilities in these states is no simple matter.

Kraus and Stoddard (1989), using national health survey data, point out that people living outside of cities report more activity limitations than those living in cities (Table 4-3).

Table 4-3 Activity Limitations of Persons Living Within and Outside Cities

Extent of Limitation	People Not in Cities	People in Cities
Not limited	83.3%	86.9%
Limited in nonmajor activity	5.3	4.3
Limited in major activity	6.6	5.2
Unable to do major activity	4.7	3.7

GAINING AND MAINTAINING EMPLOYMENT

Edgar and Levine (1988) have conducted a longitudinal study of graduates of special education programs in 13 school districts to determine the extent to which exiting students in the years 1984, 1985, and 1986 were employed and remained employed. Table 4-4 shows the percentages of students of different disabilities who were employed 6 months after leaving school and the percentages who were employed 5 years after school.

It is interesting to note that at the 5 year follow-up, 7% of the moderately/severely retarded group were living independently, 19% of the mildly retarded were living independently, and 59% of the learning disabled/behavior disordered group were living independently.

As mentioned in Chapter 3, Weisgerber et al. (1989) developed a comprehensive curriculum for educators, counselors, administrators, and employers to use in developing the social-employability skills of persons with disabilities. The

Table 4-4 Follow-Up of Students after Graduation

Disability	Employment Rate at	
	6 Months	5 Years
Severe retardation	35%	—
Moderate/severe retardation	—	38%
Mild mental retardation	39%	45%
Behavior disordered	52%	—
Learning disabled	63%	—
Learning disabled/behavior disordered	—	68%

Source: From "A Longitudinal Study of Graduates of Special Education" by E. Edgar and P. Levine, 1988, *Interchange*, 8(2), p. 4. Published by the College of Education, University of Illinois at Urbana-Champaign. Copyright 1988 by Eugene Edgar and Phyllis Levine. Adapted by permission.

General Transition Model on which this curriculum is based is shown in Figure 4-3.

In this model, which focuses on transition from school and/or the community to the workplace, it is clear that the students or clients are supported by many "stakeholders" who will stand to benefit in some way from a successful work placement. It is also clear that a multidisciplinary team composed of educators and community-based service providers can make important contributions to the development of the individuals' work readiness.

The model further shows that there are three stages of preparation, placement, and support leading to a successfully held job. Each of the stages has multiple elements, each of which involves some form of personal/social competence, as detailed below:

Stage 1 relates to social-employability skills that are appropriate to have in place as one prepares to enter into the working world:

1. Self-awareness and personal development: These skills have to do with understanding one's own feelings and knowing how to handle them. Ideally, the person with a disability should be able to identify the causes of personal feelings ("getting down in the dumps," stress, frustration, embarrassment, failure), develop self-control over these feelings rather than over-reacting to them, and begin a program of self-improvement by setting goals and values, especially concerning the individual's own sense of worth. In addition to feelings, self-awareness also includes awareness of one's own strengths and the knowledge of how to use these strengths in order to achieve personal goals.

2. Learning to relate to others: These skills have to do with fundamental social interactions, such as knowing how to share personal feelings with others in appropriate ways, accepting support from others, and exercising some sensitivity to the feelings of others. Importantly, the individual with a disability needs to be able to deal with strangers who are encountered in the community, and to some extent in the workplace, in appropriate ways, particularly in terms of their reaction to rejection or teasing, allowing "personal space," and asking for directions or making other personal needs known.

3. Learning to talk with others: These skills have to do with conversations, a vital part of social adjustment. The individual should be able to start, engage in, and end conversations, appropriately interrupt to ask questions, and listen and pay attention when others are speaking.

4. Learning to live on one's own: These skills have to do with sharing living quarters and using public transportation. The individual must respect the rights and property of others, meet obligations and responsibilities, and get to destinations in a timely manner.

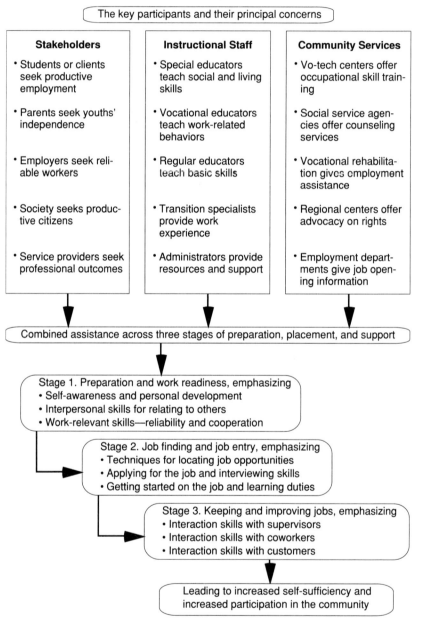

Figure 4-3 A General Transition Model. *Source*: Adapted from *Social Competence and Employability Skills Curriculum* (p. A-5) by R.A. Weisgerber, 1989, Gaithersburg, MD: Aspen Publishers, Inc. Copyright 1989 by Aspen Publishers, Inc.

5. Learning to work with others: These skills have to do with contributing in group situations, doing a fair share of the work, and being cooperative.
6. Learning to take directions: These skills include understanding the assignment, keeping track of time and progress, and completing assigned tasks.
7. Learning to be reliable: These skills involve being on time, attending regularly, and doing what is expected, such as routine duties.
8. Showing motivation: These skills involve setting reasonable goals, making a best effort toward those goals, and feeling good about accomplishments.

Stage 2 relates to social-employability skills that are critical to job-finding, interviewing, and making successful entry (in the first few weeks) into the working world:

1. Asking people about jobs: These skills involve knowing whom to ask (family, friends, and educational staff) and what to ask about.
2. Asking organizations about jobs: These skills involve talking to people in business to get their advice, getting help from agencies, and finding out about jobs listed in the newspaper.
3. Presenting oneself for an interview: These skills involve dressing appropriately, being on time for the interview, and avoiding bad posture and habits.
4. Talking during the interview: These skills involve talking about past work (or work-like) experiences, responding to questions, and telling about special skills.
5. Saying you want the job: These skills involve saying that you are interested in the work, that you will work hard, and that you'd appreciate the chance.
6. Knowing when and where to report for work: These skills involve knowing not only the location but also the procedure for checking in and out, and knowing the work schedule. At first glance, these skills may not seem to be social in nature, but they do affect employability simply because a failure to do these things correctly and independently will be seen as a burden on others and reflect negatively on the selection of the person with a disability to join the work force.
7. Getting to work on time: These skills involve getting up on time, allowing enough time to get to work, and getting help when the normal routine is interrupted for some reason.
8. Following work rules: These skills involve calling in when you are sick, respecting the rights and privacy of others (e.g., knocking on closed doors, not reading memos addressed to others), and observing safety and clean-up rules.

9. Knowing the job: These skills involve knowing what to do, how to do it, and when to do it.

Stage 3 relates to social-employability skills that are going to be needed to maintain success on the job, particularly those social-employability skills that involve the supervisor, the coworkers, and the customers:

1. Showing the supervisor that you like to work: These skills involve accepting jobs willingly, initiating new tasks (with permission), and completing tasks willingly.
2. Following directions: These skills involve listening and paying attention, getting clarification of directions if they are not completely clear, and following through on specific directions.
3. Asking for help: These skills involve asking for help at appropriate times (when there is a real need), making realistic assessments of one's own ability with respect to the assigned task (not promising what you can't deliver), and asking for help in the right way and from the right person.
4. Talking to the supervisor: These skills include discussing issues affecting performance, discussing personal matters that may have an impact on the job, and choosing the right time and place to have these discussions.
5. Working on a team: These skills involve participating willingly in group situations, doing a fair share of the work, and working at an appropriate rate.
6. Talking with coworkers: These skills involve knowing the right time and place to have conversations, having friendly conversations, and talking about the job in appropriate ways.
7. Talking with customers: These skills involve politeness, choosing appropriate topics to talk about, and answering questions appropriately.
8. Serving the customers: These skills involve helping the customers in appropriate ways, being careful not to make mistakes, and representing the company well.

Goal Setting and Preparation

Considering the strengths and weaknesses that each individual has, what are reasonable goals? It is essential that the person with a disability be directly involved in setting goals that have meaning to him or her. It is equally important that the goals are attainable and that they are set high enough to encourage the person to strive to reach them.

High-functioning individuals should be encouraged to take primary responsibility for setting their own goals and taking steps to achieve them. They can benefit from consultation, but the advisor should exercise caution about imposing personal judgments, especially ones that discourage the individual. For example, intellectually able persons with disabilities should be encouraged rather than discouraged if they elect to pursue a career field that challenges them.

Low-functioning individuals will need help not only in setting appropriate goals but also in understanding the near-term steps that are involved in attaining those goals. For example, the low-functioning individual may want to live in a shared living facility in the community, which is a worthwhile goal. He or she may not realize, however, the implications of that goal in terms of participation in housekeeping responsibilities, the management of money, or other fundamental elements that must be in place if the goal is to be realized.

Job Requirements Analysis

The *Dictionary of Occupational Titles* (DOT) has been a major tool for job analysis and career counseling for many years. Used by the United States Employment Service, the 1977 (fourth) edition listed 12,099 occupations (aggregations of jobs) organized into occupational groups using a coding system of three digits, with the first digit being the broadest grouping into nine categories, the second digit designating divisions, and the third digit designating occupational group. The nine occupational categories are

1. professional, technical, and managerial occupations
2. clerical and sales occupations
3. service occupations
4. farming, fishing, forestry and related occupations
5. processing occupations
6. machine trades occupations
7. bench work occupations
8. structural work occupations
9. miscellaneous occupations

The DOT also takes into account the occupational demands for "worker functions," using a three-digit worker trait code. The fourth digit in the overall six-number code always refers to the data-related tasks that are to be performed on the job. The fifth digit always refers to the people-related tasks, and the sixth digit refers to the things-related tasks. The components of each of these three types of tasks are as follows:

- data: information, knowledge, and conceptions of an intangible nature, collected by observation, investigation, interpretation, visualization, and mental creation, including numbers, words, symbols, ideas, concepts, and verbalization. Jobs involve synthesizing, coordinating, compiling, computing, copying, and comparing data

- people: dealing with human beings (or animals). Jobs involve mentoring, negotiating, instructing, supervising, diverting, persuading, speaking/signaling, serving, and taking instruction/helping
- things: inanimate objects such as machines, equipment, or products. Jobs involve setting up, precision working, operating/controlling, driving/operating, manipulating, tending, feeding/offbearing, and handling

In addition to the worker functions above, the list of variables in the DOT includes consideration of training times (i.e., general educational development, specific vocational preparation), aptitudes (e.g., motor coordination, verbal aptitude), temperaments (e.g., influencing people, performing under stress), interests (e.g., scientific, creative), physical demands, and working conditions (e.g., humidity, temperature, fumes).

The process of assessing the aptitudes of workers with disabilities has focused for many years on the job sample approach. Rosenberg (1973) indicated that it began in 1951 at the Williamsport Technical Institute (Pennsylvania), where clients were diagnosed over a 4-week period in an informal trial-and-error mode in various occupations in the training shops. In 1958, the May T. Morrison Center for Rehabilitation (San Francisco) began using work samples and evaluated 25 tasks in semi- and unskilled manual work, skilled and mechanical work, clerical, sales, and service areas.

Also in 1958, Rosenberg (1973) pointed out, the Philadelphia Jewish Employment and Vocational Service (JEVS), with support from the U.S. Department of Labor, developed 28 work samples to measure "potential skills" in 14 general industrial activities (e.g., packing, electrical, textiles and tailoring, layout design and drafting). Most important about the JEVS approach was the grading of tasks in terms of their complexity and the rating of quality of work performed on a five-point scale for nine aptitudes: general intelligence, verbal ability, numerical ability, clerical ability, motor coordination, form perception, spatial relations, finger dexterity, and manual dexterity.

By the 1970s, commercial work evaluation systems were being widely used to assess the client's ability to use various tools and accomplish small "assigned" tasks (e.g., solder, connect pipes) (Weisgerber, 1980). The Singer-Graflex Vocational System used a film strip and synchronized tape cassette to guide the client in work tasks in 10 different occupations. Another commercial approach, the TOWER System, involved 94 work tasks across 14 vocational areas. For example, the area of "workshop assembly" included tasks as follows: counting, number and color collating, folding and banding, weighing and sorting, counting and packing, washer assembly, inserting, lacing and tying, and art paper banding (Rosenberg, 1973). Presently, the Match-Sort-Assemble Series (Exceptional Education, 1990) provides an evaluation system for severely disabled individuals.

While there is little doubt that these detailed and lengthy work-sample evaluations give counselors a great deal of information about the client, it is much harder to make the case that such an elaborate approach is essential for a meaningful, successful placement. Typically, more information is gathered than really is relevant to the decision options at hand. There is no point in assessing job readiness in an occupation if there are no job openings and none expected in that occupation in the community.

In addition, many of the work sample evaluations have a work-like look to them, but they have little real-world relevance. For example, assembling piping using a small, upright panel with pipes and joints affixed to it is merely a shallow simulation of what the real plumber's job entails. These types of tasks, with the simulation constantly being assembled and disassembled, lack the compelling, motivating character of real-world, productive work.

Similarly, it is discouraging to observe a group of mentally retarded individuals sitting around a table, ostensibly being assessed in sorting and filing skills as they indifferently and dejectedly manipulate colored buttons, shuffle well-worn envelopes, and group different-sized washers. These are activities more nearly associated with sheltered workshops than with competitive work environments and provide little insight into the prospects for successful transition from the former to the latter. Not surprisingly, considerable attention has been given to eliminating sheltered workshops to the extent possible and instead placing severely disabled individuals in supported employment work situations in competitive business settings (Gardner, Chapman, Donaldson, & Jacobson, 1988).

By and large, current thinking is to focus on work assessments that are known to be relevant to a specific job family (1) in which the individual has expressed interest, (2) for which he or she has the cognitive capacity, and (3) in which work opportunities are available. Often, these work opportunities are "developed" by specialists in the service-providing staff (Mcloughlin, Garber, & Callahan, 1987), and high emphasis is given to precisely determining the employer's needs and expectations (Bellamy, Rhodes, Monk, & Albin, 1988). After pre-placement training in job-relevant tasks, such as using time cards, and role playing of interactions that are known to be associated with the job, such as taking directions from a supervisor, the client is placed in a community-based competitive work environment and given appropriate support from a job coach during the initial training period (Rusch, 1986; Wehman & Moon, 1988).

Every job has its own set of tasks and requirements. Efforts to analyze the essential elements of jobs are not new. In 1972, for example, Goodwill Industries of Wisconsin (Dahlke & Douglas, 1972) assisted by the Wisconsin

Employment Service, compiled a comprehensive collection of job descriptions drawn from the DOT. Each of the jobs listed (244 are included) existed in the Goodwill Industries program. Direct observation was used as the way of establishing the list of requirements as well as for developing suggestions for how the job could be restructured so that it could be performed by "handicapped and disadvantaged personnel."

For example, in the Goodwill analysis, a carpenter's helper engages in a variety of activities, such as the following:

• selecting and sawing lumber with power and hand saws
• nailing sheeting to studs after a building is framed
• dismantling shoring and bracing from forms
• digging holes and trenches to support posts and other structural members

According to the Goodwill analysis, the carpenter's helper job typically requires walking, standing, climbing, stooping, pulling, pushing, kneeling, reaching, lifting up to 100 pounds, carrying, seeing, alertness, responsibility, strength, accuracy, finger dexterity, manual dexterity, the use of both hands, and the ability to read, write, and understand simple instructions. The Goodwill staff stated that an eighth grade education is desirable and that the worker had to be able to work under the following conditions: inside, outside, cold, heat, humidity, wetness, dust, constant noise, sudden noise, high places, alone, and with others.

As with most early job analyses, the Goodwill project in Wisconsin placed a great deal of emphasis on the physical demand aspects of jobs and made limited suggestions about accommodative changes that could be made. Additionally, little attention was given to factors of work attitude and the ability to relate to others, including the supervisor, other workers, and strangers (particularly customers). In examining early attempts at job analysis, one is likely to get the impression that the work is carried out isolated from human interaction, with the worker mechanically using his or her tools to produce products. That may be true in some manufacturing contexts, where assembly tasks may be carried out in relative isolation, but it is not the case in the vast numbers of jobs that are dependent on personal-social competence at least as much as physical capacity.

Placement of Mentally Retarded Workers

There are a number of considerations affecting the successful placement of mentally retarded individuals in jobs that are suited to their skill levels. One consideration that cannot be ignored is the location of the job and whether transportation to and from the job can be managed (with training). A second consideration is the intellectual demand imposed by the job. Can it be learned or can the job be modified in some way? A third consideration is the social context in which the work is to be performed and the extent to which the mentally retarded worker will be expected to interact with one or many people, even with strangers.

Jacobs, Larsen, and Smith (1979) prepared a handbook for job placement of mentally retarded persons in which 20 personal-social skill requirements that affect placement are grouped as follows:

Social skills
1. *Self expression*—take simple directions and communicate questions
2. *Sociability*—accept criticism, exchange greetings, no excessive shyness or aggressiveness
3. *Work independence*—carry out duties without constant supervision
4. *Appearance and hygiene*—cleanliness, neatness and appropriate clothing
5. *Teamwork*—coordination with other workers

Time factors
6. *Pace*—work at a consistent pace for short periods
7. *Attendance*—reliability and punctuality
8. *Simultaneity*—performing multiple activities
9. *Timing*—awareness of scheduling and elapsed time

Performance skills
10. *Accuracy*—performance within tolerance levels
11. *Dexterity*—fine manipulations of hands and fingers
12. *Choices*—decision making appropriate to the task
13. *Direction*—follow simple directions and procedures
14. *Memory*—remembering procedures, locations, and nomenclature
15. *Caution*—to work safely and be aware of hazards
16. *Neatness*—work in an orderly manner
17. *Concentration*—attend to task despite environmental distractions

Tolerance
18. *Repetition*—psychological strength to stick to repetitive work
19. *Perseverance*—relatively continuous performance
20. *Stamina*—physical strength and endurance

For job analysis, a simple three-point scale is then applied to each of the above skill requirements to indicate the extent to which each skill is exhibited (expected to occur) in an occupational area, job group, or specific job. The scale points are "minimal, moderate, or major."

Jacobs et al. (1979) provided rating profiles for merchandising occupations (15 different jobs), office occupations (9 job groups and 49 jobs), agricultural/fishing/forestry occupations (11 jobs), skilled trades (29 jobs), and processing/manufacturing occupations (37 jobs).

The mentally retarded individual can be evaluated for appropriateness for the job by rating him or her against the 20 requirements listed previously. Using this rating approach, one or more counselors might identify requirements in which there is a marked discrepancy between the job requirement and the individual's skill repertoire. Discrepancies must be addressed either through training or through modification of the job. If training or modification of the job cannot be accomplished, the appropriateness of the job for that person is in doubt.

Job Accommodation

Generally speaking, the more that the job entails tasks that are rated as "major," the more likely that the job will exceed the capacity of the mentally retarded person. However, this is not a substitute for consideration of each case on an individual basis.

Suppose, as an example, that the occupational area is horticulture and the mentally retarded worker is to serve as a helper both in gardening work and in greenhouse work. Suppose too that the individual hired for this work is able to be trained to perform the gardening work, such as operating a rototiller (requiring a certain amount of physical strength), and can be guided in transplanting small plants into gardens in an appropriate, careful manner (requiring direction taking and dexterity). However, the greenhouse work involves planting seeds in flats to produce a consistent number of plants evenly spaced in even rows. The task requires awareness of abstract concepts, such as even spacing, and mathematical patterning, such as rows of six and columns of eight to produce four dozen plants. This may be beyond the capacity of the mentally retarded person being considered for the job.

A simple job aid could be made that would greatly simplify the counting and spacing requirement. The supervisor could prepare a wooden frame the same size as the flat to be planted, place nails at appropriate distances around the perimeter of the frame, and tie strings to the nails so that a template with 48 "holes" is created. Then, with a piece of cardboard (cut the width of the flat) as a movable cover or mask, the mentally retarded person could begin at one end of the flat, expose one row by sliding the cardboard cover, plant each hole, and repeat the action for each remaining row.

As in the example just given, job accommodation through the use of a job aid is often an easy solution to a seeming mismatch between job requirements and individual ability.

Training Modifications

Some jobs may have the appearance of complexity simply because there are multiple steps involved. Unless the steps involve a high degree of judgment (leading to alternative courses of action), it is often possible to train persons with mild retardation to perform them. The training of mentally retarded persons is usually best accomplished by breaking down an overall task into "manageable" steps that can be demonstrated, comprehended, and followed consistently.

The training procedure that has been shown to be most effective is (1) to demonstrate each step in the task, (2) have it rehearsed by the trainee until mastered at an acceptable criterion level, and (3) then combine small sets of steps while the instructor closely monitors the trainee. Simple reminders, such as checklists, can help to keep the sequence straight.

Jacobs et al. (1979) suggested that job-specific concepts or generalizations should be (1) presented, (2) reinforced, and (3) extended. For example, to teach "simple indoor cleaning" they identify four distinct phases of the concept presentation step:

1. knowledge of the tools used for cleaning tasks
2. suggested use of the tools
3. care and cleaning of the tools
4. suggested sequence of steps in cleaning a room, tool by tool

To reinforce the concept, the trainee would apply the concepts, reinforcing the positive actions, correcting unsatisfactory ones, and demonstrating some decision making (if appropriate) in the sequence of tasks.

To extend the concept, the context or situation in which the behaviors are carried out would be changed. For a room-cleaning task, extending the concept might include what to do about personal belongings in a motel room, or what to do if a room is occupied.

Jacobs identified basic skills that are common in the job categories listed in the handbook, though all are not essential for all the jobs listed:

- read and write
- arrange in order
- sort by category
- combine liquids and dry materials
- count and record numbers
- count money and make change
- repeat a visual pattern
- perform simple calculations

- communicate verbally
- use telephone
- tell time
- read dials, gauges and meters
- trace
- locate or identify by number, word, or symbol*

- secure with tape
- write messages
- measure
- manipulate small objects
- tie with string or rope

Each basic skill can be applied in various ways. For example, the basic skill of telling time is applied to getting to work on time, using a time clock to record hours worked, understanding lunch and break periods, and maintaining a delivery or route schedule.

Core skills, according to Jacobs, are the sets of skills that are applicable to all jobs in a particular job group, such as clerical or manufacturing occupations. Thirty-six such skills occur repeatedly:

- fold
- assemble
- package and wrap
- lift and carry
- transport
- pack or crate
- stamp and label
- stuff envelopes
- mix and blend ingredients
- indoor cleaning, make beds
- dress/undress another person
- use common kitchen utensils
- use cash register or calculator
- use standard office supplies
- receive and transmit messages
- use hand tools

- bundle
- fasten
- cut
- load and unload
- stack and shelve
- open and unpack
- run errands
- affix postage
- use heat and heating units
- set and clear tables
- make beds
- perform kitchen clean up
- find streets and addresses
- hand stitch
- iron
- dig and shovel

---

*Source: From *Handbook for Job Placement of Mentally Retarded Workers: Training, Opportunities, and Career Areas*, 3rd ed. (pp. 43-46) by A.M. Jacobs, J.K. Larsen, and C.A. Smith, 1979, New York: NY: Garland STPM Press. Copyright 1979 by American Institutes for Research in the Behavioral Sciences. Adapted by permission.

- use garden tools
- handle cleaning solutions

- handle live animals and fish
- type*

Detailed skills exist within each of the core skills above. The core skill "use standard office supplies" implies the use of a stapler, staple remover, paper punch, rubber stamp, scissors, ruler, glue, paper clips, tape, erasers, correction tape or fluid, and handling carbon paper, in order to perform general office tasks such as stapling documents or preparing packages for mailing.

There is abundant evidence that mentally retarded individuals want to work and are capable of being involved in making choices about the work they want to do. At the same time, the mentally retarded have generally good records of attendance, longevity, and production in jobs for which they are well matched. Brolin (1976) pointed out that one of the major problems with mentally retarded workers has been the tendency of employers to underestimate what they can learn and do.

There is abundant evidence that competence on the job must be complemented with other competencies in the community at large. Kiernan and Stark (1986) proposed the use of what they term "the Pathways Model" for integrating adults with disabilities into employment and the community. They recognized that beyond employment per se, the individual will need to be able to deal with problems of finances and community adjustment if he or she is to benefit from the integration process.

Finding and Getting Hired for Jobs

Wehman and Hill (1981) presented a model for job placement of moderately and severely disabled individuals. For these individuals, a considerable amount of help is necessary to find a job in the competitive job market. Much of the emphasis in their approach rests on (1) matching the client with the job requirements and (2) on-the-job training, advocacy, and staff withdrawal. Strategies that they have found helpful in the placement of individuals with moderate and severe disabilities include

- informing coworkers about the client's disability
- reinforcing nondisabled workers and supervisors

---

*Source: From *Handbook for Job Placement of Mentally Retarded Workers: Training, Opportunities, and Career Areas,* 3rd ed. (pp. 47-52) by A.M. Jacobs, J.K. Larsen, and C.A. Smith, 1979, New York: NY: Garland STPM Press. Copyright 1979 by American Institutes for Research in the Behavioral Sciences. Adapted by permission.

- providing parental support in problem situations
- maintaining regular contact at the work site
- assisting the client in completing the required work

Hollenbeck and Smith (1984) surveyed 569 employers to determine how they customarily solicited applicants, how they perceived the applicants that came to their firms in terms of preparation, what they thought of the interview skills of the applicants, and what their major problems were with applicants. They found that

- The most common methods employers used for attracting applicants were (1) advertisements (71.5%), (2) announcing to current employees (69.3%), (3) asking for referrals from schools (59.8%), and (4) asking for referrals from the state employment service (54.3%). Given this pattern, individuals with disabilities (or their advocates) should pay particular attention to these avenues for finding out about jobs.
- The employers felt that youthful applicants were best prepared in industrial vocation education and least prepared in English writing ability. Over 10 times as many employers were negative about applicants' English writing as were positive about it.
- Employers were disappointed at the poor performance of young people in filling out applications and in presenting themselves properly (dress and manner) at interviews.
- Major problems reported by the employers were (1) poor work habits and poor work ethics, (2) poor job search skills, and (3) poor attainment of basic skills.

Overall, the employers' views about youthful applicants were less than enthusiastic. One said,

We now generally avoid hiring young people. We have found that hiring older workers who are desperately in need of jobs because they have families, financial responsibilities and are permanently laid off from companies that are closing or have closed their facilities, we can (1) avoid training costs, (2) avoid absenteeism costs, (3) select the best employees . . . , (4) avoid turnover since older workers stay with our company, (5) avoid workers' compensation claims since our older workers tend to be more safety conscious, (6) avoid labor relations problems since older workers tend to respect authority more, and (7) gain from their experience and knowledge. (Hollenbeck & Smith, 1984, p. 33)

It is important to keep in mind that the survey by Hollenbeck and Smith applied to the general population and not simply to persons with disabilities. Nevertheless, it is possible to learn from this study about the things that employers value—things that they expect of the people that come to work for them.

Harold Krents (1980), the blind lawyer whose life has been portrayed in the mass media, has voiced a sound philosophy for securing employment for persons with disabilities. He said, "No citizen should be constantly required to do vastly better than those in the majority in order to achieve maximum employment potential" (p. 8). Moreover, according to Krents, "Employment opportunities can be achieved in a spirit of cooperation rather than confrontation." In other words, *how* you go about doing what needs to be done makes a difference.

Rosenthal (1990) is a reporter with a learning disability whose writing is slow and illegible; however, he submits his stories already typed, so the writing does not affect his performance. There are different ways to get things done. Some ways make things easier, some ways make things harder. The ideal way is to implement what business people call a "win-win" strategy. A win-win strategy is one in which the person with a disability benefits and so does the other person (or persons) involved in the process or activity.

How does this work in practice? First, the person with a disability must be able to offer something the employer wants. The employer does not expect someone to come in and do the job without instruction, but he or she wants someone who is honest, loyal, and can be counted on—someone who can get the job done. Whether the job is extremely simple or repetitive or challenging and requiring technical expertise, this expectation holds true.

The candidate for employment must convince the employer that he or she will be that kind of employee. If the first contact with the employer is made through a third party, as in the case of a severely disabled individual who will need supported employment placement, this point must be promised along with promises of special assistance by a job coach to the extent that it is needed.

Once hired and on the job, the person with a disability needs to know that he or she is valued by others because of the things that he or she does. Positive reinforcement rather than criticism is important. When other workers at the job site personally value the person who is disabled, they go out of their way to encourage, support, and involve them in ways that benefit everyone in the company. As a technique for reaching a job placement goal, the win-win strategy can be very effective.

BECOMING A VALUED EMPLOYEE

It is not enough to be hired. Employment can be very short lived if the supervisor or employer finds that he or she has made a mistake. There is evidence that employers of persons with disabilities are generally well satisfied with those individuals' work (Marriott Foundation for People with Disabilities, 1990). But employers are business people—they are in business to make a profit, not to run a social welfare program. That means they examine the work performance of all employees, including ones with disabilities, in terms of the work performed for the pay received, and the presence or absence of problems associated with their employment.

Salomone and Paige (1984) looked at the employment problems of blind and visually impaired adults. The persons they interviewed cited several kinds of problems:

- *Negative public perception of blindness* was mentioned by 45% of the persons interviewed. "There are a lot of people out there that stereotype you."
- *Diminished self concept* was mentioned by 38% of the sample. "Employers have to get a sense of how you carry yourself."
- *Employer reluctance to hire.* "Employers worry that if something happens to me their insurance rates will go up."
- *Limited transportation.* "I was more nervous about how I would get around if I got the job than I was about the job interview."
- *Poor career planning and inadequate vocational training.* "I'd like to get some kind of rehabilitation training or technical training but it seems that I am having a hard time getting into any of the programs."
- Also mentioned were: *no personal contact with positive role models, uncertainty and confusion regarding educational potential,* and various comments about *ineffective counselor help.**

Persons with disabilities can be among the best employees, or they can be seen as a liability. Which way they are perceived often depends on one of three things:

1. whether accommodations or adaptations are needed, recognized, and put in place
2. whether the employee demonstrates appropriate social-employability skills
3. whether the employee demonstrates individual abilities on the job

*Source: From "Employment Problems and Solutions: Perceptions of Blind and Visually Impaired Adults" by P.R. Salomone and R.E. Paige, 1984, *Vocational Guidance Quarterly*, December, pp. 147-156. Copyright 1984 by Department of Education, San Diego County, CA. Adapted by permission.

Accommodations and Adaptations To Enhance Performance

The first class of accommodations that must be addressed are those related to getting the person with a disability to the work site and home again. Is the individual able to drive himself or herself? If not, is public transportation available? Does the transportation go to the right place, and can it be physically accessed? If public transportation is not available or accessible, who will be responsible for providing the needed transportation? Is it a special service of some kind, or will it be a friend or relative? If the latter is the case, how reliable will that service be, day in and day out? Finally, is the transportation affordable?

The answers to these questions define the present status of the individual. Certainly, if the answers suggest that transportation is not a problem, all is well and good. However, if there are potential problems, it is clear that some accommodation will be needed. If the person does drive, is there a marked parking space at a location that is reasonably close to the work station? If the person does not have a car but could drive, is it possible that a specially equipped vehicle (e.g., one with hand-operable controls, extensions on brake pedals and accelerator, a wheelchair ramp and safety system for a van) can be made available so that he or she can become self-reliant in transportation? If so, this may be the best solution over the long term, and a case might be made for obtaining the vehicle with help from rehabilitation services.

If the individual needs to use public transportation, does he or she need training to use it? Again, rehabilitation services can arrange for the training. If public transportation is not the answer, what kind of special transportation should be arranged? Possibilities include an accessible mini-bus commercial service or perhaps a carpooling arrangement with another employee.

Another class of accommodation that needs to be considered is the location and design of the building and work station(s). Depending on the mobility of the individual with disabilities, elevator access may be needed. Some accommodations may be appropriate at the work station itself. If a wheelchair is being used, there must be space to move it around and position it for access to the working surface. There must also be a wheelchair-accessible lavatory (inward, outward, and within the room) and there should be wheelchair access to public phones. If the individual is of short stature, provision must be made to either add height (stepstool or other aid) or subtract height (lowered work surfaces, storage, and seating).

A third class of accommodations concerns adjustments that will facilitate the work itself. Persons with hearing impairments or deafness will not need physical accommodation but may benefit from having access to adaptive equipment for telecommunications, particularly a TDD device or amplifying equipment connected to the phone. Persons with mental retardation may benefit from small accommodations of the job-aid type, such as posted checklists of work routines or specially adapted job-relevant devices (e.g., color-coded marking, measuring sticks cut to size).

Depending on the nature of the work, persons with vision impairments or blindness may require adaptive equipment too, such as computer equipment with speech output or Braille output, or special devices to facilitate the reading of inkprint. Similarly, persons with limited physical ability can often benefit from computer accommodations. However, in each case, access to the computer is necessarily a function of how well the match can be made between the person's capacities and the features of the computer that allow/facilitate use by persons with restricted abilities (Vanderheiden, Lee, & Scadden, 1987).

Whatever the form of accommodation, it is important to bear in mind that there is a major upswing in the advent of new technology, especially computer technology, that will continue to facilitate the employment of people with disabilities. Summarizing a number of sources of information on the rapid expansion of the assistive device industry and its significance for the "mature market" of seniors and the employable population with disabilities, Gibler (1989) pointed out that

- There are now six times as many assistive device companies offering ten times as many products as there were 10 years ago.
- The work-at-home field has been called the fastest growing form of business in the United States by the U.S. Small Business Administration.
- The General Services Administration has mandated the accessibility of computer systems to federal employees with disabilities.
- New technologies continue to be developed that increase capacity in functional areas, and they can be produced more economically as volume increases (still leaving room for a profit margin for the manufacturers and suppliers of these devices).

Three principles should be kept in mind as accommodations and adjustments are considered, regardless of whether they involve technology or not. First, reasonable accommodations are required under the law and are rarely resisted by an employer who wants to get the best work performance from an employee. Second, accommodations do not always require devices or changes in the physical plant or acquisition of new equipment. Sometimes they may be satisfied with a personal aide in certain situations, such as a provision of an interpreter when a deaf person cannot otherwise communicate in an oral environment (e.g., group meetings) or when the person with a disability must converse with someone who has difficulty understanding his or her speech.

Third, accommodations are frequently possible at a negligible cost. Even when costs are "substantial," such as the cost of a computer-based reading device or a vehicle, the investment may be defensible when the useful life of the item is compared to the years of earning power the investment makes possible.

The United States GAO (1990b) studied the literature on the costs of ensuring building access (including public buildings, educational institutions, and places of employment), employment accommodations, transit systems, and telecommunications. Citing a 1976 report by Cochran and Associates, the GAO report (1990b) stated that the average cost of making 34 business facilities accessible was less than $.01 per square foot. Citing a report on employment accommodations by Berkeley Planning Associates (1982), the GAO stated that 51% of the accommodations cost nothing, and another 30% cost less than $500. Only 8% cost more than $2000, and these generally related to audiovisual aids. Transportation cost estimates showed that public transportation access would be relatively cheap for a lift-bus approach or a user-side taxi system and considerably more for a paratransit system. Telecommunications estimates of cost were centered on the use of interstate relay centers and amplified headsets for public telephones (no site-specific data were reported).

Not infrequently, the best and cheapest accommodations can be made through re-evaluating the nature of the work itself and modifying the work assignments of the employees accordingly. Teaming and work sharing are one way to accomplish this. In addition, as described elsewhere, many types of computer work can be accomplished at the home of the employee with a disability; through the use of modems, the work can be transmitted to the main office or plant through telephone lines.

In forming work teams, it is often possible to take advantage of the complementary skills and abilities of individuals with and without disabilities to get the work done, merely by making reallocations of the work to capitalize on the skills (and avoid the disabilities) of the persons in the team. These kinds of adjustments in scheduling of the work may not be immediately apparent when the person with disabilities first starts on the job but are often quickly recognized by coworkers as they begin to work with the individual.

Finally, it is very important that persons with disabilities be directly involved in the decisions about what accommodations are needed (if any) and how they will be accomplished. In many cases they know what will help them most; in other cases they may be unaware of the availability of technology that can help them accomplish certain tasks. Outside resources can be called on to help when situations arise that do not lend themselves to obvious solutions.

In this regard, employers should not hesitate to call on the Job Accommodation Network (JAN), which is sponsored by the President's Committee on Employment of Persons with Disabilities, through its toll-free 1-800 number. JAN staff have had considerable experience in resolving "stumbling blocks" by putting the employer with "the problem" directly in touch with another employer who has already faced and solved "the problem" (Clearinghouse on the Handicapped, 1984).

Expanding Career Options through Technology

For many individuals with disabilities, the impact of technology in selecting careers cannot be overlooked. Certainly, many persons who have intellectual ability but are handicapped in some other way have been able to use computers with great success in such far-ranging occupations as word processing, graphic design in shipbuilding, economic modeling and investment analysis, and even in the search for extraterrestrial intelligence (Weisgerber, 1990). Consider, for example, how important the telephone is as a way of sharing business information instantly across great distances. Now, simply by using inexpensive TDD (telecommunication device for the deaf) equipment and fax equipment, telephone communication is feasible (and becoming widespread) among deaf persons, opening new occupational opportunities for this group.

Special technology can also affect social interaction and the choice of a workplace. For some persons with fragile health conditions (e.g., respirator-dependent medical condition, degenerative muscular condition), the difficulty of traveling to and from work and moving about at the worksite can be overwhelming. Formerly, this need to travel was enough to negate the possibility of gainful employment for persons with special problems of this sort. Presently, microcomputers and modems make it possible for many types of work to be accomplished remotely instead of at the main worksite.

Although remote computing changes the nature and amount of interpersonal interaction that occurs with coworkers, it does not eliminate it altogether. For example, Joe Hogg is a very successful computer engineer who lives and works in Phoenix (Weisgerber, 1990). He works for a large firm involved in computer manufacture, but although he lives only a mile from the plant Joe works at home in his office—a converted garage. Joe needs a full-time personal care attendant, but he interacts using his computer and associated equipment with confidence and a high level of expertise. Joe is quadriplegic and due to his cerebral palsy cannot speak, yet he is in constant communication with colleagues at work via a highly adapted computerized workcenter (which he has paid for himself). His success at being a troubleshooter (finding bugs in new programs) has earned him the respect of his coworkers and recognition as employee of the year. Joe's value to the firm rests not in his physical presence at the plant but in the power of his brain, which he can use anywhere.

Applying Social-Employability Skills

Social interaction is a natural part of most people's lives. Socialization takes on very different forms, however, depending on the age of the participants and the context in which the interaction occurs. Hall (1986) distinguished between preadult socialization and adult socialization that is work related. In educational settings, students learn from both faculty and peers, both formally and informally. In work situations learning involves socialization over several stages of career change. Different socialization models have been proposed, but generally they share the following stages, suggested by Feldman (1981) as cited in Hall (1986):

1. anticipatory socialization: building expectations based on job interviews and preliminary exposure to the organization
2. encounter socialization: determining one's role in the work group, dealing with integration into the work group, handling conflicts in the demands of family and the organization
3. change and acquisition: resolving role demands, adjusting to group norms and values (ongoing over the career)

While these are probably sufficient to describe the general dimensions of socialization that occur for nondisabled persons, there are additional critical elements of socialization that the person with disabilities must be prepared for in employment (Calkins & Walker, 1989).

Salzberg, Agran, and Lignugaris/Kraft (1986) analyzed five types of jobs in terms of employer expectations about entry-level skills needed on the job. The jobs were all ones that are often filled by mentally retarded workers: janitors, motel maids, dishwashers, food service workers, kitchen helpers. The dimensions used in the employer evaluation were (1) 12 task-related social behaviors that affect the performance of the job tasks, (2) 7 personal-social behaviors that affect interpersonal communication, and (3) 4 behaviors related to nonsocial production. Rated highest in importance were the nonsocial production skills, followed by the task-related social interaction category and then by the personal-social category. Within the latter categories, however, it was clear that certain behaviors mattered more in one job than in another. For example, social interaction was considered to be very important where workers were in close proximity, such as in kitchen work, while the use of appropriate language and other personal-social behaviors were important where the worker interacted with customers, such as is necessary for maids and food service workers.

When persons with disabilities report to work, there are two "musts" that they face. They must prove their ability to do the work for which they were hired (more will be said about this later), and they must get along with the people they encounter in the course of doing their work. The social-employability skills that they need to draw upon in this are many and varied.

Proving Individual Abilities on the Job

Rivlin (1989) studied the achievements of professionals with disabilities holding advanced degrees. Included in the study were 129 participants, 59 disabled and a comparison group of 70 nondisabled, from rehabilitation, education, psychology, and social work professions. Rivlin found that

- The work histories of the two groups showed no significant differences.
- In terms of job search, there was no significant difference in the way that employers received professionals with and without disabilities.
- More than half of the professionals with disabilities indicated that they had encountered physical barriers, including some that had prevented them from attaining certain positions.
- Physical limitations presented a problem for some of the professionals (e.g., fatigue, fine motor skills) and affected their level of functioning.
- There was no difference in the proportion of professionals who were working full time or part time.
- The groups fulfilled similar job responsibilities.
- There was a significant difference in the salaries paid to professionals with disabilities and professionals without disabilities, with the individuals with disabilities receiving "markedly lower" pay.

Rivlin (1989) noted that there is a trend toward obtaining advanced degrees by persons with disabilities, with 2.6% of the college freshman classes in 1978 increasing to 7.4% representation by persons with disabilities in 1985.

Demonstrating the unique capacities of intellectually able persons who pursue advanced degrees, Weisgerber (1990) has profiled a number of college students with disabilities who have been studying to obtain degrees in the sciences, engineering, or math, as well as a number of working scientists, engineers, and mathematicians. The diversity of careers and disabilities represented in these profiles suggests that the range of positions in the sciences that can be successfully held by persons with disabilities is essentially unlimited, though it is important that the nature of the disability and the demands of the position be matched.

This does not mean that unusual combinations of disabilities and jobs are inappropriate, but rather that the matching process must be thoughtfully considered. For example, Manny Guitierrez is a young man with Down's syndrome who is involved in archaeological "digs" with scientists at the University of Arizona (Kotulak, 1988). His work does not entail intellectual tasks but rather the ability to label archaeological artifacts, a task in which he excels.

There is no magic formula for assuring that the match between a person with a disability and a particular job or company is going to be "right" for either the employee or the employer. When it is not, the person may need to have a different assignment within the company or relocate to another job in another company. Changing jobs is neither unusual nor necessarily a bad thing to do. But it is more difficult for persons with disabilities because their alternatives for employment are generally not as obvious or available as those for persons who are not disabled. In addition, job relocation will involve a whole new learning of how to deal with barriers (attitudinal and physical) that are associated with the new work setting. For these and other reasons, it is likely that persons with disabilities will want to keep jobs that they can succeed in doing and where they are appreciated.

Generally speaking, the immediate supervisor on a job is a very important person, because it is this person who gives assignments and judges the quality and rate of work performed. Employees with disabilities need to focus on meeting the expectations of that supervisor to the extent their disability permits. Satisfying the supervisor involves some straightforward and basic procedures:

- Be dependable by being on the job when and where expected.
- Pay close attention to the supervisor's directions, and be sure they are understood, including the time when the work is to be completed.
- Ask for help when it is needed, such as asking the supervisor for clarification of directions, but do not become dependent on others to do the assigned work.
- Stick to the job, working at a steady rate, but do not do it so fast as to bring about mistakes.
- Observe safety rules.
- Choose the right time and place to approach the supervisor about personal requests or problems.

Working with other employees presents another potential problem area for persons with disabilities. Employers do not want trouble in the work force, as it is counterproductive. Unfortunately, if problems do develop between a worker with a disability and one without disability, the latter often receives more than his or her share of the blame. All new employees have to get acquainted with people they are working with, and some do it more easily than others. Because they have been excluded from the mainstream in many ways, it cannot be taken for granted that employees with disabilities will know how to gain acceptance from their coworkers. For example, overt expressions of fondness (such as touching) are ordinarily out of place in a work site. For some persons with certain types of disabilities, this may be a habit that must be brought under control. Many times the nondisabled employees will not be familiar with the disability and will not know how they should conduct themselves to make the employee with a disability at ease and provide the right amount of support, without interfering with his or her work. The direct and best way to deal with this situation is through the use of candor and frankness in dealing with the coworkers.

Some of the ways persons with disabilities can develop positive relationships with coworkers are as follows:

- Communication, in a useful form, should be encouraged. Even persons without speech or who are not naturally expressive need to find some way to communicate in order to develop a feeling of belonging.
- At the same time, this communication must be done at appropriate times and places and should deal with appropriate topics. Workers with disabilities who "dump" on coworkers will be avoided, and workers who interfere with the work of others will be avoided.
- Carrying a fair share of the workload (within one's capacity) is an excellent way to earn the respect of coworkers.
- Respecting the property and "space" of coworkers (and the company) is essential.

Businesses stay in business only if they have customers. That is true for McDonald's franchises and it is true for manufacturers. Even government agencies have someone to serve. They all depend on good relationships with the people who use their goods and services in order to remain viable. Persons with disabilities have a right to be a part of society, and many times they are naturally going to be in circumstances where they come in contact with customers. High-functioning persons with disabilities may have little difficulty in these relationships, though difficulties may arise from time to time. Low-functioning individuals, however, will benefit from ample on-the-job training so that when they do encounter a customer (a stranger to them), they will be able to respond in appropriate ways. Returning to the main point, employers will be especially impressed if they hear customers compliment the employee with disabilities, for it will reaffirm the correctness of the employer's decision to add the individual to the work force.

MAKING A CONTRIBUTION TO SOCIETY

Satisfaction derives from self-esteem. Self-esteem comes from (among other things) being able to make a contribution to the social fabric of society. Mature individuals derive satisfaction and self-esteem from helping others who can benefit from their companionship or experience. In general, persons with disabilities do not relish the thought of constantly being "takers" and would like to be a contributing part of society. Whether they are working or otherwise "involved" in some way, they are happier and feel better about themselves.

Social and Leisure Involvement

Persons with disabilities deserve to enjoy life to the extent that their disability permits. This is a goal that is easily understood in the abstract, but not so easily accomplished. Adult involvement in social affairs takes many forms, and individuals with disabilities are not different from individuals without disabilities in that they choose to participate in social activities in different ways. Two of these, travel and athletics, serve to illustrate how these social activities can be accomplished.

Travel affords individuals an opportunity to see new places and meet new people, but it is a challenge for those who cannot find their way or who need personal attendant services. One approach that works for persons with disabilities is to use a special travel service that understands and is prepared to meet their needs. People and Places, Inc., located in Buffalo, New York, offers vacation services for adults with developmental disabilities and has been doing so since 1975. Now including persons of different disabilities and from elsewhere than Buffalo, it offers a wide range of destinations throughout Europe, the Caribbean, Mexico, and the United States. Groups are restricted to eight participants, allowing attention to individual needs.

Individuals with disabilities are no longer strangers to athletic endeavors. Early on, through protest demonstrations and fund-earning projects (such as cross-country wheelchair ventures), they proved that they could do things that were physically demanding. It is not uncommon now to discover them in places where they would not have been expected a decade ago.

Skiing has become a popular activity for paraplegic and limbless individuals. Peter Axelson is a T-10 paraplegic who is extremely active in skiing, having competed as a member of the U.S. Olympic Disabled Ski Team for a number of years and having swept first place in 1986 in the slalom, giant slalom, and downhill events (he won individual events in 1985 and 1987 as well) (Tetzlaff, 1990). Special equipment has made it possible for these individuals to practice and sharpen their skills; Axelson designed the first (sitting) mono ski in 1985. Special guiding techniques have made it possible for the blind to enjoy skiing as well.

Thanks to the stimulation of the Special Olympics program, mentally retarded, blind, and other persons with disabilities are not only participating but also receiving recognition in track and field events. As is well known, competitions are now held at local, national, and even international levels.

Examination of any issue of *Paraplegia News* (the journal of the Paralyzed Veterans of America) or *RX Home Care* (the journal of home health care and rehabilitation) quickly makes clear that there is a market developing around persons using specially designed wheelchairs in basketball, tennis, track, cycling, camping, and a number of other sports and social activities. Two associations (the National Wheelchair Athletics Association and the National Wheelchair Basketball Association) have established standards for fair competition in wheelchair events and in swimming based on the degree of neurologic damage to the spine and the extent of muscle control remaining (Glenn & Snowball, 1987).

Economic Self-Sufficiency

The employment of persons with disabilities makes economic sense. Even if the costs of training are included and the recipients of the training are moderately and severely disabled individuals who are being trained for competitive employment, there is a favorable cost benefit to society (Hill & Wehman, 1983). There is also a very great benefit to the individuals involved, and that benefit is not simply a financial one.

Self-worth and dignity are enhanced when one is self-reliant. Economic self-sufficiency is one form of self-reliance. At the personal level, economic self-reliance means personal choice. It means electing to utilize resources in a variety of ways, such as hobbies, travel, or paying the mortgage on a home, computer equipment, or even attendant care. It also means that the individual will be contributing to the economy through taxes, instead of relying on supplemental income and welfare.

There are, however, various disincentives in the present system for some people (Brown, 1990). Roth (1989) spoke for many individuals with disabilities when she said, "I never expected to receive Social Security benefits at the young age of 36, but I do. And I never thought that, by accepting help from the government, I'd entered a situation where trying to return to work could cost me money" (p. 16). Roth, who has multiple sclerosis, specifically criticized the circumstances that place many persons who receive financial support through

SSDI in a position of losing that support (which includes Medicare coverage) by earning modest monthly amounts, amounts that are very low by any criterion. Pressure for change in this aspect of the law has led to increased, though still insufficient, allowances that started in January 1990. Much greater earnings allowances are needed to encourage, not discourage, persons with disabilities to enter the work force.

If self-sufficiency is accomplished and health permits, the individual with a disability needs to prolong this status as long as possible. Previously in this chapter, the point was made that some employers prefer older workers (Hollenbeck & Smith, 1984). As one's productive career winds down, there are alternatives that can extend the individual's productive life. Lazarus and Lauer (1985) name seven avenues:

1. Modified work schedules: R.H. Macy & Company does not have mandatory retirement. Many employees opt for a shortened work schedule to reduce their responsibilities.
2. Nontraditional, part-time arrangement: Minnesota Abstract and Title Company has many jobs filled by two people, including older workers.
3. Temporary employment: The Sun Company (35,000 employees) entered into a program of hiring annuitants temporarily with great success.
4. Redesigned jobs: Evans Products (16,000 employees) customizes jobs for older workers, finding them "its most stable and reliable resource."
5. Transfer or reassignment: Kellogg Company advertises jobs internally and accepts older workers' applications for lessened responsibilities.
6. New careers: Lockheed has a specialized program for teaching retirees how to start small businesses.

Finally, volunteerism (discussed in the next chapter of this book) is a way to utilize one's expertise and knowledge to help others. Persons with disabilities are often sensitive to the ways that volunteers have helped them in the past. Accordingly, they are at their productive best as adults when they are able to reach out and help others who can benefit from their help.

Chapter 5

Retirement and Disability

1. Life Stage: The Senior Years
   - Federal and Local Programs
   - Disability Policy and Socioeconomic Independence
   - The Transition to Life in Retirement
2. Quality of Life for the Elderly with Disabilities
   - Transportation
   - Housing
   - Security
   - Health
   - Work
   - Family and Friends
   - Continued Personal Enhancement

LIFE STAGE: THE SENIOR YEARS

The aging process is universal. Although it is not a popular topic for the young or for those who are at the peak of their productivity, they cannot avoid it. The future is clouded for all of us, disabled and nondisabled alike. Understandably, persons with disabilities can anticipate even greater complications in meeting their daily needs. The same can be said for many nondisabled persons for whom the aging process leads to the onset of disability and a loss of independence and self-sufficiency. Health is a fragile and critical factor.

Loss of self-sufficiency occurs naturally in later years. It can develop from a loss of physical capacity (musculoskeletal problems) or sensory capacity (loss of vision or loss of hearing), impairments that are generally not fatal. Often, adaptations can be made, assistance in the activities of daily living arranged, and life can go on in a changed manner. The individual is nevertheless "handicapped" according to the definition used by the World Health Organization (1980). Loss of self-sufficiency can also develop from a life-threatening disease, such as heart disease or emphysema. In such a situation, health problems are likely to become what Verbrugge (1989) called "increasingly one-way."

Verbrugge studied the interactions of aging and health thoroughly. She noted that static analyses of health status do not reflect its dynamic quality. Chronic illness tends to become permanent and physiological ability to restore lost function diminishes. Manton (1988), cited in Verbrugge (1989), found that women have higher incidence rates of disability over time, and men are more likely to restore function over time.

Verbrugge described a "model trajectory of events over time" as involving (1) the clinical onset of chronic disease, followed by (2) problems in household management tasks (IADL) and discretionary activities, followed by (3) difficulty in personal care (ADL), followed by (4) institutionalization and, ultimately, death.

Verbrugge also noted that "men simply reach death sooner than women do, apparently skipping intermediate stages of disability and/or spending less time in them" (page 68).

In any case, the proportion of persons in society who have reached retirement age or older steadily increases. Katchadourian (1987) put this age increase in perspective: 2000 years ago in Rome the average life expectancy was 22; in 1900 in the United States it was 49.2; in 1985 it was 74.7. Currently life expectancy is around 85 years of age. Assuming that preventive medicine continues to extend the life span, projections suggest that by the year 2000, 20-year-olds could expect their retired life to increase to 28% of their adult life (Torrey, 1982).

Birren (1986) suggested that growing up and growing old are complementary phenomena—that the way we age may be a translation of the way we grow up, biologically, psychologically, and socially. In this model growing up is an organizing activity, while aging is a disorganizing activity. Birren pointed out that puzzling questions arise when one looks at genetic coding and asks why it is that an inherited disposition toward Alzheimer's disease typically is not actuated in the body until later in life. In reply, Birren stated, "Some genes that have late life expression in disease may have served a desirable function in earlier life. The term *pleiotropism* refers to this multiple function, which bears on the important point that normal development and aging require the proper timing of genetic expression."

As inexorable as aging may be, it does not follow that the senior years are necessarily "lost years" or ones in which feelings of usefulness and satisfaction must be given up. On the contrary, things are getting better, and they will continue to do so as society begins to appreciate and utilize the potential contributions that our older population can make.

Federal and Local Programs

President Franklin D. Roosevelt, in 1934, in the midst of the Depression, told the Congress,

> I am looking for a sound means which [I] can recommend to provide at once security against several of the great disturbing factors in life—especially those which relate to unemployment and old age....These three great objectives—the security of the home, the security of livelihood, and the security of social insurance—are, it seems to me, a minimum of the promise that we can offer to the American people. (Achenbaum, p. 275)

Achenbaum analyzed how these three principles have been reflected, with some difficulty and shortcomings, in Social Security policy. Originally, only workers who had contributed into the system were entitled to benefit from its provisions. Though this was relaxed, there were many differences in eligibility rules and monthly allowances from place to place. For example, the average monthly allowance in California was $31.36, much higher than the national average of $18.36 and about 10 times what it was in Mississippi. For all its inadequacies, however, Social Security was seen as a "floor" for protection against one's anticipated needs as the aging process moved one from independence to a condition of dependence.

The Older Americans Act of 1965 was an affirmation of Roosevelt's vision of services to elderly citizens. In it, Congress declared,

> The Congress hereby finds and declares that, in keeping with the traditional American concept of the inherent dignity of the individual in our democratic society, the older people of our Nation are entitled to, and it is the joint and several duty and responsibility of the governments of the United States . . . to assist our older people to secure equal opportunity to the full and free enjoyment of the following objectives.

> 1. An adequate income in retirement in accordance with the American standard of living.
> 2. The best possible physical and mental health which science can make available, and without regard to economic status.
> 3. Suitable housing, independently selected, designed, and located with reference to special needs and available at costs which older citizens can afford.

4. Full restorative services for those who require institutional care.
5. Opportunity for employment with no discriminatory personnel practices because of age.
6. Retirement in health, honor, dignity—after years of contributing to the economy.
7. Pursuit of meaningful activity within the widest range of civil, cultural, and recreational opportunities.
8. Efficient community services which provide social assistance in a coordinated manner and which are readily available when needed.
9. Immediate benefit from proven research knowledge which can sustain and improve health and happiness.
10. Freedom, independence, and the free exercise of individual initiative in planning and managing their own lives.

As clear and lofty as these objectives were, it is equally true that our social system as presently implemented has not fulfilled the promise of the act. That does not diminish the importance of the objectives, for they were reaffirmed by the National Commission on Social Security reform in 1983, which decided against modifying the system to reflect individual financial need (a welfare scheme), or to make payout dependent on contributions made (an annuity scheme).

There is a continuing debate over the solvency of the Social Security system. On the one side are those claiming near bankruptcy, who point out the tremendous dollar-flow in the system and look ahead to the time when the "ba-by-boomers" age into eligibility. On the other side are those, like Senator Daniel Patrick Moynihan, who look at the recent surpluses in the system and the reserve of funds and say it is "unnecessary." Social Security has clearly been politicized. From the point of view of the disability community, however, there is consider-able concern over the adequacy of payments and the need for reform to eliminate work disincentives.

Many would argue that there is overattention to bureaucratic constraints and not enough attention to the reality of the persons with special needs who also happen to be of advancing years. For example, it is painfully obvious that society has failed to serve the neediest people of all, the homeless aged and those who have chronic health care problems.

We know (Butler, 1985) that 95% of the older persons in the United States live in the community, not in institutions. May (1986) reminded us of the resistance displayed by most elderly people to going to an institution to receive care. He pointed out that while the sick go to institutions to get well, the elderly generally see entry into institutional care to be a one-way trip, only to be followed by death. The elderly can remember the time, only a few decades ago, when physicians came to the home to provide care. Now the economics of home visits is such that they only occur in extreme cases. Unfortunately, too many older persons do not take care of themselves in self-administered ways (e.g., nutrition, medication), and without motivation or external intervention they are unlikely to change.

May (1986) argued that courage, not battlefield courage, but resoluteness, by those who have come face-to-face with the realities of their declining years is essential to their own good and the good of society. He pointed out the need for humility on the part of caregivers, who hold the potential for arrogance of power and all too often use it. He also referred to integrity in events and patterns that give meaning to a person's life—"How one eats, cleanses oneself, greets one's fellow, rises to challenge, and shuts down the day—these repeated actions signal the way in which one connects with the ultimate"(p. 56).

Disability Policy and Socioeconomic Independence

Fox and Willis (1989) compiled, in two special supplements to volume 67 of the *Milbank Quarterly*, a series of articles pertaining to disability among the elderly, particularly with regard to their economic and health circumstances. It is probably the most thorough inspection of this complex topic currently available. In Supplement 1, Chirikos (1989) examined the economic impact of disability in the United States. Using reasoning familiar to economists and policy analysts, Chirikos pointed out that "aggregate economic losses" due to disabilities establish a guideline for the "value of resources" that are allocated to interventions for persons with disabilities. In this respect, he considered "disability losses" to reflect "primary market time" (the inability to engage in work), "secondary market time" (limiting effects on the earning power of others in the household), and "net consumption" (spending by and for persons with disabilities), all of which have an impact on the economy.

Chirikos (1989) estimated that at a national level the economic losses (due to disability) for persons with moderate disabilities are $54.1 billion and for persons with severe disabilities, $122.6 billion. In contrasting employability versus dependency, it is estimated that the losses for persons with disabilities of working age (15 to 64) are about $111.5 billion; for those outside those ages (0 to 14 and 65 and over), the estimated loss is $65.2 billion. If we look specifically at persons in the transitional age ranges (where productive working frequently stops), Chirikos estimated that disability in the age range of 45 to 64 years results in a loss of $72.762 billion (of which $55.38 billion applies to males and $17.382 billion applies to females). This is contrasted with the age range of 65 to 74 years, where the economic losses are estimated to be substantially less—$29.858 billion (of which $18.408 billion applies to males and $11.450 billion applies to females).

Translating and summarizing these estimates, however rough they may be, Chirikos (1989) suggested that they represent "an enormous toll on the American economy." These losses amounted to about 6.9% of the gross national product in 1980. Alternatively, Chirikos pointed out, the losses can be characterized as "a tax of about $800 levied on each and every American" or "a potential bonus to the economy of some $6,880 for each prevalent case of functional disablement that could have been prevented or postponed in that year"(p. 83).

Given the economics just presented, it is small wonder that a government policy directed at spending large sums in the area of disability makes "economic sense." Areas in which targeted intervention seem especially worthy of consideration on economic grounds are (1) interventions related to the health and physical condition of men in the age range of 45 to 65, to extend their productive worklife, and (2) programs of respite care for spouses of the disabled elderly, to allow spouses to be active in the secondary market (Chirikos, 1989).

The Transition to Life in Retirement

The transition to retirement in the senior years is not just something that happens automatically at the age of 65. The average age at which retirement occurs has moved steadily downward, reaching an average age of 59 as of June 1985 (Deutscher, 1988). Figure 5-1 shows two distinct stages in retirement, with service needs shifting due to failing health and the resulting need for greater personal care and assistance.

During early retirement, many older persons are electing to move away from colder climates in the Northeast to the South and West, where retirement communities are not uncommon. For persons with limited mobility the absence

Time Frame	Service Delivery Team	Services Delivered
Initial retirement	Social service staff, employers, family and friends	Social networks, living needs, leisure pursuits, self-enhancement
Advanced retirement	Social services, medical and convalescent staff, family and friends	Economic security, health care, social interaction

Figure 5-1 The Senior Years: Inter-Relationships and Dependencies

of snow and ice can be very important. That is not to say that moving is a lightly considered undertaking, for, as Walter (1985) has indicated, the elderly are half as likely to move as younger families. Aside from the cost implications of moving, the key consideration for older persons is the loss of established support networks (both formal and informal). There is a strong need to rebuild these support systems in the new location if well-being is to be maintained. According to Stahl and Potts (1985), "the greater the social isolation, the greater the adverse impact of chronic disease" (p. 323).

Johnston and Hoover (1982) summarized the quality of life for the older population as a whole as growing older, healthier, better educated, and more independent with respect to living arrangements and marital status. They are also less poor. In looking to the general question of whether the elderly are "satisfied" with the quality of their lives, Johnston and Hoover cite data from the General Social Surveys, conducted by the National Opinion Research Center. On "general happiness," 42.2% of the males in the 65 to 89 years age bracket express a favorable response, a higher percentage than at any other period of their lives. However, women in this age bracket show a 34.6% favorable response, which is lower than at all other ages except the 18 to 29 years bracket. For specific domains of "own health," positive satisfaction is 49.5% for men, 43.1% for women; for "family life," 74.7% for men and 70.9% for women; for "hobbies," 52.9% for men, 58.3% for women; for "friendships," 70.2% for men, 75.8% for women; and for "place of residence," 63.9% for men, 65.8% for women.

McCrae and Costa (1984) referred to retirement as "a critical life choice," one of a series of changes over the life course—changes that are facilitated if there is also continuity. They take the view that personality, cultural age norms, and expectations interact in determining the life course of the individual. In any case, there is wide consensus that the decisions involved in the transition out of the productive years and into the "golden years" are complex and highly dependent on the circumstances of one's personal situation.

According to Guillemard (1982), retirement has five variations:

1. withdrawal retirement, in which the individual withdraws from social interaction in previously established networks
2. "third-age retirement," in which a new stage in life is recognized, and the individual actively pursues creative outlets
3. leisure retirement, in which the individual becomes absorbed in leisure activities such as travel and the theater
4. protest retirement, in which the individual becomes politically oriented, often defending the interests of the elderly
5. acceptance retirement, in which the individual surrenders to the expected norm behavior of excessive television watching

According to Guillemard (1982) the individual's access to assets (financial resources, biological situation, and capital of social relations) and to potentialities (educational level, position held during the productive years, and extraprofessional skills) is an important determinant of which course of retirement will be taken. Withdrawal retirement follows from a lack of resources, while the conversion of resource capital leads to third-age retirement or leisure retirement.

Svanborg (1985) examined the biomedical and environmental influences on aging. He stated that there is a general notion that life has only two phases: (1) growth and functional improvement and (2) somatic withering (atrophy) and functional decline. For certain functions (basal oxygen consumption and perceptual speed), these may be true, but there is also evidence to show four phases:

1. growing and functional improvement
2. a constant, nearly level period
3. a functional decline at the rate of 1% a year
4. a rapid decline following the onset of manifestations of aging

Persons with disabilities may find that the critical change in life stage is signaled by a worsening in health status such that the individual with a disability no longer can maintain full- or even part-time employment in competitive environments.

For others with disabilities, the change may be triggered when they reach a preset retirement age, but it is at least as likely that it is triggered by their perception of work gratification in their jobs.

Lazarus and Lauer (1985) looked at the conditions that are associated with working past the age of retirement. They found that it is not the physical demands of the job that lead to the decision to retire but rather the absence of the opportunity to be creative, to do interesting work, and to see the end results of one's work.

In the Public Agenda Foundation study (1982), 67% of the individuals who wanted to work after the age of 65 wanted to work part time. The Harris and Associates study (1981) for the National Council on Aging found that 50% of workers over 55 wanted part-time work, 46% wanted at-home work, 38% wanted job-sharing, 29% wanted flex-time, 24% wanted full-time work, and 21% wanted a 4-day week.

Retirement may be triggered by a decline in capacity that precludes functioning in a productive manner in the community mainstream. Because certain disabilities may lead to or involve complications that affect the expected life span, this transition may occur at a younger age than would normally be expected in the nondisabled population.

Although attendant care may already be in place for many severely disabled individuals who are productively employed, it is likely to be needed for a much larger share of the elderly disabled as they live out their senior years. Simply put, what they will need is personal assistance in independent (noninstitutional) living. Chappel and Havens (1985) referred to this intermittent provision of informal or formal care as "interdependence."

One of several models for the provision of needed services may be put in place: consumer directed, agency directed, or jointly directed. Ulicny and Jones (1988) state that the consumer-directed model places the full responsibility for managing the level and nature of attendant services on the consumer. In the agency-directed model the agency provides attendants working under a supervising nurse rather than under the consumer. In the joint direction model the responsibilities are mixed.

If the individual has been functioning effectively and his or her functional capacity (intellectually and physically) does not preclude it, a consumer-directed model is preferable. With this approach personal dignity can be maintained through self-direction and self-reliance to the extent possible.

In the senior years, there is increased need for coordination between social services and health services staffs and increased need for social support from volunteers or friends who can help the individual with a disability enjoy his or her senior years with friendship and dignity.

QUALITY OF LIFE FOR THE ELDERLY WITH DISABILITIES

The term "quality of life" has been used throughout this book to suggest that well-being is more than physical—it is also social and economic. As we think of the quality of life for persons with disabilities, it is especially important to think in terms of how the quality of their lives is affected by the environment around them. We have emphasized the attitudinal barriers that persons without disabilities often unthinkingly impose on persons with disabilities by excluding them from opportunities or through inconsiderate words or actions. Quality of life is also influenced by the amount of difficulty that is encountered in daily affairs. There is little enjoyment to be gained from continuous encounters with physical barriers that stand in the way of the most fundamental life activities.

Zola (1989) pointed out that more infants with disabilities are living to adulthood because of medical, therapeutic, and technological advances, and they are being joined by nondisabled adults who develop chronic conditions and thus join the ranks of persons with disabilities. He viewed the central problem as a question of fit between impairments and practically every feature of the environment, whether social, political, economic, or physical. He argued that treating people with special needs as a separate "problem" is inappropriate. We all share the common problem of making the environment livable. Zola pointed to three areas where environmental change could benefit all: transportation, housing, and work.

Transportation

Accessibility to transportation is more than a wheelchair problem (though it certainly is that) or a problem for the blind or the mentally retarded (whose legs may be functional but whose travel skills may be limited). It is also a problem for frail elderly individuals, many of whom have chronic conditions but still have transportation needs and do not drive themselves.

Changes in mass transportation systems are expensive, however, and though previous regulations issued by the Department of Transportation in 1977 and 1979 had the intent of ensuring broad improvements in access, they were challenged by the transit industry and nullified by court rulings. Subsequent legislation in 1983 was weak, and in the interim primary attention has been given to costs, with a "cost cap" being introduced that eased the burden on transportation providers. Fortunately, in 1990 real progress is beginning to be made in selected, informed communities and at the national level, in part due to the efforts of advocacy groups. The Americans with Disabilities Act passed by Congress gives special attention to transportation. In keeping with this act, the Department of Transportation has given notice in the *Federal Register* of its intent to improve access to public transportation so that service for persons with and without disabilities is "equivalent" when viewed in its entirety.

Housing

The design of housing to meet the needs of persons with disabilities and the elderly involves much more than access to and egress from the building. Zola (1989) refers to a "built environment" that includes the design of doorways, tables, sink and counters, closets, railings, parking areas, and so forth. There is a tendency to think that only persons with disabilities need specially designed homes. Some do, some don't. But what is often forgotten is that as nondisabled people age, they are exposed to the possibility of a disabling condition arising or to onset of a chronic health condition.

Zola (1989) pointed out that 25% of those who are over the age of 65 and have disabilities would like to move from their current homes. But there is evidence that 40% of the moves of people into nursing homes could have been avoided with housing modifications. Among the most important of these adaptations are those relating to personal hygiene—toileting, bathing, and grooming.

In the late 1970s, estimates made by the Battelle Memorial Institute of the added costs associated with making housing accessible varied from .25% to 4.2%, depending on whether the "livability" features are included in the original design or are renovations. If they were routinely included in home designs, it is likely that actual costs would be in the lower part of this range. Even the more expensive accommodations, like elevators, represent a less expensive alternative to institutional care.

One approach to the problem of shelter involves the mixing of the elderly nondisabled with adults with disabilities, not necessarily seniors, in low-cost housing (Butler, 1990). The Monsignor Lyne Community is just such a 20-unit apartment complex, newly constructed in San Francisco. Developed by a combination of private initiative (Catholic Charities) and public assistance (a $496,000 grant from the mayor's office and a $1,180,000 loan from the federal Department of Housing and Urban Development), it is one of a number of similar projects comprising 1200 built or renovated living units. Although San Francisco is known as one of the highest-cost places to live in the United States, the monthly cost for living in a new apartment in the Monsignor Lyne Community is $200 per month—a substantial contrast to the $1000 per month that is common in the nearby community. Emile Schmidt, a 67-year-old retired cook now living at the project, says, "I think it's great to mix everybody. If everyone living in the place is over 65, they become old. This way is better." Charles Patterson, a former hotel manager who lost his home and money after he had an accident that damaged his spinal cord, finds time to think about others now. From his own wheelchair, he helps an older lady learn how to use her electric wheelchair. He says, "We're all in the same boat here. Finally finding a place to live is such a relief. Getting into this place is a blessing, a miracle" (Butler, 1990).

Security

Recent data show that the proportion of the general, largely nondisabled, population who have incomes at the poverty level is dropping substantially (Radner, 1986). Older women who live alone have a greater probability of being poor than elderly people in general. Some 80% of the elderly who live in their own homes own them, and 80% of those own them outright (Deutscher, 1988). These are good signs, though they may not be as evident with the elderly disabled.

Nevertheless, the trend toward increased financial security for the elderly population has led to a series of what Deutscher calls "elder bashings"—attacks by the media (see the May 1986 *Washington Post* editorial, "Pandering to the Elderly," and the June 1985 article in the *Atlantic Monthly*, "Justice Between Generations") that focus on the Social Security system and the discounts afforded the elderly in preference to the young. Other journalists are taking the opposite stance, e.g., the different view reported in the *Washington Post* in January 1987).

Katchadourian (1987) characterized the two ages of youth and retirement as "dissaving," where the consumption of income exceeds income. This is in contrast to the middle age, which he characterized as positive saving, where income exceeds consumption. To the extent that one's income (or the possibility of earning an income) does decrease, a fundamental concern can arise as to whether the necessities of life can be afforded. Persons with disabilities differ widely in their incomes during their productive years. Some live very well, on a par with nondisabled colleagues, while others just make ends meet. A frequently overlooked point is that many persons with disabilities are not in a position to save excess income as a hedge against the future. In the years where savings normally would accrue, persons with disabilities are more concerned about meeting the current costs of housing, food, and basic necessities such as heat and light, and their ability to pay for needed personal services.

Health

Functionality is positively correlated with health and, as mentioned previously, with quality of life. It is therefore no surprise that health and safety were highly rated by both men and women in the middle-year and elderly age groups in the Flanagan (1982) study of the quality of life, mentioned in Chapter 1.

An analysis of public use data tapes was carried out (supplied by the National Health Interview Survey, National Center for Health Statistics) to determine the prevalence of different types of disabilities. For the period 1983 to 1985 (a 3-year average), the prevalence of chronic conditions across the age brackets was as shown in Table 5-1.

Table 5-1 summarizes some of the different physical and mental conditions that tend to restrict functioning when many persons reach their senior years. In examining the table, one can see that, with several exceptions, there is a general increase in the incidence rate of impairments and chronic conditions across each age bracket. For example, the trend for blindness in both eyes is 0.6 or less than 1 out of 1000 persons under the age of 45, moving up to 2.1 at 45 to 69 years, 5.9 at 70 to 84 years, and 45.4 at 85 years and over.

Mental retardation is a clear exception, with the rate declining from 6 persons per 1000 in the below age 45 bracket to 2 per 1000 at 45 to 69 years, to 1.3 per 1000 at 70 to 84 years, and to a negligible number in the 85 years and over group, indicating the effects of mortality but not the addition of new cases. Eyman, Grossman,Tarjan, and Miller (1987) reported on longevity for mentally retarded persons who are institutionalized, based on 50 years of admissions data, and plotted the factors that are associated with mortality risk for these patients.

Table 5-1 Prevalence of Selected Chronic Conditions and Impairments, Expressed as Rates per 1000 Persons in Each of Four Age Brackets

Chronic Condition	Under 45	45–69	70–84	85+
Impairments				
Absence of arm(s)/hand(s)	0.1*	1.0*	1.5*	—
Absence of leg(s)	0.4*	2.6	2.9*	12.2*
Absence of fingers, toes, feet	4.4	14.8	20.6	7.6*
Complete extremity paralysis	0.9	5.8	11.0	18.2*
Cerebral palsy	1.4	0.5*	0.4*	—
Partial extremity paralysis	0.6	3.7	13.5	18.2*
Paralysis of other sites	0.5	1.8	2.9*	—
Curvature of back or spine	16.9	24.4	30.8	36.0
Other impairment of back	30.9	66.1	54.9	54.0
Impairment of upper extremity	8.9	21.4	30.1	32.5
Impairment of lower extremity	35.8	63.1	72.6	112.6
Other orthopedic impairment	1.0	2.3	2.2*	3.5*
Speech impairment	10.6	9.1	10.7	6.8*
Blindness	0.6	2.1	5.9	45.4
Cataracts	1.8	29.9	175.8	325.1
Glaucoma	1.3	13.2	43.8	62.0
Other visual/retinal disorders	22.6	52.5	112.6	198.3
Deafness	2.0	12.5	35.8	106.6
Other hearing impairment	37.2	154.8	279.4	377.4
Other chronic conditions				
Emphysema	0.8	24.0	42.3	19.0*
Epilepsy	4.9	3.8	3.4*	4.5*
Intervertebral disk disorders	9.3	37.8	24.1	16.3*
Kidney disorders	10.2	23.8	27.5	50.3
Mental retardation	6.0	2.0	1.3*	—
Multiple sclerosis	0.4*	1.3*	0.6*	—
Osteomyelitis/bone disorders	6.5	25.5	32.6	29.1*
Rheumatoid arthritis	1.8	14.3	12.5	17.1*

* Figure has low statistical reliability or precision (relative standard error exceeds 30%).

Source: Adapted from *Data on Disability from the National Health Interview Survey, 1983-1985*. An InfoUse Report (pp. 34-35) by M.P. LaPlante, 1988, Washington, D.C.: U.S. National Institute on Disability and Rehabilitation Research. (Tabulations from public use tapes.)

Speech impairment does not show a consistent trend, nor does epilepsy, both of which remain relatively constant across the age brackets. Several conditions show a particular age bracket in which incidence is higher, indicating onset of the disorder. When that age bracket is followed by a significant physical decline, such as occurs with emphysema, it suggests that the older population cannot tolerate the condition well.

Montgomery and Borgatta (1987) remind us that the costs of medical care are rising rapidly and that that presents a special problem for the elderly with reduced financial means. Specifically, in 1981 Medicare accounted for only 45% of the health expenditures of the aged, and Medicaid accounted for another 14%, leaving a considerable out-of-pocket cost remaining (Special Committee on Aging, 1983). The implications for the poor are severe; 25% of their annual income goes to medical care, in marked contrast to the 2.5% paid by elderly persons whose incomes are at three times the poverty level (Blumenthal, Schlesinger, & Drumheller, 1986). Persons with disabilities, on average, are not likely to have high incomes in their senior years.

Tanenbaum (1989) cited 1987 data from Ohio to illustrate the complexity and inadequacy of health coverage for elderly citizens. Some 38,000 people with Medicaid, a figure that represents 30% of those eligible due of their disabilities, receive no cash assistance. Too affluent to qualify for SSI, these people have "spent down" their personal resources (savings and income) on medical necessities.

Medicare is the medical entitlement that accompanies the SSDI program. Tanenbaum compares the two programs in terms of assistance given to those needing home health care. Medicare is intended as a short-term buffer when skilled care is needed. Medicaid does not require that the person be homebound or that the care be skilled. However, it must be provided by a home health agency, prescribed by a physician, and monitored by him or her. People with disabilities can be covered under both Medicare and Medicaid; in fact, there is an estimated overlap of 20% between the two programs (Gornick, Greenberg, Eggers, & Dobson, 1985).

Svanborg (1985) points out that impairments, disability, and handicap due to age itself, such as the onset of incontinence, present special practical problems that must be dealt with. He adds that the aging process can result in physician underdiagnosis since certain symptoms become less pronounced (e.g., rise in body temperature with infections) or overdiagnosis (e.g., age-related changes in blood pressure and glucose level diagnosed as hypertension and diabetes, respectively).

Data in the National Health Interview surveys, 1983 to 1985, show on average that there is a steady increase in the percentage of people who need help in performing fundamental activities of daily living (ADL) and instrumental activities of daily living (IADL) over the life span (LaPlante, 1988) (Table 5-2).

ADL include activities that involve personal self-care, such as bathing and toileting, dressing, eating, walking, getting in and out of bed, and getting outside. IADL include those activities associated with living at home independently. The two areas are closely related. This is true for both work-related and nonwork activities.

Work

It would appear from the data above that the amount of assistance needed for work-related activities is relatively constant over the years. In other words, for those who are able to work, the need for assistance does not increase substantially with age. In contrast, the need for assistance in nonwork activities moves upward with increased age, reflecting the general onset of disabilities. Some of these disabilities prevent working but do not prevent living in the community with assistance.

Family and Friends

The concept of having one's family look after one is highly culture dependent. In some foreign cultures the elderly are respected, even revered, and their wisdom is highly valued. Ensuring their welfare is viewed as a welcome duty. In the United States, where greater mobility has spread family members geographically, this separation has distanced children from their parents, and less support is available or given. In many families, the drive to earn a sizable income in order to meet mortgage payments and live well has led both the man and woman to work, leaving less time available for the care of aging parents.

These practical and cultural constraints must be kept in mind when the issue of family responsibility is raised in providing care for persons who are in their senior years, including those with disabilities. Steinmetz (1988a) noted that although there is a clear legal responsibility for a parent to provide care for a child until the age of 18 (and often through college), there is no reciprocal requirement. Nevertheless, it is apparent that adult children are the primary support system available to most elderly relatives.

Equally important, the quality of this support is highly related to the relationship of the parent(s) to the children as they were growing up (Steinmetz, 1988b). There seems to be a strong intergenerational pattern relative to abuse; when the child was abused, either physically or emotionally, this behavior is more likely to be returned to the parent, in a similar form, as the power roles change. Steinmetz reported that in 104 interviews with family caregivers who were

Table 5-2 Percentage of People Needing Daily Living Assistance

	Percentage Needing IADL or ADL Assistance	
Age Group	Work-Related Activities	Non-Work Activities
18–24	7.5	1.8
25–44	6.7	3.8
45–64	6.3	5.5
65–69	6.9	8.0

Source: Adapted from *Data on Disability from the National Health Interview Survey, 1983–1985.* An In-foUse Report (p. 57) by M.P. LaPlante, 1988, Washington, D.C.: U.S. National Institute on Disability and Rehabilitation Research.

caring for 199 elders, 12% were physically abusive, 13% were psychologically abusive, 17% forced food or medicine, and 41% were verbally abusive.

Continued Personal Enhancement

As an alternative to either continued employment or idleness, some senior citizens have turned to volunteerism. To the extent that their condition permits, persons with disabilities can join their nondisabled counterparts in helping others, including other persons with disabilities or chronic health problems. In this regard, the Harris and Associates survey (1981) found that 4 million volunteers were over the age of 65. Lazarus and Lauer (1985) pointed out the benefits of volunteerism:

1. Volunteers are less lonely (65% of those who were volunteers said "almost never").
2. Volunteers believe their help is vital to those who are served (30% felt their clients would be lonely without them).
3. The benefits exceed expectations (23% said they experienced personal growth).

We agree with Lazarus and Lauer (1988) that the challenge is to get the elderly person to make the first step. Among the techniques they suggest for this are the following:

1. Treat the older volunteer on both a professional and a personal level.
2. Marshal the skills, interests, and experience of senior volunteers.
3. Provide flexibility and diversity in volunteer options.

4. Educate the public on the phenomenon of volunteerism.
5. Apply motivational concepts to volunteer programs.

Robert Butler (1985), in his capacity as director of the National Institute on Aging, argued for the importance of federal and societal policy that encourages vigorous, productive lives in the senior years. He suggested that the United States use its technological expertise to facilitate the health and productivity of older persons, and that there should be a rethinking and redefinition of the meaning of productivity.

In conclusion, in the 1980s we saw increased awareness on the part of the public of the potential productivity of persons with disabilities in all professions and trades. We know that productivity is not easily accomplished by them, but we also know that it yields tremendous rewards to each individual in terms of self-esteem, self-satisfaction, and social interaction. As the life span increases for persons with disabilities, they will continue to need support from a society that accepts their limitations and values their participation. As nondisabled individuals age and become disabled in one or more ways, they too need the same understanding, support, and chance for participation.

In essence, we believe in the inherent worth of the individual at each stage in the life span. Just as we care about the person with disabilities who is an infant, a toddler, a child in school, a youth entering the working world, or a productive adult, we care about the senior whose life is neither worthless nor complete.

We subscribe to the view expressed by the participants in the Salzburg Seminar of 1983 (Butler & Gleason, 1985), who suggested that "when they are independent, creative, and contributing to society, the elderly confer economic and social benefits that must be counted as productivity and that society must acknowledge and reward" (pp. 131-132).

Finally, it is our own view that persons with disabilities are, more often than not, remarkable people in unique ways. We can learn with them (and from them) how to strive for and attain a quality of life that is satisfying and rewarding. To accomplish this, society must attend to the special needs of persons with disabilities at all ages, including the unborn child and the old and infirm. We must do a better job of coordinating the multidisciplinary efforts of professionals in each of the life stages.

We must provide a caring and continuing system of intervention and support that

- bridges the transitions across life stages
- is responsive to individual differences and abilities
- affords the individual an opportunity to develop a sense of worth and dignity through employment and community participation

- encourages personal and social interaction, as well as close friendships, between nondisabled persons and persons with disabilities

Reflecting on the content of this book, it should now be apparent that "disability" is a relative term. In some respects, it is an "eye of the beholder" problem, in that nondisabled persons frequently tend to view persons with disabilities in a manner that projects their own assumptions and fears onto the way in which they interact with them. All too often this leads to judgments that are ill conceived and inappropriate. We must, as a society, recognize their worth and acknowledge the right they have to learn, develop skills, become productive, experience integrated social interaction, enjoy leisure pursuits, develop close personal relationships, and sustain health and economic well-being as they move through the life stages. To the extent that we refrain from interfering and creating unrealistic barriers and instead apply a strategy that is mentor oriented and supportive, we will help them to enlarge their already important roles in society.

Rehabilitation Research and Training Centers Supported by the National Institute on Disability and Rehabilitation Research

As of 1990, the National Rehabilitation Information Center listed centers at the following locations, with these stated purposes:

- Rehabilitation Research and Training Center in Prevention and Treatment of Secondary Complications of Spinal Cord Injury, University of Alabama/Birmingham: to develop methods of treatment of secondary spinal injury and related problems
- Rehabilitation Research and Training Center on Enhancing Employability of Individuals with Handicaps, University of Arkansas: to develop a model for a comprehensive rehabilitation facility to promote employability of persons with disabilities
- Rehabilitation Research and Training Center on Vocational Rehabilitation of Individuals with Deafness/Hearing Impairments, University of Arkansas: to identify, develop, and disseminate new techniques for rehabilitation of the deaf and hearing impaired
- Native American Rehabilitation Research and Training Center, Northern Arizona University: to survey Native American populations with disabilities and to analyze their labor market conditions
- Native American Rehabilitation Research and Training Center—Improving Rehabilitation of American Indians, University of Arizona: to design and establish culturally sensitive programs for rehabilitation of Native Americans with disabilities
- Rehabilitation Research and Training Center in Progressive Neuromuscular Diseases, University of California at Davis: to improve the rehabilitation of persons with progressive neuromuscular disease

- Rehabilitation Research and Training Center on Mental Health Rehabilitation of Individuals with Deafness, University of California at San Francisco: to improve mental health assessment and treatment for persons with deafness

- Rehabilitation Research and Training Center on Aging, Rancho Los Amigos Medical Center, Downey, California: to conduct research on the rehabilitation of older persons with age-related disability

- Rehabilitation Research and Training Center for Access to Rehabilitation and Economic Opportunity, Howard University: to conduct research on the incidence of disability among economically disadvantaged persons

- Rehabilitation Research and Training Center for Children's Mental Health, University of South Florida: to improve the delivery of services to children and adolescents with severe emotional disorders

- Pacific Basin Rehabilitation Research and Training Center, University of Hawaii: to conduct research, training, and dissemination of information on rehabilitation problems of individuals with disabilities in the Pacific Basin

- Rehabilitation Research and Training Center for Treatment of Secondary Complications of Spinal Cord Injury, Northwestern University: to conduct research on the prevention and treatment of secondary complications of spinal cord injuries

- Rehabilitation Research and Training Center on Improving the Functioning of Families Who Have Members with Disabilities, University of Kansas: to conduct research on improving the functioning of families who have members with disabilities

- Rehabilitation Research and Training Center for Independent Living, University of Kansas: to conduct research on the enhancement of independent living centers

- Rehabilitation Research and Training Center: Rehabilitation for Persons with Long-Term Mental Illness, Boston University: to conduct research, training, and dissemination of information on ways to enable people with long-term mental illness to participate fully in community life

- Rehabilitation Research and Training Center in Rehabilitation and Childhood Trauma, Tufts-New England Medical Center: to improve care of injured children and work toward prevention of injuries

- Rehabilitation Research and Training Center on the Social and Psychological Development of Children and Youth with Disabilities, University of Minnesota: to carry out a set of research studies that focus on the psychosocial-developmental aspects of disability and chronic illness, service delivery issues, and policy issues

- Rehabilitation Research and Training Center—Improving Community Integration for Persons with Mental Retardation, University of Minnesota: to improve the community integration of persons with mental retardation
- Missouri Arthritis Rehabilitation Research and Training Center, University of Missouri at Columbia: to study techniques for rehabilitating persons severely disabled by arthritis
- Rehabilitation Research and Training Center on Blindness and Low-Vision Rehabilitation, Mississippi State University: to identify and classify transitional problems encountered by blind and visually impaired youth
- Rehabilitation Research and Training Center on Rural Rehabilitation Services, University of Montana: to establish a rural center to improve the lives and enhance the independence of rural persons with disabilities
- Rehabilitation Research and Training Center for Accessible Housing, North Carolina State University at Raleigh: to provide improved quality in environments for persons with disabilities and to increase the availability of accessible housing
- Rehabilitation Research and Training Center for Community Integration of Persons with Traumatic Brain Injury, State University of New York (SUNY) at Buffalo: to establish a center on community integration of persons with traumatic brain injury
- Rehabilitation Research and Training Center in Rehabilitation of Traumatic Brain Injury and Stroke, New York University Medical Center: to provide a rehabilitation research and training center for traumatic brain injury and stroke
- Rehabilitation Research and Training Center on Community Integration Resource Support, Syracuse University: to identify and evaluate state-of-the-art practices for operating community residences for children and adults with mental retardation
- Rehabilitation Research and Training Center—Rehabilitation of Psychiatrically Disabled Individuals, Yeshiva University: to do research and training directed toward the improved rehabilitation of people with long-term psychiatric disabilities
- Rehabilitation Research and Training Center on Multiple Sclerosis, Yeshiva University: to provide a rehabilitation research and training center on multiple sclerosis to help restore physical, vocational, psychological, and social function
- Consortium Development for a Rehabilitation Research and Training Center on Community Integration of Elderly Persons with Mental Retardation and Other Developmental Disabilities, Cincinnati Center for Developmental Disorders, Cincinnati, Ohio: to provide research development and imple-

mentation to help integrate older people with mental retardation into community life and to disseminate results of research

- Rehabilitation Research and Training Center—Community Referenced Technologies for Nonaversive Behavior Management, University of Oregon: to develop a practical technology of behavior management that may be used in typical settings
- Rehabilitation Research and Training Center to Improve Services for Families of Children or Youth with Serious Emotional Disturbances, Portland State University: to conduct research that has practical application in the development, evaluation, and improvement of services for families whose children have emotional disorders
- Rehabilitation Research and Training Center for Rehabilitation of Elderly Disabled Individuals, University of Pennsylvania: to conduct research and training on the rehabilitation of elderly individuals and the study of the relationship between their psychosocial and medical needs
- Rehabilitation Research and Training Center on Neural Recovery and Functional Enhancement, Thomas Jefferson Medical College: to establish a center to provide an advanced training program in neural recovery and functional enhancement and to validate instruments to assess physical function and rehabilitation outcomes
- Rehabilitation Research and Training Center in Community Oriented Services for Persons with Spinal Cord Injury, Baylor College of Medicine: to do research and provide training in community services for persons with spinal cord injury and to develop and test innovative post-acute rehabilitation models
- Rehabilitation Research and Training Center in Independent Living, Institute for Rehabilitation and Research, Houston, Texas: to promote the independence of persons with disabilities through research, training, and technical assistance
- Rehabilitation Research and Training Center on Improving Supported Employment Outcomes for Individuals with Developmental and Other Severe Disabilities, Virginia Commonwealth University: to improve employment outcomes for individuals with developmental and other severe disabilities
- Rehabilitation Research and Training Center on Severe Traumatic Brain Injury, Virginia Commonwealth University: to generate data and develop a program of services for individuals with brain injury
- Rehabilitation Research and Training Center in Traumatic Brain Injury, University of Washington: to establish a rehabilitation research and training center in traumatic brain injury

- Rehabilitation Research and Training Center on New Directions for Rehabilitation Facilities, University of Wisconsin at Stout: to conduct research on new directions for rehabilitation facilities
- Rehabilitation Research and Training Center in Improving the Management of Rehabilitation Information Systems, West Virginia University: to develop a program for needs analysis, program development, and training in rehabilitation technology

Rehabilitation Engineering Centers Supported by the National Institute on Disability and Rehabilitation Research

As of 1990, the National Rehabilitation Information Center listed centers at the following locations, with these stated purposes:

- Rehabilitation Engineering Center on Rehabilitation Technology, Rancho Los Amigos Medical Center, Downey, California: to facilitate the flow of rehabilitation technology from research laboratories to manufacturers/vendors and on to the end user
- The Smith-Kettlewell Rehabilitation Engineering Center, Smith-Kettlewell Eye Research Foundation, San Francisco, California: to develop sensory aids and new technology for blind, visually impaired, and multihandicapped individuals
- Rehabilitation Engineering Center for Technology Resources, Institute for Human Resource Development, Glastonbury, Connecticut: to develop and disseminate innovative models for the delivery of engineering services to persons with disabilities
- Rehabilitation Engineering Center on Prosthetics and Orthotics, Northwestern University: to develop a national resource for information on prosthetics and orthotics, to develop training and education materials, to advance the application of materials in the field, and to establish standards for their use
- Rehabilitation Engineering Center on Rehabilitation Technology Transfer, Electronic Industries Foundation, Washington, D.C.: to improve the flow of technology through the transfer process and to develop models for effective commercialization of rehabilitation products
- Rehabilitation Engineering Center on Evaluation of Rehabilitation Technology, National Rehabilitation Hospital, Washington, D.C.: to develop evaluation protocols, provide technical assistance, and conduct evaluations and state-of-the-art studies

- Rehabilitation Engineering Center on Augmentative Communication, University of Delaware: to develop communication aids, interface methods, educational materials, and a database
- Rehabilitation Engineering Center on Modifications to Worksites and Educational Settings, Cerebral Palsy Foundation of Kansas, Wichita, Kansas: to promote the use of technology to enhance the autonomy of severely disabled persons
- Rehabilitation Engineering Center on the Quantification of Human Performance, Massachusetts Institute of Technology: to develop computer-based instrumentation that can be used to quantify the effects of various surgical and therapeutic interventions
- Rehabilitation Engineering Center on Technology Resources, South Carolina Vocational Rehabilitation Department: to develop models for the delivery of rehabilitation engineering services, primarily to rural areas
- Rehabilitation Engineering Center on Technological Aids for the Deaf and Hearing Impaired Individuals, the Lexington Center, Inc., Jackson Heights, New York: to perform state-of-the-art studies on hearing aid technology and alternate technologies and to develop standards
- Rehabilitation Engineering Center in Functional Electrical Stimulation, Case Western Reserve University: to develop and test functional electrical systems for the restoration of neural control
- Rehabilitation Engineering Center for Quantification of Human Performance, Ohio State University: to develop innovative methods of applying technology to quantify human performance
- Rehabilitation Engineering Center for Improved Wheelchair and Seating Design, University of Virginia, Charlottesville, Virginia: to evaluate technology for wheelchairs and seating and to encourage their maximum utilization
- Rehabilitation Engineering Center in Low Back Pain, University of Vermont: to identify causes of low back pain and to develop methodologies for low back pain assessment
- Rehabilitation Engineering Center on Access to Computers and Electronic Equipment, University of Wisconsin: to study access to communication, control, and information processing systems by persons with disabilities and to disseminate information on solution strategies

In addition, there are a number of rehabilitation research and development centers supported by the Veterans Administration and basic and applied research projects related to the needs of persons with disabilities that are supported in whole or in part by the United States Department of Health and Human Services, the National Institutes of Health, the Social Security Administration, the National Science Foundation, private foundations (such as the Robert Woods Johnson Foundation), and various state-level departments.

References

Achenbaum, W. (1986). The meaning of risks, rights and responsibility in aging America. In T. Cole & S. Gadow (Eds.), *What does it mean to grow old?* Durham, NC: Duke University Press.

Agran, M., Martin, J., & Mithaug, D. (1989). Achieving transition through adaptability instruction. *Teaching Exceptional Children, 21*, 5–7.

Algozzine, B., Crews, W., & Stoddard, K. (1986). *Analysis of basic skill competencies of learning disabled adolescents. Final report. University of Florida.* (ERIC Document Reproduction Service No. EC 191 775). Gainesville, FL: University of Florida.

Algozzine, B., Maheady, L., Sacca, K., O'Shea, L., & O'Shea, D. (1990). Sometimes patent medicine works: A reply to Braaten, Kauffman, Braaten, Polsgrove, and Nelson. *Exceptional Children, 56*, 552–557.

Algozzine, B., & Ysseldyke, J. (1981). Special education services for normal children: Better safe than sorry? *Exceptional Children, 48*, 238–243.

Algozzine, B., & Ysseldyke, J. (1983). Learning disabilities as a subset of school failure: The oversophistication of a concept. *Exceptional Children, 50*, 242–246.

The American Assembly. (1960). *President's Commission on National Goals: Goals for Americans.* New York: Columbia University.

American Humane Association. (1982). *National analysis of official child neglect and abuse reporting.* Denver: Author.

American Institutes for Research. (1976). *Planning career goals (PCG) career handbook.* Monterey, CA: CTB McGraw-Hill.

Amos, K. (1980). Competency testing: Will the LD student be included? *Exceptional Children, 47*, 194–197.

Andrews, F.M., Withey, S.B. (1976). *Social indicators of well being in America: the development and measurement of perceptual indicators.* London: Plenum Publishers.

Anrig, G. (in press). Standardized testing—Now and in the future. *Harvard Graduate School of Education Alumni Bulletin.*

Association for Children and Adults with Learning Disabilities (1990). Learning disabilities programs. *CANHCgram, 22*, 3.

Baca, L., & Amato, C. (1989). Bilingual special education: Training issues. *Exceptional Children, 56*, 168–173.

Bagnato, S., Neisworth, J., & Munson, S. (1989). *Linking developmental assessment and early intervention*. Rockville, MD: Aspen Publishers, Inc.

Bailey, D. (1989). Case management in early intervention. *Journal of Early Intervention, 13*, 120–134.

Bailey, D., & McWilliam, R. (1990). Normalizing early intervention. *Topics in Early Childhood Special Education, 10*, 33–47.

Bailey, D., Palsha, S., & Huntington, G. (1990). Preservice preparation of special educators to serve infants with handicaps and their families: Implications for future research. *Journal of Early Intervention, 14*, 43–54.

Bailey, D., & Winton, P. (1987). Stability and change in parents' expectations about mainstreaming. *Topics in Early Childhood Special Education, 7*, 73–88.

Bailey, D., Winton, P., Rouse, L., & Turnbull, A. (1990). Family goals in infant intervention: Analysis and issues. *Journal of Early Intervention, 14*, 15–26.

Ballard, J. & Zettel, J. (1980). Public Law 94–142 and section 504: What they say about rights and protections. In C. Thomas & J. Thomas (Eds.), *Meeting the needs of the handicapped: A resource for teachers and librarians*. Phoenix, AZ: Oryx Press.

Barnett, D. (1983). *Nondiscriminatory multifactored assessment: A sourcebook*. New York: Human Sciences Press.

Batavia, A., & Hammer, G. (1989). Developing consumer criteria for evaluating assistive devices. In *Rehabilitation R&D Progress Reports:1989* . Baltimore, MD: Veterans Administration Prosthetics Research and Development Center.

Beauchamp, K. (1989). Meta-analysis in early childhood special education research. *Journal of Early Intervention, 13*, 374–380.

Beckoff, A. & Bender, W. (1989). Programming of mainstream kindergarten success in preschool: Teachers' perceptions of necessary prerequisite skills. *Journal of Early Intervention, 13*, 269–280.

Bellamy, G.T., Rhodes, L., Monk, D., & Albin, J. (1988). *Supported employment: A community implementation guide*. Baltimore, MD: Paul H. Brookes Publishing Co.

Bendell, R.D., Stone, W., Field, T., & Golstein, S. (1989). Children's effects on parenting stress in a low income, minority population. *Topics in Early Childhood Education, 8*, 58–71.

Bennefield, R., & McNeil, J. (1989). *Labor force status and other characteristics of persons with a work disability: 1981 to 1988 (Current Population Reports*, Special Studies, Series P-23, No. 160). Washington, DC: U.S. Government Printing Office.

Bennett, A. (1987). *Schooling the different: Ethnographic case studies of Hispanic deaf children's initiation into formal schooling*. Jackson Heights, NY: The Lexington Center.

Berkowitz, E. (1989). Domestic politics and international expertise in the history of American disability policy. *The Milbank Quarterly, 67*(Suppl. 2), 195–227.

Binder, A., & Shapiro, B. (1988). Licensed to care. *Parenting, 2*, 72–73.

Birren, J. (1986). The process of aging: Growing up and growing old. In A. Pifer & L. Bronte (Eds.), *Our aging society: Paradox and promise*. New York : W.W. Norton & Co.

Blackman, J. (1989). *Medical aspects of developmental disabilities in children birth to three*. Rockville, MD: Aspen Publishers, Inc.

Blankenship, C. (1985). Using curriculum-based assessment data to make instructional decisions. *Exceptional Children, 52*, 233–238.

Blumenthal, D., Schlesinger, M., & Drumheller, P. (1986). The future of Medicare. *New England Journal of Medicine, 314*, 722–728.

Botvin, G. (1983). Prevention of adolescent substance abuse through the development of personal and social competence. In T. Glynn, C. Leukefeld, & J. Ludford (Eds.), *Preventing adolescent drug abuse: Prevention strategies.* (National Institute on Drug Abuse). Washington, DC: U.S. Government Printing Office.

Braaten, S., Kauffman, J., Braaten, B., Polsgrove, L., & Nelson, C. (1988). The regular education initiative: Patent medicine for behavioral disorders. *Exceptional Children, 55,* 21–27.

Bracey, G. (1990). Computerized testing: A possible alternative to paper and pencil? *Electronic Learning, 9,* 16–17.

Bremner, R. (1970). *Children and youth in America: A documentary history* (Vol. 1). Boston: Harvard University Press.

Bristol, M., & Gallagher, J. (1986). Research on fathers of young handicapped children. In J. Gallagher and P. Vietze (Eds.) *Families of handicapped persons.* Baltimore, MD: Paul H. Brookes Publishing Co.

Brolin, D. (1976). *Vocational preparation of retarded citizens.* Columbus, OH: Charles E. Merrill Publishing Co.

Brown, D. (1990, January 21). Putting the handicapped to work. *Washington Post.*

Bruder, M., & Walker, L. (1990). Discharge planning: Hospital to home transitions for infants. *Topics in Early Childhood Special Education, 9,* 26–42.

Bryan, J., & Bryan, T. (1988). Where's the beef? A review of published research on the adaptive learning environment model. *Learning Disabilities Focus, 4,* 9–14.

Burkhauser, R., & Hirvonen, P. (1989). United States disability policy in a time of economic crisis: A comparison with Sweden and the Federal Republic of Germany. *The Milbank Quarterly, 67*(Suppl. 2), 166–194.

Burnett, S. (1989). Drugs and drinking takes toll on disabled. *The Times* (San Mateo, CA), Health and Science Section, p. A8.

Bush, B. (1989). No liberty without literacy. *ACLD California Chapter Newsletter (Mid Peninsula),* Fall.

Butler, K. (1990, February 5). Elderly, disabled get "elegant" low-cost housing. *San Francisco Chronicle,* p. A14.

Butler, R. (1985). Health, productivity, and aging: An overview. In R. Butler & H. Gleason (Eds.), *Productive aging: Enhancing vitality in later life.* New York: Springer Publishing Co.

Butler, S., Magliocca, L., Torres, L., & Lee, W. (1984). Grading the mainstreamed student: A decision making model for modification. *The Directive Teacher, 6,* 6–9.

Byrnes, M. (1990). The regular education initiative debate: A view from the field. *Exceptional Children, 56,* 34–349.

Calkins, C., & Walker, H. (1989). *Social competence for workers with developmental disabilities.* Baltimore, MD: Paul H. Brookes Publishing Co.

Campbell, A., Converse, P.E., & Rodgers, W.L. (1976). *The quality of American life.* New York: Russell Sage Foundation.

Campbell, P. (1989). Quality indicators in early intervention: What makes a program of highest quality? *The Networker, 2,* 4–7.

Campeau, P., & Ananda, S. (1989). *Study of anticipated services for students with handicaps exiting from school* (Final report, AIR-66901). Palo Alto, CA: American Institutes for Research.

Carnine, D., & Kameenui, E. (1990). The general education initiative and children with special needs: A false dilemma in the face of true problems. *Journal of Learning Disabilities, 23,* 141–148.

Carter, J., & Sugai, G. (1988). Teaching social skills. *Teaching Exceptional Children, 20,* 68–71.

Casto, G., & Mastropieri, M. (1986). Strain and Smith do protest too much: A response. *Exceptional Children, 53,* 266–268.

Center for the Study of Reading. (no date). *10 ways to help your children become better readers.* Urbana-Champaign, IL: University of Illinois.

Chappel, N., & Havens, B. (1985). Who helps the elderly person: A discussion of informal and formal care. In W. Peterson & J. Quadagno (Eds.), *Social bonds in later life.* Beverly Hills, CA: Sage Publications.

Cheatham, J., Regalbuto, M., Krouskop, T., & Winningham, D. (1987). *Proceedings of the IEEE/EMBS, 9,* 1100–1101.

Chirikos, T. (1989). Aggregate economic losses from disability in the United States: A preliminary assay. *The Milbank Quarterly, 67*(Suppl. 2), 59–91.

Clearinghouse on the Handicapped. (1984, July/August). JAN: A new service for employers. *Programs for the Handicapped, 6.*

Conn-Powers, M., Ross-Allen, J., & Holburn, S. (1990). Transition of young children into the elementary education mainstream. *Topics in Early Childhood Special Education, 9,* 91–105.

Council of Chief State School Officers. (1988). *Early childhood and family education: Foundations for success.* Washington, DC: Author.

Dahlke, M., & Douglas, R. (1972). *Job descriptions and physical demand requirements with job restructuring for the handicap.* Milwaukee, WI: Goodwill Industries of Wisconsin, Inc., Work Evaluation Department.

Davis, W. (1989). The regular education initiative debate: Its promises and problems. *Exceptional Children, 55,* 440–446.

Davis, W. (1990). Broad perspectives on the regular education initiative: Response to Byrnes. *Exceptional Children, 56,* 349–351.

Deaf Counseling, Advocacy, and Referral Agency. (1990). *DCARA News.* San Leandro, CA: Deaf Counseling, Advocacy, and Referral Agency.

de Haas, C., & Weisgerber, R. (1978). *Environmental sensing–selection and matching. Environmental sensing–training guidelines. Environmental sensing–evaluation of attained performance.* Palo Alto, CA: American Institutes for Research. (Three in a series of technical reports in the environmental Sensing, Selection, Evaluation and Training System [ESSETS])

DeJong, G., Batavia, A., & Griss, R. (1989). America's neglected health minority: Working-age persons with disabilities. *The Milbank Quarterly, 67*(Suppl. 2), 311–351.

Deno, S. (1985). Curriculum-based assessment–The emerging alternative. *Exceptional Children, 52,* 219–232.

Department of Education (1989). State grants program for technology-related assistance for individuals with disabilities (34 CFR Part 345, August 9), *Federal Register, 54 (* 152), 32770.

Department of Education and Department of Health and Human Services. (1988). *Meeting the needs of infants and toddlers with handicaps.* Washington, DC: Author.

Department of Transportation. (1990a). Nondiscrimination on the basis of handicap in air travel (14 CFR Part 352). *Federal Register, 55 (* 44), 8008–8083.

Department of Transportation. (1990b). Nondiscrimination on the basis of handicap in air travel (14 CFR Part 352) *Federal Register, 55 (* 64), 12336–12342.

Deutscher, I. (1988). Misers and wastrels: Perceptions of the depression and yuppie generations. In E. Steinmetz (Ed.), *Family and support systems across the life span.* New York: Plenum Press.

Division for Early Childhood. (1989). Policy developments. *DEC Communicator 16*.

Dowdy, C., Carter, J., & Smith, T. (1990). Differences in transitional needs of high school students with and without learning disabilities. *Journal of Learning Disabilities, 23*, 343–348.

Dunst, C., & Trivette, C. (1989). An enablement and empowerment perspective of case management. *Topics in Early Childhood Special Education, 8*, 87–102.

Dunst, C., Trivette, C., & Cross, A. (1986). Roles and support networks of mothers of handicapped children. In R. Fewell & P. Vadasy (Eds.), *Families of handicapped children: Needs and supports across the life span*. Austin, TX: Pro-Ed, Inc.

Eagle, E. (1989). Improving the options of handicapped students in mainstream vocational education. *TASPP Bulletin, 1*, 2–3.

Edgar, E., & Levine, P. (1988). A longitudinal study of graduates of special education. *Interchange, 8*, 3–5.

Ensher, G., & Clark, D. (1986). *Newborns at risk: Medical care and psychoeducational intervention*. Rockville, MD: Aspen Publishers, Inc.

ERIC/OSEP Special Project on Interagency Information Dissemination (1988a). Curriculum-based assessment. *Research Brief for Teachers*. Brief T2, ERIC Clearinghouse on Handicapped and Gifted Children, December, p. 1–2.

ERIC/OSEP Special Project on Interagency Information Dissemination (1988b). Social integration of handicapped students: Cooperative goal structuring. *Research Brief for Teachers*. Brief T1, ERIC Clearinghouse on Handicapped and Gifted Children, December, p. 1–2.

Espinosa, L., & Shearer, M. (1986). Family support in public school programs. In R. Fewell & P. Vadasy (Eds.), *Families of handicapped children: Needs and supports across the life span*. Austin, TX: Pro-Ed, Inc.

Evans, S. (1980). The consultant role of the resource teacher. *Exceptional Children, 46*, 402–404.

Everson, J., Barcus, M., Moon, S., & Morton, M. (Eds.). (1987). *Achieving outcomes: A guide to interagency training in transition and supported employment*. Richmond, VA: Virginia Commonwealth University.

Exceptional Education. (1990). *Match-sort-assemble series*. Seattle, WA: Author.

Eyman, R., Grossman, H., Tarjan, G., & Miller, C. (1987). *Life expectancy and mental retardation*. Washington, DC: American Association on Mental Retardation.

Fairweather, J. (1989). Transition and other services for handicapped students in local education agencies. *Exceptional Children, 55*, 315–320.

Family Enablement Project. (1989). *Family-centered assessment instruments/reference guide to the family-centered research and practice literature/dissemination materials and products*. Morganton, NC: Family, Infant, and Preschool Program, Western Carolina Center.

Feldman, D. (1981). The multiple socialization of organizational members. *Academy of Management Review, 6*, (June).

Fewell, R. (1986). Supports from religious organizations and personal beliefs. In R. Fewell & P. Vadasy (Eds.), *Families of handicapped children: Needs and supports across the life span*. Austin, TX: Pro-Ed, Inc.

Figueroa, R. (1989). Psychological testing of linguistic-minority students: Knowledge gaps and regulations. *Exceptional Children, 56*, 145–153.

Flanagan, J. (1979, September). *Life's last 20 years: How to improve them*. Paper presented at meeting of the American Psychological Association, New York.

Flanagan, J. (1982). Measurement in the quality of life: Current state of the art. *Archives of Physical Medicine and Rehabilitation, 63*, 56–59.

Fowler, S., Hains, A., & Rosenkoetter, S. (1990). The transition between early intervention services and preschool services: Administrative and policy issues. *Topics in Early Childhood Special Education, 9,* 55–65.

Fox, C. (1989). Peer acceptance of learning disabled children in the regular classroom. *Exceptional Children, 56,* 5–59.

Fox, D. (1989). Financing health services for the chronically ill and disabled, 1930–1990. *The Milbank Quarterly, 67*(Suppl. 2), 257–287.

Fox, D., & Willis, D. (1989). Disability policy: Restoring socioeconomic independence. *The Milbank Quarterly, 67 (* Suppl. 2), 1–12.

Fradd, S., & Correa, V. (1989). Hispanic students at risk: Do we abdicate or advocate? *Exceptional Children, 56,* 105–110.

Frey, K., Fewell, R., & Vadasy, P. (1989). Parental adjustment and changes in child outcome among families of young handicapped children. *Topics in Early Childhood Education, 8,* 38–57.

Fuchs, D., & Fuchs, L. (1988). Evaluation of the adaptive learning environments model. *Exceptional Children, 55,* 115–127.

Fuqua, R., Hegland, S., & Karas, S. (1985). Processes influencing linkages between preschool handicap classrooms and homes. *Exceptional Children, 51,* 307–314.

Gallagher, J., Scharfman, W., & Bristol, M. (1984). The division of responsibilities in families with preschool handicapped and nonhandicapped children. *Journal of the Division of Early Childhood, 8,* 3–12.

Gallagher, P., & Powell, T. (1989). Brothers and sisters: Meeting special needs. *Topics in Early Childhood Education, 8,* 24–37.

Gallimore, R., Weisner, T., Kaufman, S., & Bernheimer, L. (1989). The social construction of eco-cultural niches: Family accommodation of developmentally delayed children. *American Journal on Mental Retardation, 94,* 216–230.

Gardner, J., Chapman, M., Donaldson, G., & Jacobson, S. (1988). *Toward supported employment: A process guide for planned change.* Baltimore, MD: Paul H. Brookes Publishing Co.

Gartner, A., & Lipsky, D. (1987). Beyond special education: Toward a quality system for all students. *Harvard Educational Review, 57,* 367–395.

Gaylord-Ross, R., Forte, J., Storey, K., Gaylord-Ross, C., & Jameson, D. (1987). Community-referenced instruction in technological work settings. *Exceptional Children, 54,* 112–120.

Germann, G., & Tindal, G. (1985). An application of curriculum-based assessment: The use of direct and repeated measurement. *Exceptional Children, 52,* 244–265.

Gibler, C. (1989). Rehabilitation, technology, and industry's role. In L. Perlman & C. Hansen (Eds.), *Technology and employment of persons with disabilities: A report on the 13th Mary E. Switzer memorial seminar.* Alexandria, VA: National Rehabilitation Association.

Glenn, A., & Snowball, H. (1987). Classification of wheelchair athletes. In R. Steeley, & W. Gerry (Eds.), *RESNA '87: Meeting the challenge. Proceedings of the 10th Annual Conference on Rehabilitation Technology.* Washington, DC: Association for the Advancement of Rehabilitation Technology.

Goodall, P., & Bruder, M. (1986). Parents and the transition process. *The Exceptional Parent, 15,* 22–24, 26–28.

Gornick, M., Greenberg, J., Eggers, P., Dobson, A. (1985). Twenty years of Medicare and Medicaid: Covered populations, use of benefits, and program expenditures. In *Health Care Financing Review, 1985 Annual Supplement* (p. 13–59). Washington, DC: U.S. Department of Health and Human Services.

Gottwald, S., & Thurman, S.K. (1990). Parent-infant interaction in neonatal intensive care units: Implications for research and service delivery. *Infants and Young Children, 2,* 1–9.

Graff, J., Ault, M., Guess, D., Taylor, M., & Thompson, B. (1989). *Health care for students with disabilities.* Baltimore, MD: Paul H. Brookes Publishing Co.

Granat, M., Smith, A., Keating, J., Andrews, B., & Delargy, M. (1989). Implementation of a functional electrical stimulation (FES) walking system for the incomplete spinal cord injured patient. In *Rehabilitation R&D Progress Reports: 1989.* Baltimore, MD: Veterans Administration Prosthetics Research and Development Center.

Green, A., & Stoneman, Z. (1989). Attitudes of mothers and fathers of nonhandicapped children. *Journal of Early Intervention, 13,* 292–304.

Gresham, F. (1981). Social skills training with handicapped children: A review. *Review of Educational Research, 51,* 139–176.

Gresham, F., & Elliott, S. (1990). *Social skills rating system.* Circle Pines, MN: American Guidance Service, Inc.

Grisham, D. (1985). *Computerized vision training* (First annual report, AIR 38501-12/85). Palo Alto, CA: American Institutes for Research.

Grisham, D., McLaughlin, D., Rubin, D., Bacon, T., Silverman, C., & Joers, J. (1986). *Video visual skills user's guide* (Project product, AIR 38502-12/86). Palo Alto, CA: American Institutes for Research.

Gross, R., Cox, A., & Pollay, M. (1983). Early management and decision making for the treatment of myelomeningocele. *Pediatrics, 72,* 450–458.

Guillemard, A. (1982). Old age, retirement, and the social class structure: Toward an analysis of the structural dynamics of the latter stage of life. In T. Hareven & K. Adams (Eds.), *Aging and life course transitions: An interdisciplinary perspective.* New York: Guilford Press.

Guralnick, M. (1990a). Major accomplishments and future directions in early childhood mainstreaming. *Topics in Early Childhood Special Education, 10,* 1–17.

Guralnick, M. (1990b). Social competence and early intervention. *Journal of Early Intervention, 14,* 3–14.

Haber, L. (1987). *State disability prevalence rates: An ecological analysis of social and economic influences on disability.* Washington, DC: National Institute on Disability and Rehabilitation Research.

Haight, S., & Molitor, D. (1983). A survey of special education teachers consultants. *Exceptional Children, 49,* 550–551.

Hall, R. (1986). *Dimensions of work.* Beverly Hills, CA: Sage Publications.

Hamblin-Wilson, C., & Thurman, K. (1990). The transition from early intervention to kindergarten: Parental satisfaction and involvement. *Journal of Early Intervention, 14,* 55–61.

Hanline, M., & Deppe, J. (1990). Discharging the premature infant: Family issues and implications for intervention. *Topics in Early Childhood Special Education, 9,* 15–25.

Hanline, M., & Knowlton, A. (1988). A collaborative model for providing support to parents during their child's transition from infant intervention to preschool special education public school programs. *Journal of the Division for Early Childhood, 12,* 116–125.

Hanline, M., Suchman, S., & Demmerle, C. (1989). Beginning public preschool. *Teaching Exceptional Children, 21,* 61–62.

Harris, L., & Associates. (1981). *Aging in the eighties: America in transition.* Washington, DC: National Council on Aging.

Hartley, M., White, C., & Yogman, M. (1989). The challenge of providing quality group child care for infants and young children with special needs. *Infants and Young Children, 2,* 1–10.

Hayward, B., & Wirt, J. (1990). Handicapped and disadvantaged students: Access to vocational education. *TASPP Bulletin, 1,* 1–3.

Hentoff, N. (1985). The awful privacy of Baby Doe: Should infants born with treatable or manageable handicaps be "allowed to die? One civil libertarian says no." *Atlantic Monthly, 255,* 54.

Heriza, C., & Sweeney, J. (1990). Effects of NICU intervention on preterm infants: Part 1—Implications for neonatal practice. *Infants and Young Children, 2,* 31–47.

Herr, S. (1989). Disabled clients, constituencies, and counsel: Representing persons with developmental disabilities. *The Milbank Quarterly, 67*(Suppl. 2), 352–379.

Higher Education and Adult Training for People with Handicaps. (1988). Focus on college admissions tests. *Information from HEATH, 8,* 1, 10–11.

Higher Education and Adult Training for People with Handicaps. (1989). *Resource Directory.* Washington, DC: American Council on Education.

Hill, M., & Wehman, P. (1983, Spring). Cost benefit analysis of placing moderately and severely handicapped individuals into competitive employment. *Journal of the Association for the Severely Handicapped, 8,* 30–38.

Hoier, T., & Foster, S. (1985). Methods of assessing children's social skills: Current status and future directions. *Journal of Special Education Technology, 7,* 18–27.

Hollenbeck, K., & Smith, B. (1984). *Selecting young workers: The influence of applicants' education and skills on employability assessments by employers.* Washington, DC: U.S. Department of Education. (ERIC Document Reproduction Service No. ED 245 115.)

Holmes, S. (1990, May 23). House approves bill establishing broad rights for disabled people. *New York Times,* pp. 1, 10.

Horowitz, D., & Hausdorff, J. (1989). Design of a human-machine interface of a voice-controlled vocational robotic work station. In *Proceedings of the 12th Annual RESNA Conference* (pp. 117–118). San Jose, CA: Association for the Advancement of Rehabilitation Technology.

Huefner, D. (1988). The consulting teacher model: Risks and opportunities. *Exceptional Children, 54,* 403–414.

Hume, J., & Dannenbring, G. (1989). A longitudinal study of children screened and served by early childhood special education programs. *Journal of Early Intervention, 13,* 133–145.

Hutinger, P. (1988). Linking screening, identification, and assessment with curriculum. In J. Jordan, J. Gallagher, P. Hutinger, & M. Karnes (Eds.), *Early childhood special education: Birth to three.* Reston, VA: Council for Exceptional Children and Division for Early Childhood.

Infant Health and Development Program. (1990). Intervention helps low birthweight babies improve mental ability. *Report on Educational Research,* June, 7.

Jacobs, A., Larsen, J., & Smith, C. (1979). *Handbook for job placement of mentally retarded workers.* New York: Garland STPM Press.

Jaffe, D. (1988). Ultrasonic head-controlled wheelchair and interface. Palo Alto, CA: Veterans Administration Medical Center.

Jenkins, J., Pious, C., & Jewell, M. (1990). Special education and the regular education initiative: Basic assumptions. *Exceptional Children, 56,* 479–491.

Johnson, L., & Murphy, M. (1990). Siblings of children with handicapping conditions. *DEC Communicator, 16,* 3.

Johnson-Martin, N., Attermeier, M., & Hacker, B. (1990). *The Carolina curriculum for preschoolers with special needs.* Baltimore, MD: Paul H. Brookes Publishing Co.

Johnson-Martin, N., Jens, K., & Attermeier, M. (1986). *The Carolina curriculum for handicapped infants and infants at risk.* Baltimore, MD: Paul H. Brookes Publishing Co.

Johnston, D., & Hoover, S. (1982). Social indicators of aging. In M. Riley, R. Abeles, & M. Teitelbaum (Eds.), *Aging from birth to death: Vol. 2. Sociotemporal perspectives.* Boulder, CO: Westview Press.

Jones, R. (Ed.). (1983). *Reflections on growing up disabled.* Reston, VA: Council for Exceptional Children.

Kaiser, A., & Hemmeter, M. (1989). Value-based approaches to family intervention. *Topics in Early Childhood Education, 8,* 72–86.

Kamman, R., Christie, D.A. Irwin, R.M., & Dixon, G. (1979). Properties of an inventory to measure happiness (and psychological health). *New Zealand Psychologist, 8,* 1.

Karnes, M., & Stayton, V. (1988). Model programs for infants and toddlers with handicaps. In J. Jordan, J. Gallagher, P. Hutinger & M. Karnes (Eds.). *Early childhood special education: birth to three.* Reston, VA: Council for Exceptional Children and Division for Early Childhood.

Karr, A. (1990, May 23). Disabled-rights bill inspires hope, fear. *The Wall Street Journal,* pp. B1–B2.

Katchadourian, H. (1987). *Fifty: Midlife in perspective.* New York: W.H. Freeman & Co.

Kauffman, J., Braaten, S., Nelson, C.M., Polsgrove, L., & Braaten, B. (1990). The regular education initiative and patent medicine: A rejoinder to Algozzine, Maheady, Sacca, O'Shea, and O'Shea. *Exceptional Children, 56,* 558–560.

Kaufman, M., Agard, J., & Semmel, M. (1985). *Mainstreaming learners and their environment.* Cambridge, MA: Brookline Books.

Kelley, J. (1982). *Social-skills training: A practical guide for interventions.* New York: Springer Publishing Co.

Keough, B. (1988a). Improving services for problem learners: Rethinking and restructuring. *Journal of Learning Disabilities, 21,* 19–22.

Keough, B. (1988b). Perspectives on the early education initiative. *Learning Disabilities Focus, 4,* 3–5.

Kiernan, W., & Stark, J. (1986). *Pathways to employment for adults with developmental disabilities.* Baltimore, MD: Paul H. Brookes Publishing Co.

Kilgo, J., Richard, N., & Noonan, M.J. (1989). Teaming for the future: Integrating transition planning with early intervention services for young children with special needs and their families. *Infants and Young Children, 2,* 37–48.

Kirk, J. (1989). Special education is working. *The Special Edge: California Resources in Special Education, 4,* 1.

Kjerland, L. (1986). *Early intervention tailor made.* Eagan, MN: Project Dakota, Inc.

Kotulak, R. (1988, July 10). Arizona archaeologists dig out hidden talents of handicapped. *Chicago Tribune,* p. 8.

Kraus, L., & Stoddard, S. (1989). *Chartbook on Disability in the United States.* Washington, DC: National Institute on Disability and Rehabilitation Research.

Krauss, M. (1990). New precedent in family policy: Individualized family service plan. *Exceptional Children, 56,* 388–395.

Krents, H. (1980). The human dimension to affirmative action for the handicapped. In *Affirmative action for the handicapped. A handbook for employment opportunity specialists of the federal contract compliance programs.* Washington, DC: U.S. Department of Labor.

Kronick, D. (1989). The regular education initiative. *ACLD Newsbriefs, 24*, 3–6.

Landerholm, E. (1990). The transdisciplinary team approach in infant intervention programs. *Teaching Exceptional Children, 22*, 66–70.

Lazarus, M., & Lauer, H. (1985). Working past retirement: Practical and motivational issues. In R. Butler & H. Gleason (Eds.), *Productive aging: Enhancing vitality in later life.* New York: Springer Publishing Co.

Lerner, J. (1981). *Special education for the early childhood years.* Englewood Cliffs, NJ: Prentice-Hall.

Levine, P., Allen, L., & Wysocki, K. (1986). *The follow-up study: An annotated bibliography.* Seattle, WA: Child Development and Mental Retardation Center, University of Washington.

Lieberman, L. (1990). REI: Revisited… again. *Exceptional Children, 56*, 561–562.

Lilly, M. (1977). The merger of categories: Are we finally ready? *Journal of Learning Disabilities, 10*, 115–121.

Lovitt, T., & Ballew, C. (1988). *Self-management tactics.* Seattle, WA: University of Washington.

Madden, N., & Slavin, R. (1982). *Count me in: Academic achievement and social outcomes of mainstreaming students with mild academic handicaps* (Report No. 329). Baltimore, MD: The Johns Hopkins University.

Mallory, B. (1986). Interactions between community agencies and families over the life cycle. In R. Fewell & P. Vadasy (Eds.), *Families of handicapped children: Needs and supports across the life span.* Austin, TX: Pro-Ed, Inc.

Manton, K. (1988). *Sex differences in functional impairment in the U.S. elderly population: The interaction of specific diseases, functional impairments, and mortality.* Paper presented at the Population Association of America Meetings, 1988, Center for Demographic Studies, Duke University, Durham, NC.

Marriott Foundation for People with Disabilities. (1990). Employment of people with disabilities: A sound business decision. *The Special Edge, 4*, 8–9.

Marston, D., & Magnusson, D. (1985). Implementing curriculum-based measurement in special and regular education settings. *Exceptional Children, 52*, 266–276.

May, W. (1986). The virtues and vices of the elderly. In T. Cole & S. Gadow (Eds.), *What does it mean to grow old?* Durham, NC: Duke University Press.

McCollum, J., McLean, M., McCartan, K., & Kaiser, C. (1989). Recommendations for certification of early childhood special educators. *Journal of Early Intervention, 13*, 195–211.

McCrae R., & Costa, P. (1984). Aging, the life course, and models of personality. In N. Schock, R. Greelich, R. Andres, D. Arenberg, P. Costa, Jr., E. LaKatta & J. Tobin (Eds.), *Normal human aging: The Baltimore longitudinal study of aging.* (National Institutes of Health Publication No. 84-2450). Washington, DC: U. S. Department of Health and Human Services.

McCrostie, M., & Peacock, A. (1984). Disability policy in the United Kingdom. In R. Haveman (Ed.), *Public policy toward disabled workers.* Ithaca, NY: Cornell University Press.

McCubbin, H., Sussman, M., & Patterson, J. (Eds.). (1983). *Social stress and the family.* New York: Haworth Press.

McDermott, P., & Watkins, M. (1983). Computerized vs. conventional remedial instruction for learning-disabled pupils. *The Journal of Special Education, 17*, 81–88.

McDonald, L., Kysela, G., Siebert, P., McDonald, S., & Chambers, J. (1989). Parent perspectives: Transition to preschool. *Teaching Exceptional Children, 22*, 4–8.

McKinney, J., & Hocutt, A. (1988). Policy issues in the evaluation of the regular education initiative. *Learning Disabilities Focus, 4*, 15–23.

McLaughlin, M., Valdiviseo, C., Spence, K., & Fuller, B. (1988). Special education teacher preparation: A synthesis of four research studies. *Exceptional Children, 55*, 215–221.

McLeod, R. (1990, March 19). 12-Nation survey ranks U.S. low in child welfare. *San Francisco Chronicle*, pp. A1, A18..

Mcloughlin, C., Garber, J., & Callahan, M. (1987). *Getting employed, staying employed: Job development and training for persons with severe handicaps*. Baltimore, MD: Paul H. Brookes Publishing Co.

Meisels, S.J., Harbin, G., Modigliani, K., & Olson K. (1988). Formulating optimal early childhood intervention policies. *Exceptional Children, 55*, 159–165.

Meyen, E., & Schumaker, J. (1981). *Curriculum development for social behavior*. Institute for Research in Learning Disabilities, Lawrence, KS: University of Kansas.

Meyer, L., & Evans, I. (1989). *Nonaversive intervention for behavior problems: A manual for home and community*. Baltimore, MD: Paul H. Brookes Publishing Co.

Minskoff, E., Sautter, S., Sheldon, K., Steidle, E., & Baker, D. (1988). A comparison of learning disabled adults and high school students. *Learning Disabilities Research, 3*, 115–123.

Montgomery, R., & Borgatta, E. (1987). Values, costs, and health care policy. In E. Borgatta & R. Montgomery (Eds.). *Critical issues in aging policy: Linking research and values*. Beverly Hills, CA: Sage Publications.

Moore, M., Strang, E.W., Schwartz, M., & Braddock, M. (1988). *Patterns in special education service delivery and cost*. Washington, DC: Decision Resources Corporation.

Murphy, M., & Vincent, L. (1989). Identification of critical skills for success in day care. *Journal of Early Education Intervention, 13*, 221–229.

National Early Childhood Technical Assistance System (1983). *Guidelines and recommended practices for the individualized family service plan*. Washington, DC: Association for the Care of Children's Health.

National Regional Resource Center Panel on Indicators of Effectiveness in Special Education. (1986). *Effectiveness indicators for special education*. Hampton, NH: Center for Resource Management, Inc.

Nelson, G., & Stowitschek, J. (1988). Supported employment: Program features compared to outcomes. In W. Schill (Principal Investigator), *Transition research on problems of handicapped youth: Occasional paper number 2*. Seattle, WA: University of Washington.

Nelson, R., Fischer, J., & Rubenstein, J. (1985). Education and career preparation. *Journal of Adolescent Health Care, 6*, 136–140.

Neubert, D., Tilson, G. Jr., Ianacone, R. (1989). Postsecondary transition needs and employment patterns of individuals with disabilities. *Exceptional Children, 55*, 494–500.

Nosek, M., & Fuhrer, M. (1989). New models for delivery of personal assistance services. In *Rehabilitation R&D Progress Reports: 1989*. Baltimore, MD: Veterans Administration Prosthetics Research and Development Center.

Odom, S., & Chandler, L. (1990). Transition to parenthood for parents of technology-assisted infants. *Topics in Early Childhood Special Education, 9*, 43–54.

Odom, S., & McEvoy, M. (1990). Mainstreaming at the preschool level: Potential barriers and tasks for the field. *Topics in Early Childhood Special Education, 10*, 33–47.

Office of Human Development Services (1990). Fiscal year 1991 federal allotment to states for developmental disabilities basic support and protection and advocacy formula grant programs (Document No. 90–7580). *Federal Register, 55*(63), 12285–12286.

Office of Special Education and Rehabilitative Services. (1989). Model approaches to providing technology assistance. *OSERS News in Print, 2,* 6–7, 14.

O'Neil, S. (1976). *Occupational survival skills: Implications for job maintenance and mobility.* Urbana-Champaign, IL: University of Illinois.

Palfrey, J., Singer, J., Walker, D., & Butler, J. (1986). Health and special education: A study of new developments for handicapped children in five metropolitan communities. *Public Health Reports, 101,* 379–388.

Panel on the Quality of American Life. (1980). *The quality of American life in the eighties.* Washington, DC: U.S. Government Printing Office.

Parke, R. (1986). Fathers, families, and support systems. In J. Gallagher & P. Vietze (Eds.), *Families of handicapped persons.* Baltimore, MD: Paul H. Brookes Publishing Co.

Permobil. (1990). Permobil given high marks by MCET. *Permobil News, 2,* 1.

Peters, D. (1988). Head Start's influence on parental and child competence. In S. Steinmetz (Ed.), *Family and support systems across the life span.* New York: Plenum Press.

Phelps, L.A., & Lutz, R. (1977). *Career exploration and preparation for the special needs learner.* Boston: Allyn and Bacon, Inc.

Popovich, K. (Ed.). (1989). First steps. *Centerpoint: A Newsletter for Health Care Professionals and Clients Served by the Rehabilitation Engineering Center, Children's Hospital at Stanford, 2,* 1.

President's Committee on Employment of the Handicapped. (no date). *Out of the job market: A national crisis.* Washington, DC.

Public Agenda Foundation. (1982). *Jobs in the 1980s and 1990s.*

Pugach, M., & Johnson, L. (1989a). The challenge of implementing collaboration between general and special education. *Exceptional Children, 56,* 232–235.

Pugach, M., & Johnson, L. (1989b). Prereferral interventions: Progress, problems, and challenges. *Exceptional Children, 56,* 217–226.

Radner, D. (1986). Changes in the money income of the aged and nonaged, 1967–1983. Department of Health and Human Services, Social Security Administration, *Studies of income distribution.* Washington, DC: U.S. Government Printing Office.

Raymond, C. (1990). Scientists urge federal standards in child care. *The Chronicle of Higher Education, 36,* A7, A15.

Rehabilitation Research and Training Center. (1990). Range of supported employment options available and range of individuals served by supported employment programs. *RRTC*-Virginia Commonwealth University, Winter, 1990.

Reller, D., & Weisgerber, R. (1987). *Perspectives on how disabled persons have experienced breakthroughs with computers.* Palo Alto, CA: American Institutes for Research.

Report on Educational Research. (1990, May 16). Bank Street research says schools ignore behavior disorders. *Report on Educational Research,* p. 7.

Research Triangle Institute. (1990). What's the problem? *Hypotenuse, January/February/March,* 10–12.

Reynolds, M., Wang, M., & Walberg, H. (1987). The necessary restructuring of special and regular education. *Exceptional Children, 53,* 391–398.

Rimland, I. (1985). A parent speaks to the professionals. *ACLD Newsbriefs,* May/June, 19, 21.

Rivlin, B. (1989). Professionals with and without disabilities: Recent study compares employment trends. *NARIC Quarterly, 2,* 1, 8–10.

Rochlin, J. (1989, February). *Employment: Issues and the challenge*. Paper presented to the Rehabilitation Services Administration (Region IX), San Diego, CA.

Rosenberg, B. (1973). The work sample approach to vocational evaluation. In R. Hardy & J. Cull (Eds.), *Vocational evaluation for rehabilitation services*. Springfield, IL: Charles C Thomas, Publisher.

Rosenthal, D. (1990). Learning disability doesn't mean unable to learn. *CANHCgram, 22*, 1, 7.

Rossi, R. (1990). Demographic accounting for special education. *Social Indicators Research, 22*, 1–30.

Rossi, R., & Wolman, J. (1988). A model accounting plan for special education. *The Journal of Special Education, 21*, 57–73.

Roth, W. (1989, September 17). Let us work. *Parade Magazine*, p. 16.

Rueda, R. (1989). Defining mild disabilities with language-minority students. *Exceptional Children, 56*, 121–129.

Rule, S., Fiechtl, B., & Innocenti, M. (1990). Preparation for transition to post-preschool environments: Development of a survival skills curriculum. *Topics in Early Childhood Special Education, 9*, 78–90.

Rusch, F. (1986). *Competitive employment issues and strategies*. Baltimore, MD: Paul H. Brookes Publishing Co.

Rusch, F., & Schutz, R. (1981). Vocational and social work behavior. In J. Matson & J. McCartney (Eds.), *Handbook for behavior modification with the mentally retarded*. New York: Plenum Press.

Sainato, D., & Lyon, S. (1989). Promoting successful mainstreaming transitions for handicapped preschool children. *Journal of Early Childhood Intervention, 13*, 305–314.

Salomone, P., & Paige, R. (1984). Employment problems and solutions: Perceptions of blind and visually impaired adults. *Vocational Guidance Quarterly, December*, 147–156.

Salzberg, C., Agran, M., & Lignugaris/Kraft, B. (1986). Behaviors that contribute to entry-level employment: A profile of five jobs. *Applied Research in Mental Retardation, 7*, 299–314.

Sargent, L. (1981). Resource time utilization: An observational study. *Exceptional Children, 47*, 420–425.

Schill, W.J., McMartin, R., & Matthews, K.A. (1988). Employer perspectives and handicapped employees experiences: An empirical analysis. In W.J. Schill (Principal Investigator), *Transition research on problems of handicapped youth: Occasional paper number 2*. Seattle, WA: University of Washington.

Schmitt, P., Cartledge, G., & Growick, B. (1988). Addressing the transition and social skill needs of learning disabled adolescents and adults. *NARIC Quarterly, 1*(Spring), pp. 1–6.

Schreiber, F. (1973). *Sybil*. New York: Warner Books.

Scotch, R. (1989). Politics and policy in the history of the disability rights movement. *The Milbank Quarterly, 67*(Suppl. 2), 380–400.

Scuccimarra, D., & Speece, D. (1990). Employment outcomes and social integration of students with mild handicaps: The quality of life two years after high school. *Journal of Learning Disabilities, 23*, 213–219.

Sexton, D., Hall, J., & Thomas, P. (1984). Multisource assessment of young handicapped children: A comparison. *Exceptional Children, 50*, 556–558.

Sheldon, J., Sherman, J., Schumaker, J., & Hazel, J.S. (1984). Developing a social skills curriculum for mildly handicapped adolescents and young adults: Some problems and approaches. In S. Braaten, R. Rutherford, & C. Kardash (Eds.), *Programming for adolescents with behavioral disorders*. Reston, VA: Council for Exceptional Children.

Sherman, S., & Robinson, N. (1982). *Ability testing of handicapped people: Dilemma for government, science, and the public.* Washington, DC: National Academy Press.

Singer, J., & Butler, J. (1987). The Education for All Handicapped Children Act: Schools as agents of social reform. *Harvard Educational Review, 57,* 125–152.

Slavin, R., Madden, N., & Leavey, M. (1982). *Combining cooperative learning and individualized instruction: Effects on the social acceptance, achievement, and behavior of mainstreamed students.* Paper presented at the annual convention of the American Educational Research Association.

Smith, C., & Greenberg, M. (1981). Step-by-step integration of handicapped preschool children in a day care center for nonhandicapped children. *Journal of the Division for Early Childhood. April,* 96–101.

Smith, J. (1988). Social and vocational problems of adults with learning disabilities: A review of the literature. *Learning Disabilities Focus, 4,* 46–58.

Smith, R., & Leslie, J. (1990). *Rehabilitation engineering.* Boca Raton, FL: CRC Press.

Special Committee on Aging. (1983). *Hearing: The future of Medicare.* Washington, DC: Government Printing Office.

Specialized Training Program. (no date). Specialized training program employment projects. *Rehabilitation Research & Training Center Newsletter, 2.*

Spiegel-McGill, P., Reed, D., Konig, C., & McGowan, P. (1990). Parent education: Easing the transition to preschool. *Topics in Early Childhood Special Education, 9,* 66–77.

Staehlin, J. (1985). Inside VME: Working for the community. *VME Volunteers for Medical Engineering,* December, 1.

Stagg, V., & Catron, T. (1986). Networks of social supports for parents of handicapped children. In R. Fewell & P. Vadasy (Eds.), *Families of handicapped children: Needs and supports across the life span.* Austin, TX: Pro-Ed, Inc.

Stahl, S., & Potts, M. (1985). Social support and chronic disease: A propositional inventory. In W. Peterson & J. Quadagno (Eds.), *Social bonds in later life.* Beverly Hills, CA: Sage Publications.

Stainback, W., & Stainback, S. (1984). A rationale for the merger of special education and regular education. *Exceptional Children, 51,* 102–111.

Stainback, W., Stainback, S., Courtnage, L., & Jaben, T. (1985). Facilitating mainstreaming by modifying the mainstream. *Exceptional Children, 52,* 144–152.

Stake, R., Denny, T., & DeStefano, L. (1989). Perceptions of effectiveness: Two case studies of transition model programs. Urbana-Champaign, IL: Secondary Transition Intervention Effectiveness Institute, University of Illinois.

Steele, R., & Gerrey, W. (Eds.). (1987). *RESNA '87: Meeting the challenge. Proceedings of the 10th annual conference on rehabilitation technology.* Washington, DC: Association for the Advancement of Rehabilitation Technology.

Steinmetz, S. (1988a). *Duty bound: Family care and elder abuse.* Beverly Hills, CA: Sage Publications.

Steinmetz, S. (1988b). Parental and filial relationships: Obligation, support and abuse. In E. Steinmetz (Ed.), *Family and support systems across the life span.* New York: Plenum Press.

Stilladis, K., & Wiener, J. (1989). Relationship between social perception and peer status in children with learning disabilities. *Journal of Learning Disabilities, 22,* 624–629.

Stowitschek, J., & Salzberg, C. (1987). *Job success for handicapped youth: A social protocol curriculum.* Reston, VA: Council for Exceptional Children.

Svanborg, A. (1985). Biomedical and environmental influences on aging. In R. Butler & H. Gleason (Eds.), *Productive aging: Enhancing vitality in later life.* New York: Springer Publishing Co.

Szymanski, E., King, J., Parker, R., & Jenkins, W. (1989). The state-federal program: Interface with special education. *Exceptional Children, 56,* 70–77.

Tallman, I. (1965). Spousal role differentiation and the socialization of severely retarded children. *Marriage and the Family, 27,* 37–42.

Tanenbaum, S. (1989). Medicaid and disability: The unlikely entitlement. *The Milbank Quarterly, 67*(Suppl. 2), 311–351.

Templeman, T., Fredericks, H., & Udell, T. (1989). Integration of children with moderate and severe handicaps into a daycare center. *Journal of Early Intervention, 13,* 315–328.

Tetzlaff, S. (Ed.). (1990). Go for the gold. *Centerpoint, 2,* 2–3.

Thurlow, M., Ysseldyke, J., & Weiss, J. (1988). Early childhood special education exit decisions: How are they made? How are they evaluated? *Journal of the Division of Early Childhood, 12,* 253–262.

Toombs, M. (1989a). Being an effective advocate in the educational system. *ACLD Newsbriefs, 24,* 11.

Toombs, M. (1989b). Monitoring: The advocate's point of view. *LDA Newsbriefs, 24,* 1–3.

Torrey, B. (1982). The lengthening of retirement. In M. Riley, R. Abeles, M. Teitelbaum. (Eds.), *Aging from birth to death: Vol. 2. Sociotemporal perspectives.* Boulder, CO: Westview Press.

Turkewitz, G., & Kenney, P. (1985). The role of developmental limitations of sensory input on sensory/perceptual organization. *Developmental Behavioral Pediatrics, 6,* 302–306.

Turnbull, H., & Turnbull, A. (1990). The unfulfilled promise of integration: Does part H ensure different rights and results than part B of the Education of the Handicapped Act? *Topics in Early Childhood Special Education, 10,* 18–32.

Tyner, R. (Ed.). (1989). Drugs put baby at risk. *The ACLD Gram, August-September, 23,* 13.

Ulicny, G., & Jones, M. (1988). Consumer management of attendant services: Benefits and obstacles. *NARIC Quarterly, 1,* 6–14.

United States Employment Service (1977). *Dictionary of occupational titles.* Washington, DC: U.S. Government Printing Office.

United States General Accounting Office (1989a). *Child care: Selected bibliography* (Human Resources Division Report GAO/HRD 89-98FS). Gaithersburg, MD: Author.

United States General Accounting Office (1989b). *Early childhood education: information on costs and services at high-quality centers* (Human Resources Division Report GAO/HRD 89-130FS). Gaithersburg, MD: Author.

United States General Accounting Office (1989c). *Special education: Congressional action needed to improve chapter 1 handicapped program* (Human Resources Division Report GAO/HRD 89-54). Gaithersburg, MD: Author.

United States General Accounting Office. (1990a). *Early childhood education: What are the costs of high quality programs?* (Human Resources Division Report GAO/HRD 90-43BR). Gaithersburg, MD: Author.

United States General Accounting Office (1990b). *Persons with disabilities: Reports on costs of accommodations* (Human Resources Division Report GAO/HRD 90-44BR). Gaithersburg, MD: Author.

Vanderheiden, G., Berliss, J., Borden, P., & Kelso, D. (1989). Development of user-, professional-, and public-accessible databases on assistive and rehabilitative technology. In *Rehabilitation R&D*

Progress Reports:1989. Annual report of the Rehabilitation Research and Development Service. Baltimore, MD: Veterans Administration Prosthetics Research and Development Center.

Vanderheiden, G. Lee, C., & Scadden, L. (1987). Features to increase the accessibility of computers by persons with disabilities: Report from the industry/government task force. In R. Steeley & W. Gerry (Eds.). *RESNA '87: Meeting the challenge. Proceedings of the 10th annual conference on rehabilitation technology.* Washington, DC: Association for the Advancement of Rehabilitation Technology.

Van der Loos, M. (1989). Clinical evaluation of a vocational desktop robotic aid for severely physically disabled individuals. In *Rehabilitation R&D Progress Reports–1989.* Baltimore, MD: Veterans Administration Prosthetics Research and Development Center.

Van Dyke, D., & Fox., A. (1990). Fetal drug exposure and its possible implications for learning in the preschool and school-age population. *Journal of Learning Disabilities, 23,* 160–162.

Verbrugge, L. (1989). Gender, aging, and health. In K. Markides (Ed.), *Aging and health–Perspectives on race, ethnicity, and class.* Beverly Hills, CA: Sage Publications.

Vergason, G., & Anderegg, M. (1990). The regular education initiative and special education reform in California. *The Journal of California C.E.C., 39,* 8–9.

Viadero, D. (1990). Groups push for big boost in special-education funds. *Education Week, 9,* 21.

Walker, D., Singer, J., Palfrey, J., Orza, M., Wenger, M., & Butler, J. (1988). Who leaves and who stays in special education: A 2-year follow-up study. *Exceptional Children, 54,* 393–402.

Walter, A. (1985). The mediating role of social networks in the housing decisions of the elderly. In W. Peterson & J. Quadagno (Eds.), *Social bonds in later life.* Beverly Hills, CA: Sage Publications.

Wang, M., Gennari, P., & Waxman, H. (1985). The adaptive learning environments model: Design, implementation, and effects. In M. Wang & H. Walberg (Eds.), *Adapting instruction to individual differences.* Berkeley, CA: McCutchan.

Wang, M., Peverly, S., & Randolph, R. (1984). An investigation of the implementation and effects of a full-time mainstreaming program. *Remedial and Special Education,* 21–32.

Wang, M., & Walberg, H. (1988). Four fallacies of segregationism. *Exceptional Children, 55,* 128–137.

Wehman, P., & Hill, J. (1981). Competitive employment for moderately and severely handicapped individuals. *Exceptional Children, 47,* 338–345.

Wehman, P., Kregel, J., & Barcus, J. (1985). From school to work: A vocational transition model for handicapped students. *Exceptional Children, 52,* 25–37.

Wehman, P., Kregel, J., & Shafer, M. (1989). *Emerging trends in the national supported employment initiative: A preliminary analysis of twenty-seven states.* Richmond, VA: Virginia Commonwealth University.

Wehman, P., & Moon, M. (1988). *Vocational rehabilitation and supported employment.* Baltimore, MD: Paul H. Brookes Publishing Co.

Wehman, P., Moon, M., Everson, J., Wood, W., & Barcus, M. (1988). *Transition from school to work: New challenges for youth with severe handicaps.* Baltimore, MD: Paul H. Brookes Publishing Co.

Wehman, P., Wood, W., Everson, J., Goodwyn, R., & Conley, S. (1988). *Vocational education for multihandicapped youth with cerebral palsy.* Baltimore, MD: Paul H. Brookes Publishing Co.

Weil, M., & Karls, J.M. (1985). *Case management in human service practice: A systematic approach to mobilizing resources for clients.* San Francisco, CA: Jossey-Bass.

Weisgerber, R. (1976). *Health care needs of the handicapped: An exploratory study.* Palo Alto, CA: American Institutes for Research.

Weisgerber, R. (1980). *A special educator's guide to vocational training.* Springfield, IL: Charles C Thomas, Publisher.

Weisgerber, R. (1984a). *Implications of research and theory for the use of computers with the learning disabled.* Palo Alto, CA: American Institutes for Research.

Weisgerber, R. (1984b). *Social solutions.* Burlingame, CA: Professional Associated Resources.

Weisgerber, R. (1987, April). *An overview of CREATE research.* Paper presented to the Council for Exceptional Children, Chicago, IL.

Weisgerber, R. (1991). *The challenged scientists: Disabilities and the triumph of excellence.* New York: Praeger. Unpublished book manuscript, National Science Foundation.

Weisgerber, R., Armstrong, T., Sacks, A., & Steele, R. (1989). *Technology transfer guidebook.* Palo Alto, CA: Rehabilitation R&D Center, Veterans Administration Medical Center.

Weisgerber, R., Dahl, P., & Appleby, J. (1981). *Training the handicapped for productive employment.* Rockville, MD: Aspen Publishers, Inc.

Weisgerber, R., Dalldorf, M., Jabara, R., Feichtner, S., & Blake, P. (1989). *Social competence and employability skills curriculum.* Rockville, MD: Aspen Publishers, Inc.

Weisgerber, R., & de Haas, C. (1978). *Environmental sensing—reference compendium.* Palo Alto, CA: American Institutes for Research.

Weisgerber, R., Everett, B., Puzarne, A., & Shanner, W. (1973). *Educational evaluation of the Optacon (optical to tactile converter) as a reading aid to blind elementary and secondary students.* Palo Alto, CA: American Institutes for Research.

Weisgerber, R., & Rubin, D. (1985). Designing and using software for the learning disabled. *Journal of Reading, Writing, and Learning Disabilities, 1,* 133–138.

White, K., & Casto, G. (1985). An integrative review of early intervention efficacy studies with at-risk children: Implications for the handicapped. *Analysis and Intervention in Developmental Disabilities, 5,* 7–31.

Wiggins, S., & Behrmann, M. (1988). Increasing independence through community learning. *Teaching Exceptional Children, 21,* 20–24.

Will, M. (1984a). An advocate for the handicapped. *American Education, January-February,* 4–6.

Will, M. (1984b). *Bridges from school to working life. Programs for the Handicapped, March/April,* 1–5.

Will, M. (1985). Ms. Will speaks on the least restrictive environment. *Programs for the Handicapped,* Jan./Feb., 1–2.

Wilson, R., Mulligan, M., & Turner, R. (1985). Early childhood intervention in an urban setting. *Teaching Exceptional Children, 17,* 134–139.

Winget, P. (Ed.). (1989). San Bernardino provides support. *The Special Edge: California Resources in Special Education, 3,* 3.

Winget, P. (Ed.). (1989/1990). Parent involvement "critical" in process to provide effective programs. *The Special Edge: California Resources in Special Education, 4,* 1, 14.

Winget, P. (Ed.). (1990). Principles for family focused services. Early intervention focuses on family. *The Special Edge: California Resources in Special Education, 4,* 10.

Wise, S., & Plake, B. (1989). Research on the effects of administering tests via computer. *Educational Measurement: Issues and Practice, 8,* 5–10.

Wittenberg, C. (1971). Studies of child abuse and infant accidents. In J. Segal (Ed.), *The mental health of the child: Program of the National Institute of Mental Health.* Washington, DC: U.S. Government Printing Office.

World Health Organization. (1980). *International classification of impairments, disabilities, and handicaps.* Geneva, Switzerland: Author.

Wright, A., Cooperstein, R., Renneker, E., & Padilla, C. (1982). *Local implementation of P.L. 94-142: Final report of a longitudinal study.* Menlo Park, CA: SRI International.

Yamaguchi, G., & Zajac, F. (1989). Sensitivity of simulated human gait to neuromuscular control patterns. In *Proceedings of the XIIth International Congress of Biomechanics.* Los Angeles, CA: Department of Kinesiology, University of California at Los Angeles.

Yelin, E. (1989). Displaced concern: The social context of the work-disability problem. *The Milbank Quarterly, 67*(Suppl. 2), 114–165.

Yogman, M. (1984). Development of the father-infant relationship. In H. Fitzgerald, B. Lester, & M. Yogman (Eds.), *Theory and research in behavioral pediatrics.* New York: Plenum Press.

Zeigert, K. (1983). The Swedish prohibition of corporal punishment: A preliminary report. *Journal of Marriage and the Family, 45.*

Zola, I. (1989). Toward the necessary universalizing of a disability policy. *The Milbank Quarterly, 67*(Suppl. 2), 401–428.

Index

A

ABLEDATA, 137
Academic skills, 98–99
Accommodations for disabled
  cost factors, 174–175
  design of facilities, 173
  job accommodations, 166–167
  technology and, 174
  transportation related, 173
  work-related, 173
  work sharing as, 175
Adaptability instruction, 117
Adaptive environments, 78
Adaptive Learning Environments Model, 80
Adaptive testing, 90–91
Adulthood
  developmental aspects, 11, 12
  economic self-sufficiency, 182–183
  family support, 151–152
  federal programs, 132–134
  federal/state advocacy, 134–135
  health needs, 144–148
  independent/group living, 148–150
  mentors, 152
  post-high school transition, 130–132
  private sector involvement, 141–144

  rehabilitation, 135–138
  rehabilitation engineering, 138–141
  self-advocacy, 150–151
  social/leisure involvement, 181–182
  See also Employment in adulthood
Advocacy
  effectiveness of, 120–121
  federal/state, for disabled adults, 134–136
  parental role, 49–51
  private sector, for disabled adults, 142–144
  school-to-work-transition and, 71
  self-advocacy, 150–151
  strategic planning and, 121
  strategies employed by undergraduates, 121
Aging
  phase approach to, 192
  stability of quality of life, 3
Alcohol
  abuse by disabled, 147
  newborn effects, 54
Americans with Disabilities Act, 122, 133, 151, 194
Amphetamines, newborn effects, 55
Assertiveness, parental, 51
Assessment, educational, 88–94
  adaptive testing, 90–91

About the Author

Robert A. Weisgerber has been active in research and development in the area of disability for over 20 years. He is Principal Research Scientist and Director of the Center for Research on the Specially Challenged at the American Institutes for Research in Palo Alto, California. Holding a doctorate in education from Indiana University, he has served on the faculties of Indiana University, San Francisco State University, the University of Calgary, and several other institutions of higher education.

Dr. Weisgerber has authored a number of publications in special education, including journal articles, technical papers and reports, guidebooks, manuals, curricula, book chapters, and textbooks. Among the more recent publications are *The Challenged Scientists* (in press), the *Social Competence and Employability Skills Curriculum* (Aspen Publishers), and the *Technology Transfer Guidebook* (for the Rehabilitation Research and Development Center, Veterans Administration, Palo Alto).

Dr. Weisgerber's research in the area of disability has been wide ranging. In the area of technology, he conducted the first national evaluation of the Optacon (a device that enables the reading of inkprint by the blind), investigated the use of alternative electronic environmental sensing devices for enhancing the mobility of blind persons, and developed innovative computer software for improving the reading-related skills of learning-disabled students. In the area of social skills, he has developed several curricula, one (*Social Solutions*) related to interpersonal social skills that are broadly applied throughout life. The second, mentioned above, concerns the development of social-employability skills necessary for successful employment.